CW01217579

ARAN DESIGN
The Creative Knitter's Handbook

ARAN DESIGN
The Creative Knitter's Handbook

RITA TAYLOR

THE CROWOOD PRESS

First published in 2018 by
The Crowood Press Ltd
Ramsbury, Marlborough
Wiltshire SN8 2HR

www.crowood.com

© Rita Taylor 2018

All rights reserved. No part of this publication may be reproduced or transmitted in any form or by any means, electronic or mechanical, including photocopy, recording, or any information storage and retrieval system, without permission in writing from the publishers.

British Library Cataloguing-in-Publication Data
A catalogue record for this book is available from the British Library.

ISBN 978 1 78500 407 0

Typeset by Kelly-Anne Levey
Printed and bound in India by Parksons Graphics

CONTENTS

Acknowledgements 7

Abbreviations 8

Introduction 11

1	History	13
2	Materials and Equipment	29
3	Stitch Dictionary	39
4	Starting a Project	77
5	Aran Knitting Patterns	99
6	Tips and Techniques	129

Bibliography 140

Appendix 141

Index 142

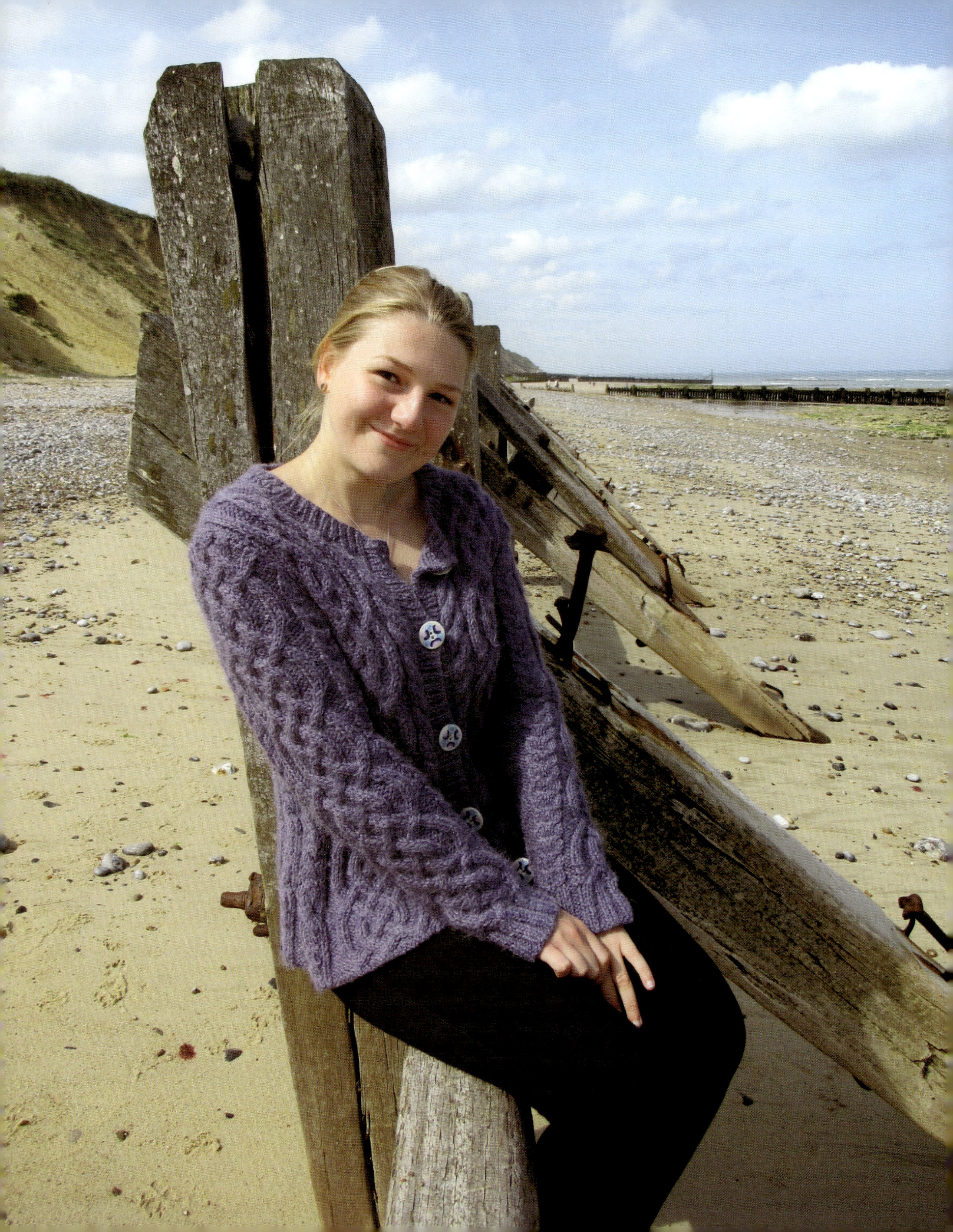

ACKNOWLEDGEMENTS

Thank you to Elly Doyle for checking the patterns, to Hilary Grundy for knitting many of the swatches, to photographers Natalie Bullock, Helen James, Marj Law, Rosemary Brown, Ron Wiebe, and to the models, Natalie, Erin and Tess. Thank you to the Knitting & Crochet Guild for permission to use photographs of some of the Aran knitwear in their collection, to the Board of Trinity College Dublin for the picture of the Aran men in their ganseys, and to Batsford Books for the image of the sweater from Gladys Thompson's book. Special thanks to my husband who has been helpful and supportive throughout this work.

Thank you to Mavis Clark for her memories of her grandmother's knitting and, last but not least, thank you to the skilful ladies of the Aran Islands who created such beautiful stitches. Without their originality this book would never have come into being.

ABBREVIATIONS

Abbreviations in Patterns

alt	alternate
approx	approximately
beg	begin(ing)
c3f	slip 2 stitches onto a cable needle and hold in front, k1, k2 from cable needle
cm	centimetres
cont	continue
dec	decrease
foll	following
g	grams
inc	increase
incto5	(k1, p1, k1, p1, k1) into the same stitch to make 5 stitches from 1
k	knit
k2tog	knit 2 together
kfb	knit into front and back of same stitch
m1	make 1 stitch by knitting into the horizontal bar between stitches
M1L	make 1 stitch in the left leg of the stitch below
M1R	make 1 stitch in the right leg of the stitch below
m	metres
mb	make bobble: k1, yo, k1, yo, k1 all into the next stitch. Turn, purl these 5 stitches, turn and knit them, turn and purl them again, then, with the right side facing, decrease back to one stitch (other ways of making bobbles are given in Chapter 6)
mm	millimetres
p	purl
p2tog	purl 2 together
p3tog	purl 3 together
patt	(work in) pattern
pfbf	purl into front, back and front of stitch
rem	remaining
rep	repeat
rev st st	reverse stocking stitch
RS	right side
sl	slip
sk2p	slip 1, knit 2 together and pass slipped stitch over the knitted stitches
ssk	slip each of the next 2 stitches independently, return them to the left needle and knit together through back loops
st st	stocking stitch
st(s)	stitch(es)
tbl	through back loop
tog	together
tw2l	Insert the right needle behind the first stitch on the left needle into the back of the 2nd stitch and knit it without dropping the stitches off the needle. Knit into the front of the first stitch and drop both stitches off the needle
tw2r	twist 2 right: knit into the back of the 2nd stitch on the left needle, take the right needle in front of the 1st stitch, then knit into the back of the 1st stitch on the left needle before slipping both stitches off the needle
WS	wrong side
yo	yarn over needle

Abbreviations in Charts

1/1LC	slip next stitch onto cable needle and place at back, k1, then k1 from cable needle
1/1RC	slip next stitch onto cable needle and place at front, k1, then k1 from cable needle
1/1LPC	slip next stitch onto cable needle and place at back, k1, then p1 from cable needle
1/1LPT	slip next stitch onto cable needle and place at back, k1tbl, then p1 from cable needle
1/1RPC	slip next stitch onto cable needle and place at front, p1, then k1 from cable needle
1/2RPC	slip next 2 stitches onto cable needle and place at back of work, k1, then p2 from cable needle
1/2LPC	slip next stitch onto cable needle and place at front of work, p2, then k1 from cable needle
1/2RC	slip next stitch onto cable needle and place at front of work, p2, then k1 from cable needle
1/2LC	slip next stitch onto cable needle and place at front of work, k2, then k1 from cable needle
1/3LC	slip next 3 stitches onto cable needle and place at back, k1, then k3 from cable needle
1/3RC	slip next stitch onto cable needle and place at front, k3, then k1 from cable needle
1/3RPC	slip next 3 stitches onto cable needle and place at back of work, k1, then p3 from cable needle
1/3LPC	slip next 3 stitches onto cable needle and place at back of work, k1, then p3 from cable needle
2/1RC	slip next stitch onto cable needle and place at back of work, k2, then k1 from cable needle
2/1LC	slip next 2 stitches onto cable needle and place at front of work, k1, then k2 from cable needle
2/1LPC	slip next 2 stitches onto cable needle and place at back, k1, then p2 from cable needle
2/1RPC	slip next 2 stitches onto cable needle and place at front, p1, then k2 from cable needle
2/1/2RPC	slip next 3 stitches onto cable needle and place at back of work, k2, slip left-most stitch from cable needle to left needle, move cable needle with remaining stitches to front of work, p1 from left needle, then k2 from cable needle
2/2LC	slip next 2 stitches onto cable needle and place at back, k2, then k2 from cable needle
2/2RC	slip next 2 stitches onto cable needle and place at front, k2, then k2 from cable needle
2/2LPC	slip next 2 stitches onto cable needle and place at front, p2, then k2 from cable needle
2/2RPC	slip next 2 stitches onto cable needle and place at back, k2, then p2 from cable needle
2/3LPC	slip next 2 stitches onto cable needle and place at front, k3, then p2 from cable needle
3/1LC	slip next 3 stitches onto cable needle and place at front of work, k1, then k3 from cable needle
3/1RC	slip next stitch onto cable needle and place at back of work, k3, then k1 from cable needle
3/1LPC	slip next 3 stitches onto cable needle and place at front, p1, then k3 from cable needle
3/1RPC	slip next 3 stitches onto cable needle and place at back, k3, then p1 from cable needle
3/2RPC	slip next 2 stitches onto cable needle and place at back of work, k3, then p2 from cable needle
3/2LPC	slip next 3 stitches onto cable needle and place at front of work, p2, then k3 from cable needle.
3/3LC	slip next 3 stitches onto cable needle and place at front, k3, then p3 from cable needle
3/3RC	slip next 3 stitches onto cable needle and place at back, k3, then p3 from cable needle
4/1LPC	slip next 4 stitches onto cable needle and place at front, k1, then p4 from cable needle
4/1RPC	slip next 4 stitches onto cable needle and place at back, p1, then k4 from cable needle
4/2RPC	slip next 4 stitches onto cable needle and place at back of work, p2, then k4 from cable needle
4/2LPC	slip next 4 stitches onto cable needle and place at front of work, p2, then k4 from cable needle
4/4LC	slip next 4 stitches onto cable needle and place at front, k4, then k4 from cable needle
4/4RC	slip next 4 stitches onto cable needle and place at back, k4, then k4 from cable needle
6/6RC	slip next 6 stitches onto cable needle and place at back of work, k6, then k6 from cable needle.
6/6LC	slip next 6 stitches onto cable needle and place at front of work, k6, then k6 from cable needle.

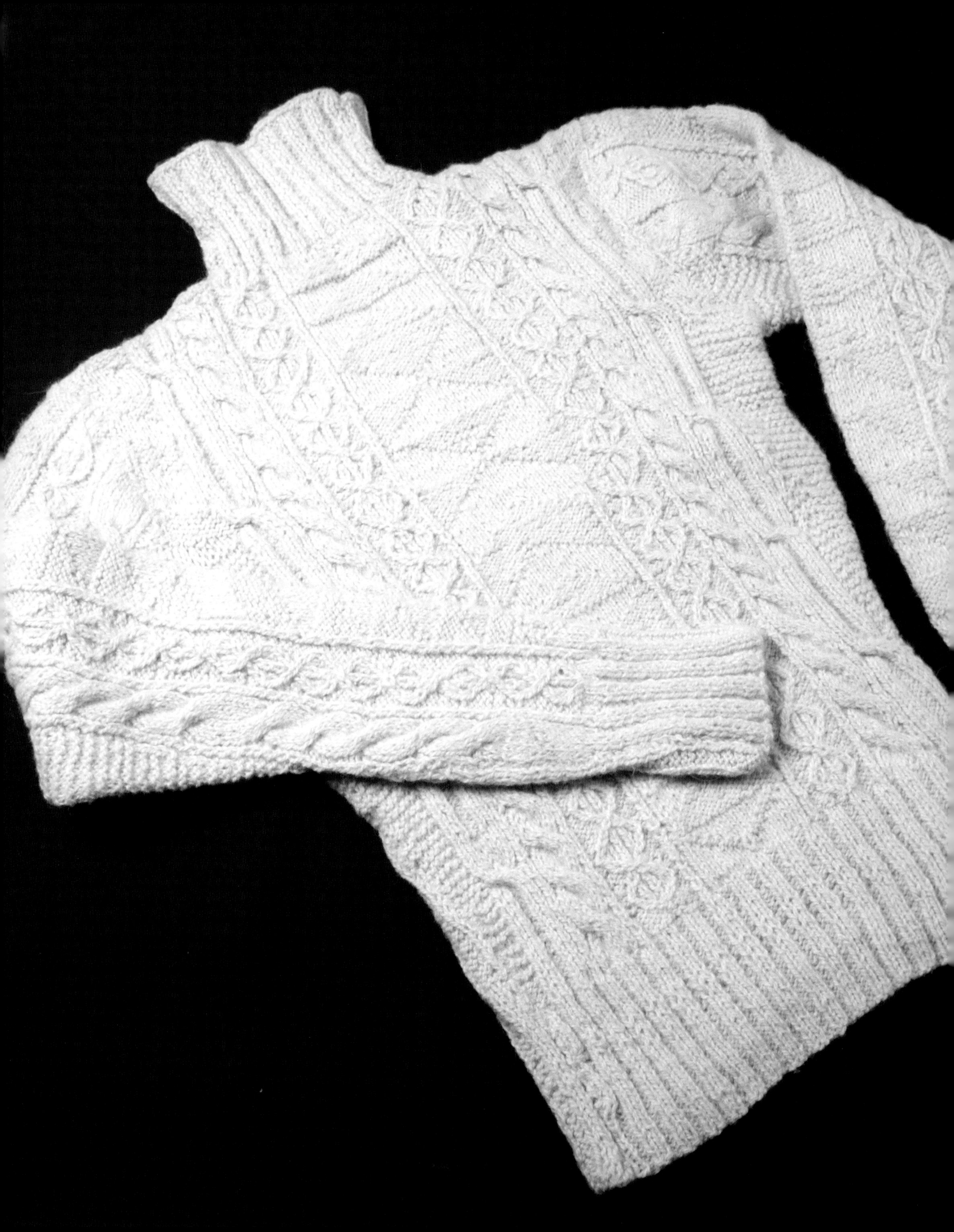

INTRODUCTION

There are many opinions on what are the origins of Aran knitting, but the truth is that it is a reasonably young tradition. However, a tradition it is, and people do have an idea of what constitutes a typical Aran sweater. It has a comfortable fit, is usually made from a fairly thick, undyed cream wool and features vertical patterns of crossing stitches, some of which look like ropes, some diamond shapes and some criss-crossed like ribbons. Traditionally there is a wide central panel flanked by bands of cables (the rope-like patterns). Some garments are decorated with bobbles. It is a unisex garment and can be made as a sweater or cardigan in all sizes to fit babies to adults.

Of late some of the central panels have become very intricate, inspired by the Celtic and Viking designs found on stones and crosses. The originators of these motifs appear to be Elsebeth Lavold in her Viking knitting books and Alice Starmore in *Fishermen's Sweaters*. There are also a number of inventive knitters who have created new cables through experimentation. While these are not 'traditional' Aran motifs, they look pleasing and beautiful and are another option for the designing of Arans, so I have included one or two here. These intertwining patterns now appear to be accepted as traditional elements in Aran design. While some may disagree about their authenticity, I see no problem with it. Artists of all kinds like to push the boundaries of their crafts, continuing to experiment in order to keep the craft alive.

What this book aims to do is help you to design an Aran sweater yourself; to become comfortable with working a variety of cable stitches and to understand how they work. The more that you experiment, the more you will discover the potential for 'inventing' new cables. This book is not so much an instruction manual, but more a guidebook to help you develop your own ideas. While there are already many existing patterns that you can follow to the letter, my aim is to get you to follow the example of the knitters of the Aran Islands and see how satisfying it is to create something that you have planned and designed for yourself.

While the book does contain a few patterns for you to work as they are, it also gives ideas for ways to change these patterns into a different design, either by changing the shape or inserting different cable motifs. It does not contain basic knitting instructions, but is aimed at the knitter who is already competent in working the commonly used stitches.

The intricacy of all the different crossovers and interlocking of stitches may at first appear too complex to work into a fresh Aran design for all but the most experienced of knitters; I hope that this book will allay some of those fears and will enable you to produce Aran knits that you will be proud of and happy to wear for many years. I hope that it will also give you some ideas of how to use Aran stitches to develop new motifs of your own.

OPPOSITE PAGE: An curragh from the Collection of the Knitting and Crochet Guild.

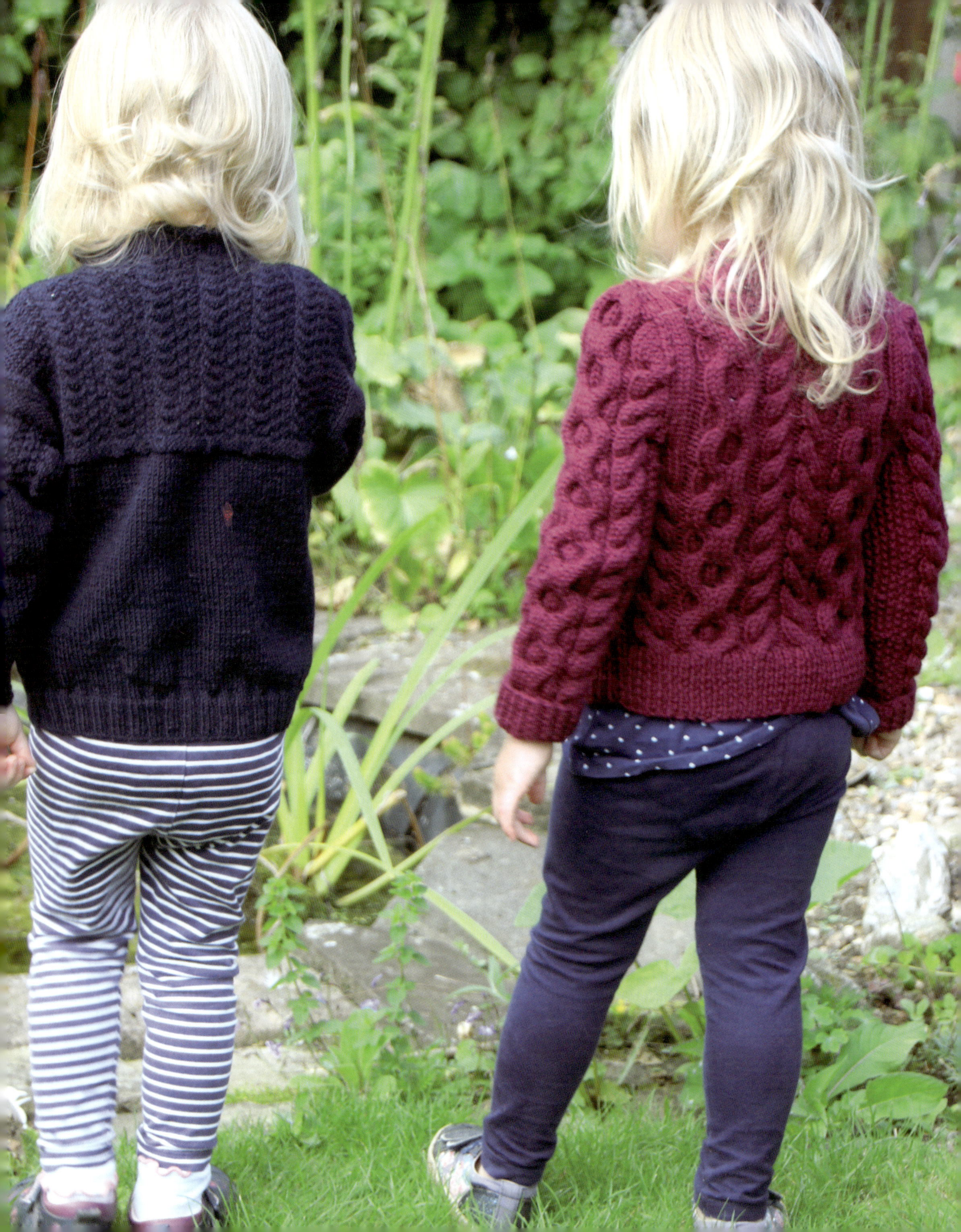

CHAPTER 1

HISTORY

> In through the front door
> Once around the Back
> Out through the Window
> And off jumps Jack
>
> Anon, an old rhyme used for teaching children to knit

The Origins of Knitting

It is impossible to know the exact history of knitting. Early pieces of knitting were usually made for practical reasons; as they wore out, they would be discarded. They were made from perishable fibres which disintegrate so easily that there are only fragments of fabric to study – no whole pieces. This makes it difficult to discern exactly how they were constructed, or for what purpose. Those items reliably dated as coming from before the eleventh century were most likely made using a technique known as naalbinding, where the yarn was passed in and out of loops made with fingers or a threaded needle. The earliest knitted example of this dates from AD 256 and was found in Syria. It is just a fragment approximately five inches square and there is no clue as to what it was part of. The successor to this technique was the peg loom – a series of sticks held in the hand or mounted on a rectangular block. It was worked as in loop knitting, with the yarn being wrapped around the peg before being lifted over a new strand above it.

There is some speculation that knitting with two needles, in the form that we know it now, dates from well before the eleventh century. This theory arose from paintings of the Virgin Mary apparently knitting a sock. However, these are paintings created in Europe in the fourteenth century and simply prove that knitting was known there at that time, not that is was being created much earlier. The earliest piece of knitting that can be dated and which appears to have been made with two hand-held needles was found in Egypt. It is a pair of socks, elaborately patterned and worked in fine cotton yarn. Some pieces of knitting, silk cushion covers and gloves were also found in 1994 in the tomb of Prince Fernando de la Cerda in northern Spain. Because he died in 1275 and these items were buried with him, their dates are accurate. The pieces are so neat and detailed that it is presumed that knitting had been practised in Europe for a long time before this.

Pieces like these that have been reliably authenticated were usually made for special occasions, especially religious ceremony, and they are fine examples of the craft. Other pieces still in existence were made by craftsmen belonging to the guilds of the Middle Ages. An apprentice would not receive the designation of Master Craftsmen until he had knitted a number of specified pieces. The main piece to be knitted before an apprentice could become a Master was a knitted carpet containing at least a dozen colours, and which was probably intended to be a wall hanging. Other items had to be made following a set of general instructions but not a precise pattern; for example,

OPPOSITE PAGE: From Fisherman's gansey to cable aran.

stockings were to be decorated with 'clocks', a form of fine cabling made by crossing or twisting two stitches. These twisted stitches would often form a small rope or diamond shape, demonstrating that crossed stitches were known in Europe in the fourteenth century at least.

Knitted socks and gloves were fairly common throughout Europe and the Middle East at this time. It was easier to use knitted rather than cut fabric because of the complex shaping required to accommodate the fingers and thumb in gloves and the heel shaping in socks, but it took until the fifteenth century for the craft to come to Britain. It was probably spread via the trade routes and was mainly used to make caps and bonnets, particularly in Coventry, Monmouth and Kilmarnock. A guild of hat knitters was established in England, with the aim of standardizing the construction of the various types of hats. The hats were made from wool rather than the silk or cotton used for gloves and stockings, as these hats were not for special occasions but for everyday wear. They were not left in their original knitted state, but were felted to make them more hard-wearing and waterproof.

The changes in fashion from long robes to doublet and hose in the sixteenth century brought about a growth in the sock knitting industry. Long stockings were now favoured rather than short or mid-calf socks. These long knitted stockings had to be tied at the tops because purl stitch, needed to make an elastic rib, had not yet been discovered.

The first pair of knitted stockings to be seen in England came from Spain and were worn by Henry VIII. He favoured them over cloth stockings because they emphasized his 'well-shaped calf'. They were also much more comfortable than the coarse cloth stockings previously worn. Queen Elizabeth I loved the texture of the silk lace stockings originally sent to her as a gift from France; she had the ladies at court taught how to knit so that they could keep her well supplied. Once royalty was seen to be wearing something, that fashion spread, and eventually the stocking industry became a vital part of the British economy. But stockings were not cheap: the Earl of Leicester paid 53 shillings and 4 pence for a pair of hose, which is more than £500 in today's currency! However, in 1589 the invention of the stocking frame by William Lee dealt a death blow to this hand knitting industry and many of the great knitting centres of Britain gradually faded away.

The Continuing Tradition of Hand Knitting

Despite the impact of the stocking frame on the British knitting industry, in parts of Britain more distant from the manufacturing towns the practice of hand knitting continued, and it is from here that we get many of our well-known traditions. Handknitted stockings continued to be an important source of income for many people – men, women and children – in the Yorkshire Dales, Scotland and Ireland. In 1588 a knitting school was created in the town of York to teach girls and young women how to make those items that were now turning out to be in great demand. Schools in other parts of the country followed soon afterward. To speed up the knitting process, many of the knitters would work with a knitting stick or sheath attached to their waist. The non-working end of the working needle would be held in place by the sheath so that the hand was free to throw the yarn more quickly. Sometimes a clew holder was also attached to the waist to hold the ball of wool while the knitter walked around.

The fashion for these comfortable handknitted stockings continued, and there was such a demand for wool that villages were destroyed in order to give the land over to sheep pasture. As late as 1805 the export of stockings from Aberdeen alone was valued at £100,000. But as a result of the mechanization of stocking manufacture with the introduction of William Lee's stocking frame, and also as fashions changed, the boom time came to an end and people began to look for other commercially viable items to knit.

In the more remote parts of Britain men and women continued to knit for themselves and their families the items that were suited to their way of life, the local conditions and the qualities of the wool produced by the local sheep. The sheep of the Shetland Islands, for example, produce wool that is capable of being spun very finely, which led to the production of the famous 'wedding ring shawls'. The native sheep of Aran and the west of Ireland, similar to the modern Galway breed, produced coarser fleece with hair and kemp that can withstand high rainfall and the Atlantic gales. The wool from these sheep was used to make hard-wearing clothing that was suited to the way of life of the fishermen and farmers.

Typical of these garments was that made famous on Guernsey. Like most areas of Britain, the island originally produced stockings for export, but the French Revolution disrupted this trade and the industry declined. However, the islanders continued to knit sweaters for the local fishermen, as they had done since the sixteenth century when they were first granted a licence to import wool. These sweaters – what we now know as ganseys – were knitted in the round, in the traditional square shape with a straight neck so that they could be reversed as they became worn. They were usually made of heavy, tightly spun worsted wool imported from England and were knitted using fine needles known as 'wires', giving a firm finish to the fabric that was said to 'turn water'. The type of yarn used and the technique of mixing knit and purl stitches also made them warm (combinations of knit and purl stitches side by side trap more air as the loops lie in different directions). This simply shaped garment, possibly based on the traditional linen smock with its patterned yoke, square sleeves and simple shape, was the favourite workwear of many of the coastal communities around Britain and Ireland. They were, and still are, traditionally knitted in the round with dyed navy blue wool. Like the smock, they were usually plain up to the yoke, where they would frequently have a pattern of cables alternated with knit and purl stitches, sometimes with a simple rib and garter stitch pattern at the armhole edge and above the welt.

The welts would often have side slits for ease of movement, but otherwise these sweaters were constructed in a similar way all around the coast of Britain. They were knitted in the round, to a basic T-shape, with underarm gussets and often one or two purl stitches to mark the position of what would otherwise be side seams. The advantage of being knitted this way was that there were virtually no seams to come undone. The sleeves were picked up from the stitches of the gusset and along the armhole edge and worked downwards, which had the added bonus of making them easy to repair when they were rotted by the salt water.

The simple decoration of a Channel Islands gansey.

The Development of Aran Knitting

The three inhabited islands in Galway Bay – Inishmore (Inis Mór), Inishmaan (Inis Meáin) and Inisheer (Inis Oírr) – are mainly formed of limestone rock. There is some fertile ground on the northern sides of the islands, but the rest is barren, often bare rock. The islands are windswept and rocky with just a few inches of topsoil. Because they are cut off from many of the everyday things that mainland people take for granted, island peoples are often resourceful. Necessity is the mother of invention, and the Aran islanders 'improved' the scanty soil

The barren coast of Inishmore.

with the addition of sand and seaweed. The island climate is relatively mild and this 'home-made' soil was good enough to produce potatoes and other vegetables, and enough grass for a few sheep to feed on.

Fishing, as well as farming, was also an important means of providing food for the Aran islanders. The men would fish from small boats, known as curraghs, and there is documentary evidence from photographs published in 2012 of them wearing what look like machine-knitted ganseys similar to those produced by the contract knitters of Guernsey. The men and women on the Aran Islands would copy these square-shaped ganseys, known as *geansais* in Ireland, and hand knit them, just as they had been accustomed to doing for the stockings and shawls and other warm garments that they made for themselves and their families. They would spin the wool on a Great Wheel and dye the wool intended for sweaters with indigo. There is no evidence of a cream Aran sweater in these pictures, taken in the mid-nineteenth century.

Life was incredibly difficult on the Islands, and as a result of the policies of the government, the farms became smaller and smaller, so were less able to support their inhabitants. In 1886 Father Michael O'Donohue, the parish priest of Aran, sent a telegram to Dublin telling the authorities how difficult it was for the people to sustain a living and that help was desperately needed. His request was heeded and the Congested Districts Board began to stimulate the fishing industry by building piers out from the islands towards the mainland, and by starting a steamer service to Galway. The Board had been set up in

---

A page from Heinz Edgar Kiewe's paper presented at Oxford in 1966

Origin of the 'Isle Of Aran' Knitting Designs by Heinz Edgar Kiewe, Oxford (Fourth Revised Edition)

Folklorists have a habit of becoming too enthusiastic about insular tradition. Since they usually live in big towns and take the importance of political geography a bit too seriously, they often mix up nationalism with the migration of symbols and designs which is usually inspired by faith and superstition rather than by local genius. Abstract Folk designs of Europe generally came with the pilgrims, missionaries, pirates and/or favourable trade winds to the northern countries from the Eastern Mediterranean where the three great religions were born.

It will be interesting from this point of view to trace the origin of the famous Aran patterns.

We have studied the designs of Aran Knitting for the past 30 years, and it is a curious fact that we must have been the beginners of this interest in Aran Sweaters in England. It was in 1936 to be precise that we purchased a peculiar whiskery looking chunk of a sweater in 'Biblical White' at St Stephen's Green in Dublin. To us it looked at that time too odd for words, being hard as a board, shapeless as a Coptic Priest's shirt and with an atmosphere of Stonehenge all around it.

We took it to Mary Thomas, our dear friend in London. At the time she was Fashion Editor of *The Morning Post* and the sight of the hide-like fabric made her most excited. 'You have found a knitted sampler of Cable stitches,' the great expert said. 'May I publish it in my new book?' She did so in the *Mary Thomas Book of Knitting Patterns* (page 62).

She described the photo as a 'magnificent example of "Crossover Motifs" arranged in pattern; it is a classical choice every pattern being of the same crossover family. The knitting is intricate but traditional of Aran and worn by the Irish Fishermen of that island.'

We were most *enthusiastic* about our discovery for at that time there was only one interlace pattern in the vocabulary of the British knitter and that was the Cablestitch used exclusively on the Jersey-Guernsey Isle by fishermen and for those 'cricket sweaters' one of the earliest of handknitted folk designs and common to the English Village Greens of Victorian days. In 1937 we saw the beautiful film *Man of Aran* by Robert Flaherty, and we made up our mind to help to revive a 'Biblical White' Fishermen's Sweater, kin to sea, storm and tough people. During the War we explored sources for congenial wool of the whiskery type of the natural sheepwool of the Aran Isles used before the War, and today we employ quite an industry of Harris Tweed Spinners on the Outer Hebrides; people who have a closer bond with the folk in Aran than with those in Glasgow, Edinburgh or Liverpool.

This is a replica of the sweater featured in Mary Thomas' book. It was knitted to a pattern that I designed for the Knitting & Crochet Guild and is in the Guild Collection.

1891 by the government to encourage economic growth and discourage emigration in rural areas where the population had outgrown the productive capacity of the land. By the 1890s, knitting was being actively encouraged on the islands as a viable way of making a living. Now it was the women, rather than the master craftsmen of the guilds, who practised the craft. While the men continued to work on the land and sea, the women took to knitting with great enthusiasm, now that they had an outlet for their work.

Dr Muriel Gahan (1897–1995) founded her shop Country Workers Limited in 1930 to promote traditional country crafts. She was very keen to keep alive the Irish country crafts, such as weaving, basket making and knitting. She felt that the people who practised these crafts deserved more respect and recognition. In December 1930 she opened the Country Shop in St Stephen's Green in Dublin as an outlet for the sale of many of the traditional Irish crafts. The shop also contained a restaurant/coffee shop and became a popular place for locals and tourists alike to visit, gossip and shop.

Tourists were keen to purchase the items she sold there, and in order to find more traditional crafts, Dr Gahan visited

Heinz Edgar Kiewe's theory

Kiewe based his assumptions on pictures from the *Book of Kells*, where he spotted a small picture of Daniel wearing what he interpreted as a *bainin* sweater (a sweater made from a specific type of yarn) and a pair of Aran stockings. He attributed the stitch patterns on Daniel's garments to those motifs found on Celtic crosses and stones, surmising that the people of the Aran Islands must have been inspired by these motifs, incorporating them into their knitting from the time the stones were created. He linked many of the patterns to a religious theme; he saw Trinity Stitch as a symbol of the Father, Son and Holy Ghost, the Tree of Life as representing growth, and Ladder stitch as a depiction of Jacob's ladder linking Earth to Heaven. He explained that the interlinking motifs were associated with the linking of man to God. He had no proof for these theories, and simply asserted that they were more than likely true.

HISTORY 17

the Aran Islands in 1935. Through her friend Elizabeth Rivers, an artist who lived on Inishmore, she was put in touch with the knitters in the area and started to buy their unusually decorative sweaters from them. These were the first Aran handknits to go on sale and one of them, displayed in the window of her shop, was spotted by Heinz Edgar Kiewe, a self-styled 'professor of textile history'. He wrote a paper on his findings in 1966.

Heinz Edgar Kiewe, a man more interested in myth and folklore than in establishing facts through primary sources, owned a wool shop, the Art Needlework Industries in Oxford. Even though he did not present his 'facts' as documented evidence, he promoted himself as an expert in the history of textiles. He surmised that knitters were working Aran patterns more than 2,000 years ago. His book *The Sacred History of Knitting*, which he published in the 1930s, helped to promote the myths and romantic notions of Aran stitches and what he felt was their ancient history. Many of these myths have continued to this day, especially those concerning the ancient clan stitches that supposedly belong to the different families in Ireland. But, as we know now, Aran knitting is not an ancient tradition; it began at the end of the nineteenth century in a bid to relieve the hardship of the poorest families on the islands. The Celtic lands have long been areas of myth and mystery, especially when they are islands! Consequently, there are lots of myths about the origins of Aran knitting and its various motifs.

The use of Celtic knot work decoration was widespread in illuminated religious manuscripts in the seventh and eighth centuries, especially in their carpet pages, which were the full-page illustrations at the beginning of each chapter. Amongst the scrolls and motifs are depictions of fantastic creatures filled with highly decorative motifs, which is where Kiewe claimed to have seen evidence of Aran knitting. All kinds of beasts and artefacts were ornamented with it. But the original Aran sweaters had no such intertwining designs; their decorative stitches were composed of vertical lines and stitches, many of which imitated the shapes of the motifs found on the fishermen's ganseys. The 1936 sweater that Kiewe saw has a panel of diamonds created in simple moss stitch, but there are no outlining travelling stitches alongside it.

The Origins of the Aran Sweater

Before around the middle of the nineteenth century you would not have seen anyone on the three Aran Islands wearing what we would now recognize as an Aran sweater. They were more likely to be wearing the type of basic gansey pullover described above, found in the fishing communities around the North Sea.

Knitted sweaters of any kind were not originally part of Aran native dress, as most clothing was made from woven flannel. Samuel Lewis, a publisher of topographical dictionaries, including one for Ireland published in 1842, made no mention of a special type of knitting on the Aran Islands. Like the writer, J. M. Synge, who had a keen interest in customs and folklore, he also noted that some of the younger men were beginning to adopt 'the usual fishermen's jersey' (the gansey, or *geansai* in Ireland) common around British

Typical cable patterns found on fishermen's ganseys around the British Isles.

and Scottish coasts at the time. This is strong evidence that these garments were well known on the Aran Islands.

Synge, and other visitors to the Islands interested in the folklore and customs, took photographs of the people of the West of Ireland and the Aran Isles. Many of the photographs taken by Synge and Alfred Cort Haddon are now kept at Trinity College Dublin, and some of them show Aran men dressed in their navy blue ganseys. A photograph of four Aran men taken in 1910 purports to show that these are examples of sweaters handknitted by the women of the islands. However, on close examination of the photographs, I am sure they are the commercially produced machine-knitted ganseys made by contract knitters in England. I have examined examples of these machine-made ganseys in the museums in Cromer and Sheringham and they are identical. The fact that three of those in the photograph are all identical to each other also proves the case to me.

However, it is undoubtedly true that some skilled women would be able to work cable patterns by hand, and we have Mavis Clark's recollections to show that this was so. The knitters would increase their repertoire of stitches by copying patterns seen on the ganseys of the boat builders and the women who came with them from England and Scotland to share their skills and stimulate the local fishing industry. This is the strongest evidence to me that the patterns on Aran sweaters originated from the navy blue knitwear already

Photograph of Aran men in their ganseys, taken by J. M. Synge in 1910. Reproduced with kind permission of Trinity College Dublin.

A machine-knitted sweater in Sheringham Museum. With thanks to Ron Wiebe.

The Irish gansey made by Mavis Clark from memory of her grandmother's pattern..

popular among fishermen from Britain, the Channel Islands and across the North Sea.

Mavis Clark, a fellow member of the Knitting & Crochet Guild who spent the 1940s in the West of Ireland, which is very similar in geological and social terms to the Aran Islands, told me of her aunt, born and bred in Ireland, who had been knitting the familiar cabled yoke pattern on these ganseys since her mother passed it down to her at the beginning of the twentieth century. The photograph shows a reproduction of this pattern that Mavis knitted for the Guild.

The pattern set-up is:
Row 1: K2, p2, k2, c4 forward and repeat.
Row 2: P2, k2, p2, p4 and repeat.
Row 3: P2, k2, p2, k4 and repeat.
Row 4: K2, p2, k2, p4 and repeat.

A Description of Life in North Mayo in the 1940s, by Mavis Clark

There was no tarmacadam roads only drovers' roads, horses and traps or sidecars were few, but some families had them. The only cars was the Doctor and the Postman. So apart from being a bit of a shock to us, it was probably the best survival kit we could ever have had.

We walked to school, four miles of track along the Atlantic coast and carried turf with us to keep the classroom fire burning during the day and a piece [snack] for lunch. It was a convent state school and very minimalistic. Slates to write on instead of exercise books. We were dressed in everything home-made, a tweed skirt, knitted knee length socks and some knitted underwear and a gansey or froke [another name for a sweater].

When June came the sheep were all sheared by hand – fleeces selected by Granny and laid out on the stone dykes in all weathers to bleach.

Galway sheep, descendents of the native sheep of the Aran islands.

It was then teased out by us children, carded by my Aunt with paddle carders and spun by Granny on her spinning wheel. This took several weeks, but she would have spun enough to weave on a Heddle type loom and this would be sent to a tailor to make specific items of clothing and while this was being done Aunt would have got the knitting needles out and started on a round of oiled wool socks, stockings, frokes, jumpers or ganseys what ever was needed. Aunt had no knitting patterns, she made it up as she went along.

Mavis' grandfather was a Blackface Sheep farmer. These sheep are similar to the Galway sheep bred on the Aran Islands now. They are a hardy breed and can be sustained on poor soil.

Like Mavis' aunt, most of the knitters on the Islands would make up their own patterns; they were already skilled at devising stitches and understood how to make the cables turn in different directions.

Cables were a popular feature of working sweaters; since the 1600s they had been used on socks and stockings, perhaps inspired by those seen on visitors from other parts of the world; cables and travelling stitches were a familiar design on Austrian and German woollen goods. Such stitches could also be produced on a knitting machine, and most of the ganseys produced commercially featured such patterns as those seen in many of Synge's photographs.

But these commercially produced garments were more expensive to buy and, where families kept their own sheep or could exchange other produce with neighbouring sheep farmers, the women of the Islands preferred to knit their

A pair of handknitted Aran socks in the Collection of the Knitting & Crochet Guild, with lovely 6-stitch rope cables at the cuffs.

This cream 'Aran' jumper only has patterning on the yoke, not all over as we associate with traditional Arans now. Note the buttons on the shoulders to enable it to go over a child's head more easily and less painfully.

own. Most of the farmers' wives on the Islands would own a spinning wheel, or they would at least have a close neighbour who did.

While they knitted practical garments for their own families, they could also subsidize their income by knitting socks and ganseys for sale. The patterns were passed on by word of mouth down the generations, so the knitters were already skilled in the working of cabled patterns on ganseys and sock tops. They worked without written instructions, using those stitch patterns that they knew by heart. Many women collected peat to bring home in baskets on their backs, knitting as they walked. Knitting is a skill that needs little equipment; it is a portable craft that can be carried out while doing other tasks. But checking a written pattern every few minutes would be tiresome and make multi-tasking like this difficult.

It is said that there was a tradition for young children to wear white sweaters, rather than the navy blue worn by their fathers, and that more intricate versions of them were worn for First Holy Communions or to Mass on Sundays. But although there are pictures of children in cream or white sweaters, no one has seen photographic evidence of sweaters with the all-over patterning that we associate with Aran knits.

From the middle of the nineteenth century, instruction books for knitting were being widely published in Britain for use in the knitting schools as well as by individuals. They included line-drawn illustrations, which were sometimes a little more fanciful than the actual stitches. Most of these books had descriptions of how to work crossed stitches.

In 1881 *The Lady's Knitting* book described the working of a cable thus: 'Take the next 2 stitches on a third needle, and keep them on the right side of your knitting, knit the next 2 stitches, and then knit off the 2 on the third needle.'

Workers with the Congested Districts Board trained knitters to create complex patterns from these stitches, and instead of the fine, dark-coloured wools traditionally used to make fishermen's jerseys, the Islanders experimented with soft, thick, undyed yarn, known as *bainin* (pronounced 'Baw neen' and meaning small white), which has a high lanolin content, making them warm even when wet. This thicker wool was knitted on bigger needles, so it was much quicker

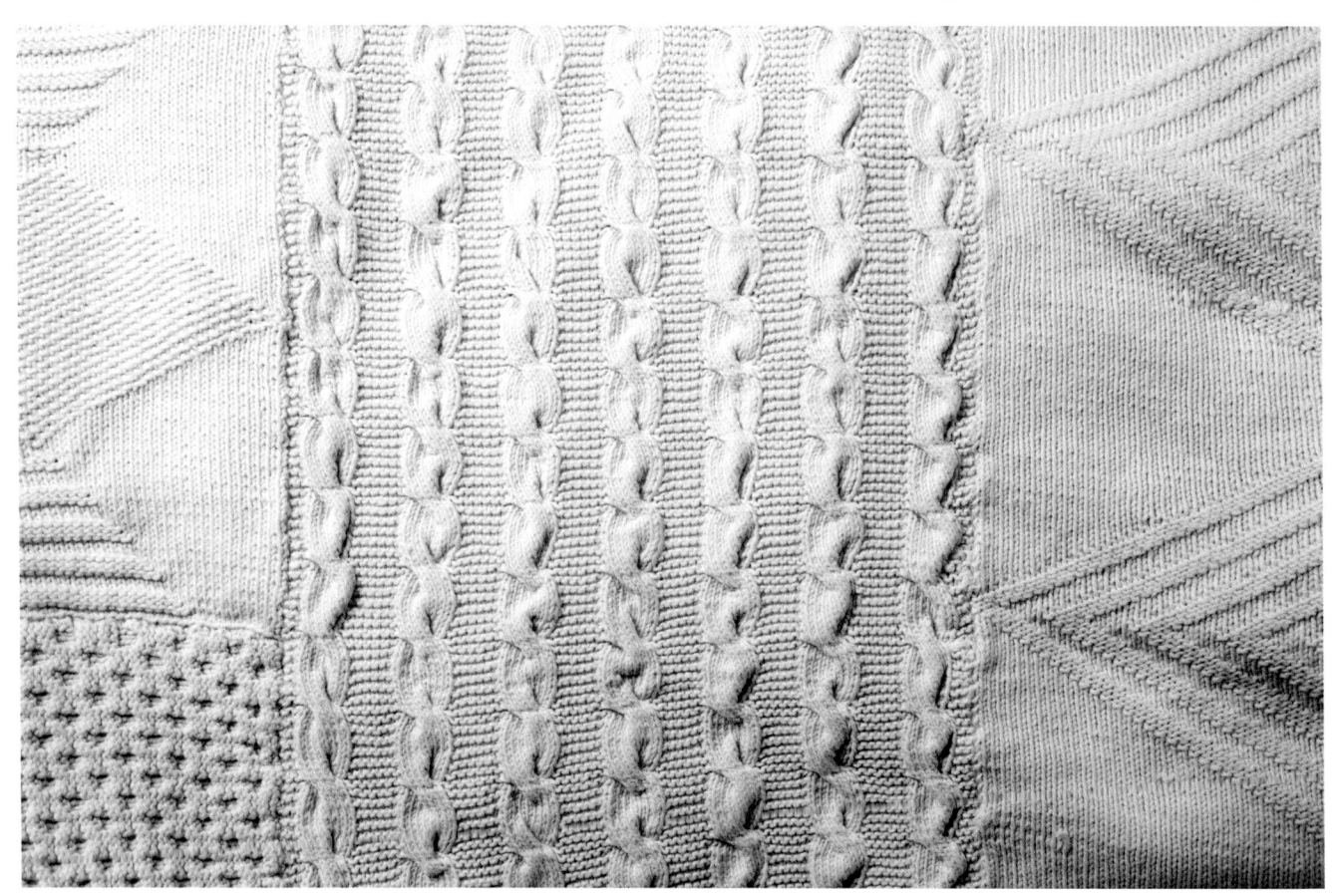

A section of a blanket with an unusual central panel of cable stitches. Reproduced with kind permission of the Knitting & Crochet Guild.

Close-up of moss stitch diamond motifs on white gansey.

to produce a garment – an important consideration when making multiple items for sale.

As they could already create various cables from the familiar patterns that they used on stocking tops and blankets, they were quickly able to learn other patterns, such as zigzags and honeycombs, by crossing the stitches in a different direction. It would not be too huge a step to devise a diamond pattern from a zigzag, or a braid from a rope-like cable. Diamond patterns in purl stitches were already familiar to them from their ganseys, and the shapes and stitch counts could be translated into knit stitches moving across a purl background instead of purl stitches on a knit background.

There is a suggestion that many of the stitch patterns came via Germany through the USA. A Bavarian lady living in New York taught some of the more complex crossing stitches to Margaret Dirrane, who had emigrated to America in 1900. But Margaret did not return to Ireland until 1908, by which time the Congested Districts Board had already begun its knitting programme and many women had surely begun to 'invent' their own stitches. However, the similarity between the diamond shapes of 'clocks' on German socks makes me think that perhaps there is some truth to this version. There are also similarities between Aran stitch designs and those of the Tyrolean cardigans with their diamonds and bobbles, but, so far, no one has come up with a story of an Austrian woman visiting Ireland in one of her colourful embroidered cardigans.

The Island women were keen to take up this means of generating a welcome addition to their income and, as all knitters know, liked to compete with one another to produce something no one had seen before. Island peoples tend to be inventive through necessity, so it would not be surprising

Pattern for a Tyrolean-style cardigan from the 1950s.

A typical Celtic motif.

if some of the women of Aran were able to produce different cables and arrangements of patterns out of their heads. Muriel Gahan encouraged them to experiment continually with these intricate stitches. She recognized their talent

This sweater from Kilmurvey has a side panel of garter stitch incorporating stitch increases. Reproduced with kind permission of the Knitting & Crochet Guild.

and bought the finished garments from them to sell in her shop. No doubt, this economic incentive encouraged them to experiment with even more elaborate stitches as they competed with one another to produce a new design. There was an increase in tourism to Ireland in the latter half of the 1930s and these unusual sweaters were seen as very desirable to take back home. The Arts and Crafts Movement during the nineteenth and early twentieth centuries, with its utilization of Irish Celtic motifs and designs, had encouraged the fashion for such handicrafts, especially those seen as coming from the more 'remote' regions. Irish Celtic motifs were familiar on all kinds of products. Influenced by John Ruskin and William Morris, people were beginning to appreciate the work of craftsmen.

The navy blue ganseys that the women were used to making were always knitted in the round. Some of the early Aran sweaters could well have been knitted in this way too. A lot of the early photos show patterns with twisted stitches, that is, formed by knitting into the back of the stitch. This technique is more awkward to make on a purl stitch, but just as quick to achieve in a knit stitch as knitting it into the front of the stitch. This does make

An Aran sweater with underarm gussets. Reproduced with kind permission of the Knitting & Crochet Guild.

24 HISTORY

A 1950s pattern for a pair of identical Arans.

An example of the type of patterns produced in the 1950s.

me think that perhaps they were knitted on four or five needles in the round to begin with. Several of the early Aran sweaters donated to Dublin Museum have the typical square shape of a gansey. Some are knitted in the round with underarm gussets, saddle shoulders and with sleeves knitted downwards from a straight armhole. Some have increases along the sides of the back and front.

Later on, sweaters were designed with shaped armholes to accord with the fashion of the time for more tailored garments and, be it set-in sleeve or raglan, it would be more awkward to knit these in the round than knitting them flat, in pieces, which is now the technique used almost universally. Garments knitted in pieces could also be worked by more than one person. Perhaps the children would knit the less intricate sleeves while their mothers worked the back and front; children could certainly knit the ribs, and children as young as five are recorded as helping with the knitting.

> While knitting an Aran sweater in the round seems unusual, there is no reason why you couldn't design a seamless sweater for yourself. You could even try knitting one top-down, but remember to choose stitch patterns that will work in the reverse direction!

As these intricately cabled sweaters began to be seen more frequently outside Ireland, some of the spinning companies took notice, and in the 1940s the first Aran knitting patterns

An example of the type of patterns produced from the 1960s onwards.

were published by Patons of Alloa. This company claims to still have a garment knitted from one of these patterns and a picture of it was published by them in 1955. Other companies also took an interest in these unusual stitch patterns and there was a proliferation of Aran knitting patterns in the 1950s, some of which can be seen in these photographs. With the lifting of wool rationing in the 1950s, most of the British wool spinners began producing patterns for Aran sweaters and cardigans for all the family and there was a proliferation

A poster advertising the film Alive and Kicking *showing a number of different Aran sweaters and featuring the pattern for the main illustration on the back.*

of Aran knitting patterns in the 1950s. It must have been a pleasure to knit without wondering if your meagre amount of wool would stretch to complete a sweater! In 1956 the American magazine *Vogue* also published patterns for men's and women's Aran sweaters. Marriner's Yarns of Keighley liked the association of their family name with the sea through the development of Aran patterns. However, there is no evidence that Aran sweaters were ever worn by sea fishermen. They would surely be too bulky and much more difficult to repair than the plain navy blue ganseys, should they become snagged and torn.

Like Muriel Gahan, other people also sought to promote the sale of Aran knits. In the 1950s Padraig Augustine O'Síocháin, a journalist with *The Irish Times*, bought a business called Galway Bay Products Ltd with a view to marketing the handknits of the Aran Islands. He persuaded the knitters to cut down on the number of stitch motifs that they used, and to make the garments more commercially acceptable by following the shape of the current fashion and keeping to standard sizes. He was a skilful businessman and may well have introduced the notion of 'clan patterns' and meanings for the different stitches as a way of increasing demand for his products. He also promoted the oft-repeated myth of using the patterns to identify fishermen lost at sea.

The demand for Aran knitwear grew significantly and the sweaters were exported all over the world. All over Ireland knitters began producing garments for men, women, children and babies – everything they could think of featuring the traditional Aran patterns.

The desirability of Aran sweaters quickly spread throughout America by courtesy of The Clancy Brothers, a quartet of Irish musicians. They wore Aran sweaters for their appearance on the *Ed Sullivan Show* in the early 1960s and they and their sweaters became a huge hit with a TV audience of over 80 million. Similar sweaters were soon being worn by such stars as Steve McQueen and Grace Kelly, and their sudden fame drove an increase in demand around the world. In addition, a film titled *Alive and Kicking*, starring Sybil Thorndike and Stanley Holloway, was made in 1959. It was set on the Aran Islands and featured lots of Aran knitwear.

At the same time, Gladys Thompson was researching fishermen's ganseys for her book *Guernsey and Jersey Patterns*. She was concerned that these patterns would be lost if they were not written down. She travelled to Dublin in 1954 to examine the sweaters held in the museum there. While there, she saw a collection of Aran sweaters that she felt should also be documented. So the book became *Patterns for Guernseys, Jerseys and Arans* when it was published in 1955. Its subtitle included the words 'fishermen's sweaters', which may be how Arans came to be associated with the sea.

The growth in their popularity of Aran knits was so rapid that the knitters of the Islands were unable to keep up with demand, so skilled knitters of Scotland were recruited to help fill in the gap. This increased the popularity of Aran knits in that country too, and they are now often associated with Scotland as well as Ireland. Aran patterned socks, especially, are frequently worn with the kilt nowadays and are known as Scottish kilt hose.

Because crossing the stitches and using thicker wool make a garment that is denser, therefore warm and relatively windproof, Aran sweaters quickly became popular as

A selection of Aran sweaters.

sportswear. Commercial patterns frequently picture them being worn by models carrying a fishing rod or standing in a boat. This ties in with the myth of the drowned Aran Island fisherman being recognized by the patterns on his sweater, which still persists among those who write popular articles about Aran knitting, as it does in tales of the gansey.

Many customers may have bought a particular decorative Aran sweater because they thought that its pattern was associated with their family name. But, as we know, these garments were not made on the Aran Islands until the beginning of the twentieth century, and any of the ancient stories surrounding them are fiction, quite possibly made up by the knitters, who were expert spinners of tales as well as of wool.

Today, hundreds of Aran sweaters are made on the Aran Islands and the mainland. A lot of them are hand-tooled on knitting machines, but are still labelled as handmade. They are readily sold through the supposed meanings attached to their stitch patterns, or to the alleged connections with family names. The reason that these myths still persist is due to marketing and 'blarney'. Aran knitwear is a staple item of trade in the Irish tourist industry, and if interesting stories can be attached to any aspect of it, it's sale potential is increased. But, as knitters ourselves, we can be sure that Aran stitches were created, not to convey any meaning or to identify a particular clan or family, but by inventive and skilful knitters who were interested to see what would happen if... New ways of crossing stitches were tried because they made an attractive, and therefore more marketable, pattern.

Even though Aran knitting may have these fanciful tales attached to it, I hope you will enjoy reading its history, and use the instructions in this book to help you create a unique and personal Aran sweater that you or your family will be pleased to wear for many a year.

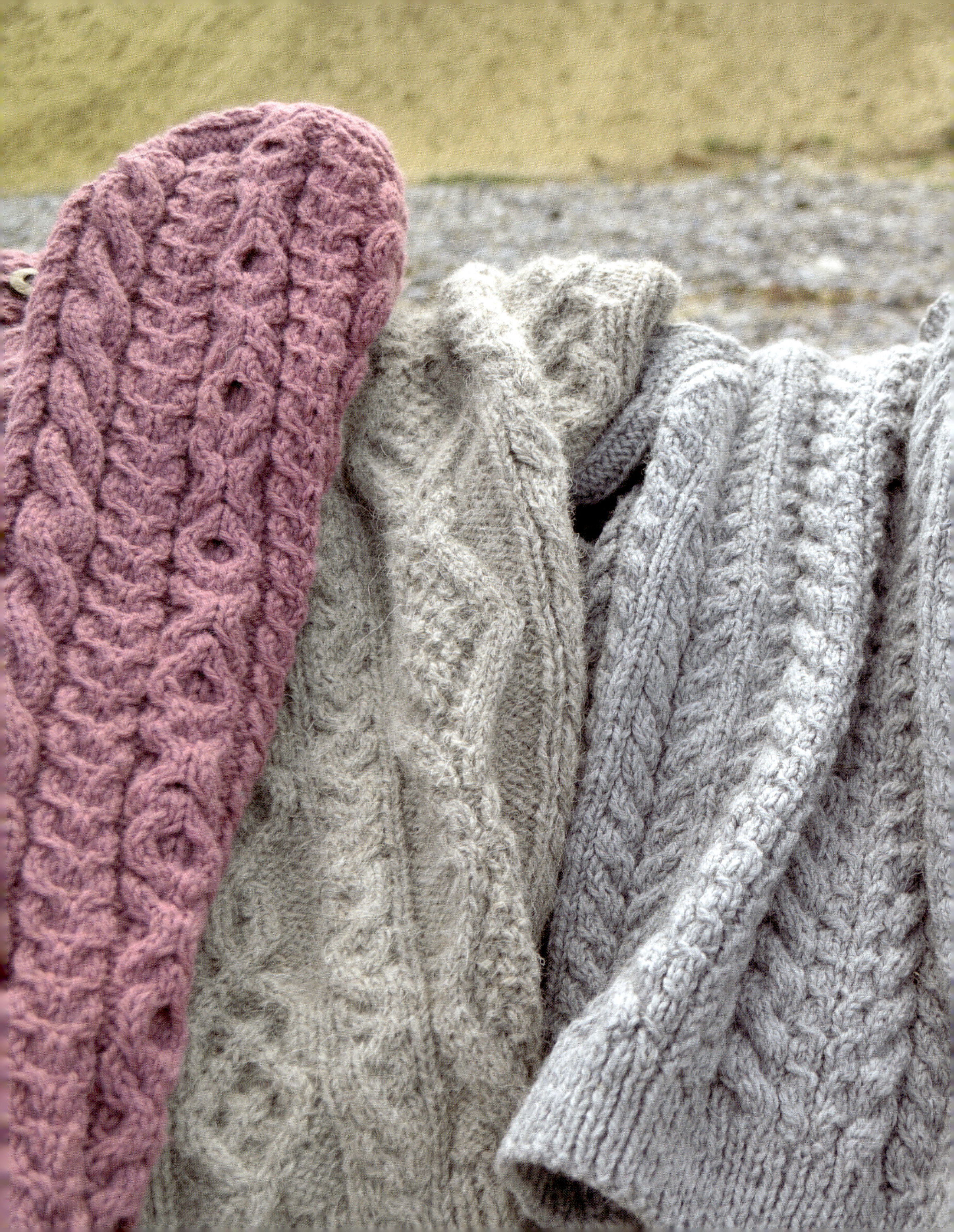

CHAPTER 2

MATERIALS AND EQUIPMENT

Yarn

There are far more yarns and fibres available now than there were one hundred or more years ago. But this wonderful richness and diversity can cause problems for the first-time Aran knitter. Cabled motifs can be worked with any yarn, but not all yarn produces a satisfactory appearance, as can be seen from the samples in this chapter. Consider the different characteristics of the yarn you would like to use, including its thickness (also known as weight), texture, colour, fibre and handle. Do not choose textured or fluffy yarns for an Aran knit or the intricacy of the cables will disappear. Also think about its aftercare. Most wool yarns are best handwashed, although some labelled 'superwash' can be washed in the washing machine. Synthetics can be machine-washed, but frequently become shapeless as a result. You might also want to consider the environmental impact of some yarns. Superwash wool is coated with plastic, and manufacturing cotton yarn, for example, requires the use of many pesticides.

In my opinion, the best yarn for an Aran knit is wool; it is warm, moisture-absorbent, fire-resistant and hard-wearing, yet, some the yarn produced from some breeds is surprisingly soft. Wool is also much more elastic than most other knitting yarns, making it ideally suited to patterns where the stitches are pulled in different directions.

OPPOSITE PAGE: *A selection of swatches.*

A basket of different Aran wools.

Chenille – a variegated polyester and rayon yarn. The design is completely lost in this multicoloured, soft yarn.

Variegated yarn – an Australian yarn made from a mixture of 70 per cent bamboo and 30 per cent cotton. As well as disguising the cables visually, this yarn also tends to flatten them out.

Mohair – the difficulty with locating the individual stitches with this yarn makes it awkward to work cables, never mind the fact that they have no depth and disappear into the fibres.

Beaded yarn – the cables show up well here but, depending on the amount of cables, the beads would make for an overdecorated garment.

While Arans were traditionally knitted in white or cream, there are more colours available these days. However, the patterns show up best in lighter colours, as can be seen in the various samples throughout book. If you are working your first Aran, it is also probably best to choose one of the lighter coloured yarns so that you can see the stitches clearly as you are working.

Apart from these examples, all of the other swatches and items in this book were knitted with wool.

These swatches are all knitted to the same patern on 4.5mm needles.

> In addition to working with ligher coloured yarn, choose a spot where you can sit comfortably and work in a good light too. This will help you to concentrate on working unfamiliar stitches.

30 MATERIALS AND EQUIPMENT

Another yarn in which the cables are lost amongst the hairiness.

Cotton – the stitches are well defined but the yarn is inelastic and loses its shape.

A loosely spun yarn that needs more concentration when working crossed stitches.

Woollen spun – the finished product looks good, but because the yarn is loosely spun, it is easy to split the stitches when working cables.

How Yarn Is Processed

Woollen v Worsted

There are two ways of constructing a yarn for knitting; they are known as woollen spun and worsted spun. Woollen-spun yarns are light and airy as well as being a little bit hairy! Worsted-spun yarns are firmer, denser and stronger, so making them ideally suited to Aran knitting. However, because worsted-spun yarn is denser than woollen-spun yarn, it has fewer metres per gram, and so more worsted-spun yarn than woollen-spun yarn is required to make the same garment.

Woollen-spun yarns are made from short fibres, but not necessarily sheep wool – they could be plant fibres or wool from other animals. Worsted-spun yarns are made from long fibres that are combed before being spun. This combing makes the fibres lie in one direction, parallel to one another, and removes any short, coarser fibres and bits of vegetation. Worsted-spun yarns are spun more tightly, with extra twist, which makes them smoother, firmer and more lustrous. Woollen-spun yarns, on the other hand, are carded back and forth, which makes the fibres lie in all directions. They are

MATERIALS AND EQUIPMENT 31

Aran cardigan, worn open for a more casual look.

Tweed – The tweed yarn above, is perhaps a little too dark to show the stitches to best advantage, but some lighter tweed and flecked yarns work well with Aran stitches.

spun lightly to preserve the bounciness and elasticity of the yarn. They look plumper than worsted-spun wool and feel lighter, but because they are not spun tightly, they can pill and break easily. Another interesting difference is that, while you will get the same number of stitches to the inch, worsted-spun yarns will need fewer rows to achieve the same tension! This can matter in Aran knitting where you want the pattern to end at a specific point, although this is not an issue if you are working in stocking stitch or garter stitch, for example.

The yarns best suited to Aran knits are those that are twisted tightly together, although not so tight that they form a crepe yarn.

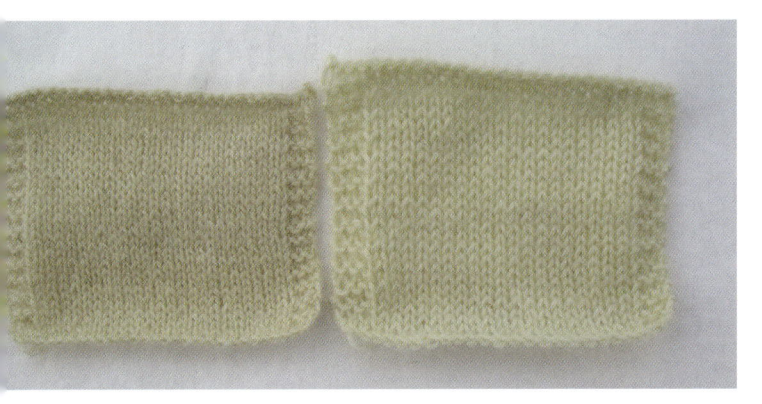

Woollen spun is on the left and worsted spun on the right.

Boreray and Southdown wool. The Boreray yarn is a much more 'whiskery' yarn, more akin to that used to make the early Arans. The Southdown yarn is much smoother.

Thickness

Arans are traditionally made with what is known as 'Aran weight' yarn. This approximates to 2 strands of 4 ply twisted together. But what does 'ply' mean? Most knitting yarns consist of two strands of spun yarn twisted together in the opposite direction to that in which they were first spun. This makes a 2 ply yarn that can be any thickness, depending on the diameter of the original spun thread. Spinning more strands together gives a thicker yarn, which will also have a rounder and loftier appearance. Aran weight yarn is usually made from between 8 and 10 plied strands, which is why it is known in some countries as 10 ply. The more plies there are, the stronger and smoother the yarn becomes, which makes it ideal to use for projects that need good definition in the stitch pattern.

However, simply because a yarn is called Aran weight does not necessarily mean that it will be interchangeable with another maker's Aran yarn. Do not think that 8 balls of one Aran weight yarn will equate to 8 balls of another make: the wool of one breed of sheep may not have the same density as that of another. A mix of wool with another fibre will also make a difference. There will probably be considerably more metres of yarn in 50 grams of a wool/acrylic mix than in 50 grams of pure Southdown. A totally synthetic yarn will have even more metres than either of these. Remember the question you were once asked in school: 'Which weighs more, a pound of feathers or a pound of lead?' Always check and compare the yardage per gram, which should be stated on the ball band.

Originally, the sweaters made on the Aran Islands would use yarn from the local sheep that were farmed there. This was much more coarse and 'whiskery' than we would like now. It was also unscoured, which gave it a degree of waterproofing.

Some Suitable Sheep Breeds

Different breeds of sheep will produce wool with different characteristics. Not all wools are good for Aran knitting and while worsted-spun yarns give the best stitch definition because of their smoothness, some sheep breeds produce wool that is just as good whether worsted spun or woollen spun.

Blue-Faced Leicester

This wool has become very popular as it is soft and semi-lustrous while also hard-wearing. It has very good stitch definition, so is ideal for any textured knits.

Galway

This is said to be the true Irish sheep. It is a white sheep, classed as a longwool, but does not have the lustre of a Wensleydale, for example. It is ideal for Aran knitting as it gives good stitch definition.

Jacob

Jacob sheep are an old, black and white breed. Their worsted-spun wool is ideal for textured knits, although some of the darker colours can be a bit coarse.

Some Southdown sheep, showing how thick and curled their fleeces are.

Modern Galway sheep, photographed in Galway where the terrain is similar to that of the Aran islands.

A Southdown ewe with her lambs.

Shetland

Shetland sheep vary in colour from creamy white to brown. Their fleece is non-lustrous and can be spun very finely. The yarn produced from it is soft and silky, and while it can be used for Aran knitting, it is not ideal for textured stitches.

Southdown

These sheep are white, producing a low-lustre yarn that gives a more matt appearance to the finished knitwear. It is smooth, light and springy, making it warm, so ideal for outdoor garments. These sheep have short-hair fleeces, so are not as good for worsted-spun yarn, but the lack of hairs in the wool means the yarn produced from it gives very good stitch definition.

Other fibres

Alpaca

Alpaca yarn does not contain lanolin, which can cause allergies in some people. It is also soft, lightweight and not itchy. But it is not as elastic as sheep's wool, which can make working some of the wider cable stitches difficult. However, it can be blended with wool and is then ideal for textured items.

Cashmere

Cashmere is extremely soft and warm for its light weight. It is not as elastic as wool and is not very durable, so is probably not a good choice for an outer garment, although it could be used for a cabled beanie.

Cotton

For summer wear, cotton would seem like the ideal choice, but the density of cotton makes a cabled garment made in it much heavier than one made in wool. It is also inelastic and has a tendency to droop when it is worn. However, a mixture of wool and cotton retains the elasticity of wool, while the cotton makes for a cooler fabric.

Silk

This is a much stronger fibre than it would first appear to be, although it can easily be damaged by sunlight. It has some elasticity, though not as much as wool, and is resistant to pilling. When combined with wool, it gives the yarn an interesting lustre that can be an advantage in textured garments.

Synthetic Yarns

These are made from various polymers which are first turned into liquid and then chemically thickened so that they can be spun into yarn. The variety of polymer used affects the characteristics of the yarn, but most of them are non-absorbent, resist felting and moth damage, and feel light and soft. However, most synthetic yarns have the disadvantage that they are not as elastic as wool and will stretch, especially after washing, thereby flattening out any textured stitches.

Needles

Knitting needles are now made in a wide variety of types, lengths, shapes and materials. The choice of which to use is a matter of personal preference, but these notes may help you to decide which are best for your purpose. Generally, needles with sharp points are good for lifting stitches to work cables and crossings, but sharp points can also split stitches, causing problems with counting. Needles that have some flexibility are more comfortable to use when working lots of crossing stitches.

Cable Needles

Cable needles are used to hold the stitches that are to be worked out of sequence, that is after those on the knitting needle. They should be the same diameter as, or slightly smaller than, the needles you are using to knit the garment. If you use a larger size cable needle, hoping that it will grip the stitches better, you could distort them. Like knitting needles, cable needles also come in various materials and in different shapes: straight like a double-pointed needle, with a kink in the middle or shaped like a letter J on its side. The shaped ones are useful where you are crossing a lot of stitches, as stitches are less likely to slip off.

Some essential knitting equipment.

Knitting Needle Size Conversion Table

MM	Old UK	US
2	14	0
2.25	13	1
2.75	12	2
3	11	-
3.25	10	3
3.5	–	4
3.75	9	5
4	8	6
4.5	7	7
5	6	8
5.5	5	9
6	4	10
6.5	3	10.5
7	2	–
7.5	1	–
8	0	11
9	00	13
10	000	15
12	–	17
16	–	19
20	–	36
25	–	50

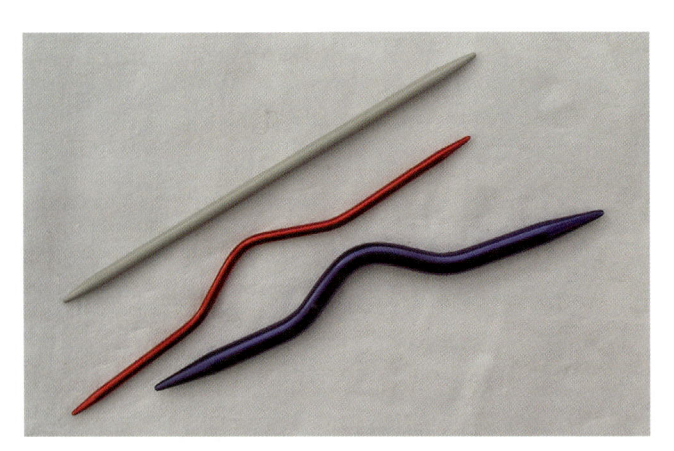

A set of differently shaped cable needles.

A selection of stitch markers.

Are Cable Needles Really Necessary?

It is possible to work cables without slipping them on to a cable needle, but this is not recommended for large numbers of crossing stitches, as some of them can begin to unravel.

There are two ways of holding the stitches: the first one involves grasping the stitches firmly with your fingers. The second leaves stitches already worked on the needles.

First Way

For example, when crossing a 4-stitch cable to the left:

Step 1: Remove 2 sts with the point of the right needle and pinch them between finger and thumb.

Step 2: Knit 2 stitches on the left needle.

Step 3: Slip the point of the left needle back through the 2 stitches you are holding and knit them onto the right needle.

Second Way

Step 1: Knit the 3rd stitch from the left needle and keep it on the needle.

Step 2: Manoeuvre the needle so that it will enter the 4th stitch on the left needle without dropping the stitch you have just worked.

Step 3: Knit the 4th stitch and move the two knitted stitches onto the right needle.

Step 4: Knit 2 stitches on the left needle.

There are some useful videos and pictures available on the Internet that will give you a clearer picture of how the above methods work.

Stitch Markers

There are two kinds of stitch markers: split ring and closed ring.

Closed-ring stitch markers slip on to the needles where you need to mark a place in the row, although you could use split-ring makers or lengths of contrasting coloured yarn in the same way. Some of the closed-ring markers are very attractive, but take care that they are not so ornate that they snag the yarn.

Split-ring markers are useful for placing at the beginning of a row where you need to make a crossing in a cable. It is then easy to count how many rows you have worked after the marker before making the next crossing.

I find stitch markers essential for Aran knitting. They are used to mark the beginning and end of each pattern panel, making it easy to keep track of the change of motif between the filler stitches.

They can also be used to mark the start of a round when working in the round on circular needles. You can also use them to keep count of the number of stitches on your needles; for example, after every 10 stitches you can add a marker to make it easier to keep count.

Use split-ring markers to mark individual stitches or rows: for example, the first and last row of a stitch pattern. We hope it won't happen, but they can also be used to hold a dropped stitch until you have time to repair it!

Swatches

Perhaps the most important tool for designing an Aran. They are essential when designing any piece of knitting, but even more so for an Aran design. Different stitches behave in different ways. Rope cables pull in more when they cross every 4th row than they do at less frequent intervals. They also pull in more when worked side by side, and more than in diamond shapes or twisted stitches where only two stitches cross each other.

Make your swatches large enough. If they are to be used for working out your tension, make them long enough so that you have relaxed into the knitting process as you make them; the tension in the first few rows will not be the same as in those at the end. Also, make the swatches wide enough; working one repeat of a cable won't show how it behaves when used several times across a piece of knitting. A different tension will be created when joining several diamonds together, with or without a cabled crossing, than when they are used alone. Some stitches, such as those where only one knit stitch is crossed, will not pull in much when worked in the body of a garment, but will do so when they are combined with purl stitches to work as a patterned rib. An example is the use of twisted cable rib for the cuffs and neckband of the ladies' cardigan in Chapter 5. It is the combination of 2 knit, 2 purl stitches that gives it the elasticity.

The start of the pattern on the saddle shouldered sweater with stitch markers between each of the motifs.

Tag attached to a knitted swatch with information on the type of yarn and the needles used.

Another way of counting the rows between crossings is to count the stitches from the back of the work. As can be seen from here, all of the stitches are displayed as stocking stitch.

Interlocking twist seen from the back, showing how it would be easier to count the stitches and rows from this side.

Sampler of different stitches and cables, showing how much they can vary in width over the same number of stitches.

MATERIALS AND EQUIPMENT 37

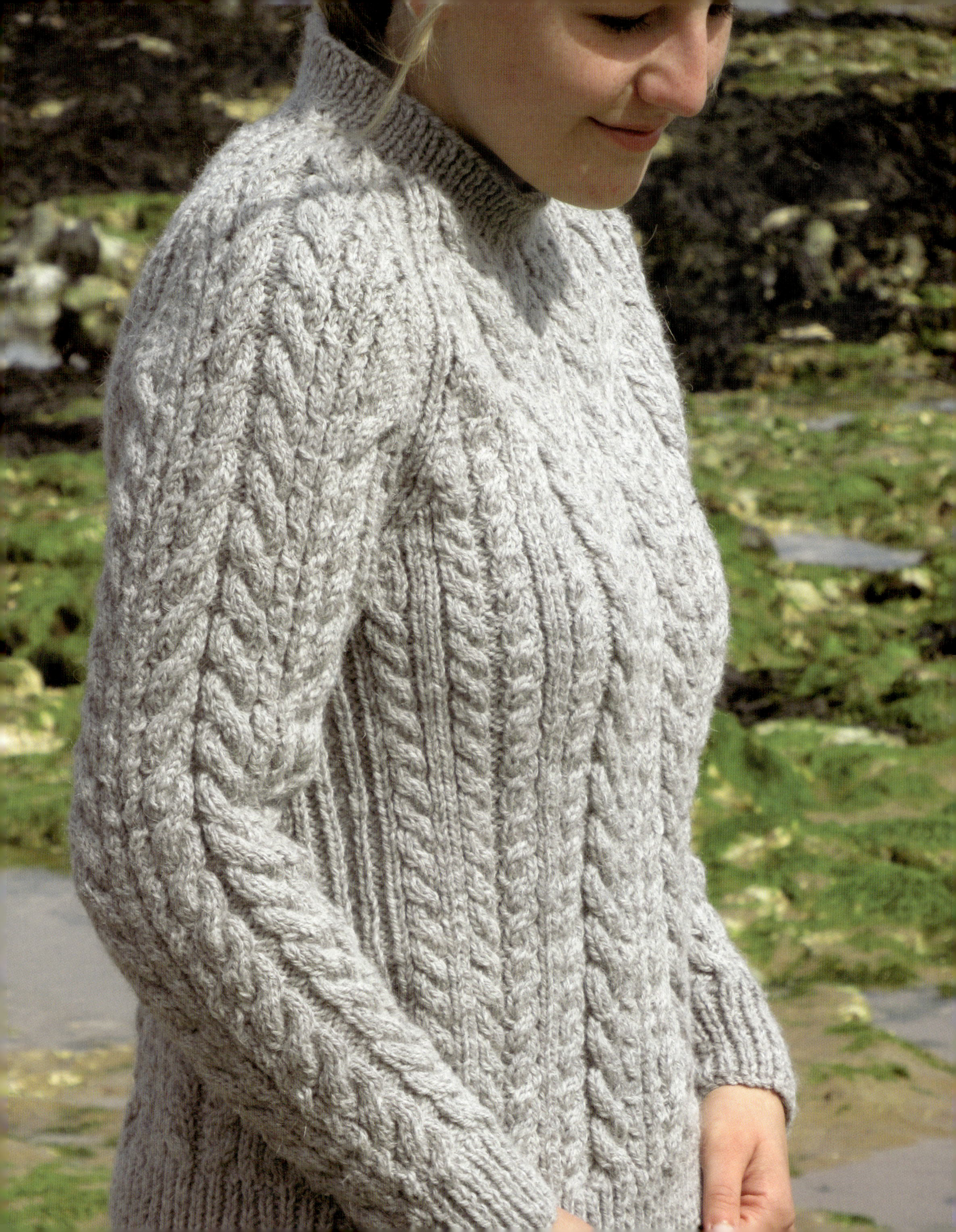

CHAPTER 3

STITCH DICTIONARY

There are hundreds of cable stitch patterns, and only a few of them are illustrated here. Those shown are the main stitches to be found in traditional Aran knits, plus a few of the 'newer' cable designs inspired by Viking and Celtic motifs.

While the overall design of a cabled garment looks complicated, the cables themselves are not difficult to do. They are all made up of the usual knit and purl stitches that you are so familiar with and are achieved by working one group of these stitches in a different order to the one in which it appears on the left needle. They can be all knit stitches, or a combination of knit and purl stitches. The latter may appear a little more intricate than if all of the stitches were knit stitches, but this usually only means moving the stitches more than once in the same group.

Most of the stitches depicted here follow the same method of working: two or more stitches in a group are crossed over each other by working the second set of stitches in the group before the first set. This makes the stitches appear to slope to the left or right. In order to do this, a third needle with points at each end, known as a cable needle, needs to be used. The first set of stitches are slipped onto the cable needle and held out of the way while the next set are worked. To make the stitches slope to the left, the stitches on the cable needle are held in front of the work while the next set of stitches are worked. To slope the stitches to the right, the stitches on the cable needle are held at the back of the work, behind the stitches that are knitted first. The stitches that are being held on the cable needle can now be knitted from the cable needle

OPPOSITE PAGE: *The raglan sleeved sweater showing the repeated cables.*

A mixture of knitted swatches.

or placed back onto the left needle before being worked according to the pattern. The following row is almost always worked as the stitches present themselves: that is, if the cabled stitches have been worked as knit stitches, they will be worked as purl stitches on the reverse side, and vice versa. Many cable patterns will be worked as knit stitches crossing knit stitches, but there are exceptions, usually in diamond-shaped patterns, where one set of stitches are knitted and another set are purled. The symbol for knit over knit is different to that for knit over purl, so be aware of this as you work through the charts.

Once you are familiar with these stitches, you will be able to work out how to alter and adapt them in order to create items of different sizes. For example, the diamond pattern on the cushion in Chapter 5 could be made smaller by reducing the number of stitches and rows in the panel before reversing the direction of the diamond. Similarly, it could be made even larger by increasing the number of stitches in that area. Many of the diamond patterns can be made more elaborate by placing cables above them before repeating the pattern, as can be seen in the panel on the Saddle Shouldered Sweater in Chapter 5. Their centres can also be filled with other stitches such as cables, smaller diamonds or, most familiarly, one of the various forms of moss stitch. Moss stitch fillers are especially attractive when the edge stitches of the piece are worked in the same version of moss stitch.

The swatches illustrated here were all knitted on wooden or bamboo needles – sometimes straight ones, sometimes interchangeables – but all were knitted with wool yarn. One or two of the swatches were knitted with a wool/silk mix and some of them with superwash wool.

Fillers and Spacers

These stitches, combinations of knit and purl, are very useful both for separating panels of cables and also for enlarging the size of a project without disrupting the pattern motifs. The most commonly used ones are variations on moss stitch, as shown in the following examples.

Moss Stitch (worked over an even number of stitches)

Row 1: *K1, p1; rep from * to end.
Row 2: *P1, k1; rep from * to end.

Moss Stitch (worked over an odd number of stitches)

Row 1: *K1, p1; rep from * to last st, k1.
Repeat this row.

Irish Moss Stitch (worked over an even number of stitches)

Row 1: *K1, p1; rep from * to end.
Row 2: *K1, p1; rep from * to end.
Row 3: *P1, k1; rep from * to end.
Row 4: *P1, k1; rep from * to end.

Double Moss Stitch (requires a multiple of 4 stitches)

Row 1: *K2, p2; rep from * to end.
Row 2: *K2, p2; rep from * to end.
Row 3: *P2, k2; rep from * to end.
Row 4: *P2, k2; rep from * to end.

Variations can be made by working 1 or 2 rows of stocking stitch between the pairs of rows, which will give what are known as broken rib patterns. Increasing the numbers of knit and purl stitches in each column gives a basketweave pattern, which is sometimes used for the central panel of a garment.

Basketweave

Basketweave patterns are simply blocks of knit and purl stitches, alternated after a few rows. A familiar example is shown below.

Row 1: *K6, p6; repeat from * to last 6 sts, k6.
Row 2: *P6, k6; repeat from * to last 6 sts, p6.
Rows 3–8: Repeat rows 1–2 three times.
Row 9: *P6, k6; repeat from * to last 6 sts, p6.
Row 10: *K6, p6; repeat from * to last 6 sts, k6.
Rows 11–16: Repeat rows 9–10 three times.
Repeat these 16 rows as often as needed.

Top left: broken rib; top right: staggered rib; bottom left: basketweave; bottom right: rice stitch.

Trinity Stitch

Another attractive stitch that can be used as a filler or a central panel is trinity stitch, also known as bramble stitch, blackberry stitch and even raspberry stitch. It is worked over a multiple of 4 stitches plus 2 edge stitches, with the pattern worked on the wrong side rows.

Row 1: Purl.
Row 2: K1, (k1, p1, k1) all into next stitch, p3tog, k1.
Row 3: Purl.
Row 4: K1, p3tog, (k1, p1, k1) all into next stitch, k1.
Repeat these 4 rows.

Trinity stitch, also known as bramble stitch, blackberry stitch and even raspberry stitch.

Choosing Stitches

When designing your Aran garment, try to keep the cable motifs in proportion to the finished size of the sweater or cardigan. A stitch such as double cross on a small sweater could overwhelm any of the other cables alongside it and look ungainly. For a child's garment, use some of the less intricate cables and perhaps work it in double knitting yarn instead of Aran weight yarn.

The system used here for describing how the cables are to be moved is based on a software program called Stitchmastery. There are other ways of describing the movement of cables with different abbreviations and symbols, but, to me, this one illustrates best whether the cables move to the left or the right, or whether you are crossing knit stitches over knit stitches or purl stitches. It is also easy to see what the finished motif will look like from the chart. At one time commercial patterns would print out the instructions for the cables in detail for each row. Row 1 of the ladies' cardigan in Chapter 5 would read:

Row 1 (RS): P2, k2, p2, C6F, p6, (k6, p4) twice, k6, p6, C4F, C4B, p4, K6, p4, C4F, C4B, p6, (k6, p4) twice, p6, C6B, p2, k2, p2.

Imagine every row being written out in this way! It is easy to lose your place among so many words and abbreviations. Being able to read a chart makes following a pattern so much easier. If you are not familiar with charts, practise working one of the rope patterns without reading the accompanying text.

C4B abbreviation

You may be more familiar with the abbreviation C4B, meaning cross 2 stitches over 2 stitches that have been left at the back. In Stitchmastery, this would be written as 2/2RC, meaning a 4-stitch cable that crosses 2 stitches over 2 others and slopes to the right. The old abbreviation Tw3F, meaning cross 2 of the 3 stitches to the right but keeping the one at the back as a purl stitch, now becomes 2/1LPC, and makes a cable where 2 knitted stitches are crossed to the left over 1 purl stitch. Tw3F is difficult to interpret without looking up its meaning each time, until you become familiar with it. However, 2/1LPC can esily be read as 2 stitches over 1 purl stitch crossing left.

Rope Cables

Rope cables are the simplest to work. They cover a fixed number of stitches with the crossings at intervals compatible with the number of stitches. The number of stitches in the cable usually corresponds to the number of rows between the points where the stitches cross, but changing the frequency of when the stitches cross gives a slightly different appearance to the cable. The cable will become more obvious and stand out more from the background the more frequently the crossing is repeated. In the past, rope cables were often worked over an odd number of stitches, with the greater number of stitches crossing over the lesser number. This was supposed to pull less on the top stitches, giving them a more even appearance. Nowadays they are usually worked over an even number of stitches, half of which are held on a cable needle while the others are worked.

The frequency with which the stitches cross over one another gives some variety to the ropes. A 4- stitch rope will usually cross every fourth row. This gives a cable that looks like a tightly twisted cord. Crossing the stitches at less frequent intervals makes a looser cable. For variety, the stitches could be crossed at different intervals in the same cable, first after four rows and then after six rows.

For most rope cables, all of the stitches will be knit stitches, but there are instances where half the stitches are knit stitches and half are worked in moss stitch, or some that are worked all in rib. Most of the cables illustrated in this book can be adapted to using different types of stitches and to different frequencies of crossings.

Working 6-stitch rope cables using a cable needle with twists to the left and right

- To make a 6-stitch rope cable that twists to the left, hold three of the stitches on a cable needle or double-pointed needle at the front of the work, knit the three stitches on the left needle, then return to the ones that were held on the cable needle and knit those.
- To make the rope cable twist to the right, hold three of the stitches to the back of the work, knit the three stitches on the left needle, then the ones that were held on the cable needle.

These two actions are used in virtually all cables.

All rope cables can be worked in either direction. Working a right-crossed rope alongside a left-crossed rope produces a different motif again. They can be worked directly next to one another or divided by a knit or purl stitch. The raglan sleeved round-neck sweater in Chapter 5 illustrates this and is a simple way of producing a complex-looking design.

Twisted Stitches

In some of the older Arans, all of the knit stitch twists were made by working into the back of the stitch. This gave the stitches a little more prominence, even more so if their purl sides were also worked into the back of the stitch, but that is a more tricky manoeuvre and not practised very often. The supposed 'fisherman's gansey' shown here may have been worked in the round in the manner of the early sweaters that the women would have been used to making. The stitches of the chain cable and the outline stitches of the diamond appear to have been worked into the backs of the stitches.

Plaited and Braided Cables

The next step on from a rope cable is a plaited cable. This is worked in exactly the same way as a rope cable but over alternate groups of stitches.

Working a 9-stitch plait

- Cross the first group of 6 stitches, then knit the next 3 stitches.
- Work 4 rows straight.
- Knit the first 3 stitches, then cross the next 6 stitches.
- Any number of stitches can be made into a plait using this technique.

Similar to plaited cables are braided cables, where the knit stitches are divided by one or a number of purl stitches. If two or more purl stitches are introduced, the crossings form a trellis-like pattern. The more purl stitches there are between the knit stitches, the wider the trellis pattern that is made.

Rope 4-stitch.

Incorporating twisted stitches as well as cables. Gladys Thompson, Patterns for Guernseys, Jerseys and Arans *(1955). Image of gansey on loan from Mrs Foreman, reproduced with kind permission of B. T. Batsford, part of Pavilion Books Company Limited.*

STITCH DICTIONARY 43

Medallions

If the crossed stitches of a rope cable are worked in alternate directions, first crossing to the left and then to the right, a pattern known as a snake, or wave cable is produced. If these snake cables are worked side by side with the crossings going in opposite directions on the same row, they will form what appears to be a circle. These are known as medallions. One of the most well known of these patterns is the variation known as the oxo cable, where stitches are crossed in the same direction twice before crossing in the opposite direction twice.

Several medallions joined side by side over a number of rows form the well-known honeycomb pattern, often used as the central panel of an Aran garment. Worked over an even number of stitches, this pattern is easy to split at the centre to convert a sweater pattern to a cardigan pattern. It is also easy to add another set of stitches to this pattern where you need to make a panel wider.

Marriage Lines

The simplest cable to work on a purl backgound is one that moves knit stitches one stitch to the left for a few rows and then back to the right for the same number of rows, forming a zigzag pattern. This pattern stitch is reminiscent of the marriage lines worked in purl stitches on a gansey, seen on the illustration of the machine-knitted gansey in Chapter 1, from which it may well have been copied. Zigzags can be worked both with only one stitch travelling or with a group of stitches travelling. If they are worked side by side with a purl stitch between them, they can make useful panels for increasing the width of a garment without needing to find alternative designs that fit into the extra stitches.

Diamonds

If the zigzags are placed opposite each other with the travelling stitches moving in opposite directions, they will form diamonds – probably the most versatile of all of the cable motifs. Diamonds can be made any number of stitches wide. The wider they are, the more rows will be needed to make them cross at the top and bottom, so take note of this when combining it with other panels that cross on the same rows. But you can also make use of this feature to more easily change the size of a garment.

A diamond panel on a cushion showing how the motifs can be joined at their crossing points.

Diamonds can be filled with a wide variety of other stitches – most frequently this is moss stitch, but you can also use small rope cables, ribs, smaller diamonds and even bobbles. They can be elongated by working a number of rows before changing direction, which gives them more of an oval appearance, and they can be crossed or left plain at the top and bottom.

Diamond panels can also be joined together at their widest points, as in the cabled cushion shown. Again, the number of crossings between meeting points can be adjusted if more rows are required to make the piece longer.

Instead of being joined together, a number of diamond panels can be worked side by side but at half drop intervals. This arrangement makes a particularly attractive centre panel and is frequently seen on Aran knits.

Ways of Working Cables

Most cables containing fewer than eight stitches can be worked without a cable needle. Two of the methods are described in Chapter 2 Materials and Equipment, but another way is to knit the stitches in the wrong order without dropping the stitches off the needles until they are all worked. This method is best worked with a needle that is made either of metal or a somewhat flexible material, such as bamboo, as it involves putting some strain on the right needle.

> **To work a 6-stitch cable sloping to the left:**
> Step 1: Pass the right needle behind stitches 1, 2 and 3 on the left needle.
> Step 2: Knit into the back of stitches 3, 4 and 5, one at a time.
> Step 3: Bring the right needle to the front, knit the first 3 stitches as usual and slip all the stitches onto the right needle.
>
> **To work a 6-stitch cable sloping to the right:**
> Step 1: Pass the right needle in front of stitches 1, 2 and 3 on the left needle.
> Step 2: Knit into the front of stitches 3, 4 and 5, one at a time.
> Step 3: Knit into the front of stitches 1, 2 and 3 and slip the stitches onto the right needle.
>
> In both cases, it helps to lift stitches 1, 2 and 3 away from the left needle slightly so that it is easier to insert the right needle.

Each of the methods – working with a cable needle, transferring the stitches before knitting them and knitting them out of order – will produce a slightly different look to the stitches as they become stretched in different ways depending on the way they are worked. They will gradually settle back over wear, but it is best not to use different methods in the same garment.

Cables where only one stitch is worked out of order can easily be worked without a cable needle. See the instructions for claw stitch and 5-stitch cable for examples of this.

Inventing Cable Stitches

Stitches can be made to cross knit over purl or purl over knit. They can be worked in stocking stitch, moss stitch, garter stitch or rib, or any combination of stitches that pleases you. They can be a simple cross or they can weave in and out of one another like braids or plaits, or across a larger number of stitches to form what we now call Celtic cables. A simple rope cable of 8 or more stitches can also be split into a smaller set of independent cables, or they can be brought back together again to reform the 8-stitch cable. Two narrow cables can be placed side by side to form what looks like a more complex design; a purl stitch between them makes them stand out more.

A single knit stitch can also be made to move across the background fabric, often to form a diamond or a pair of zigzag lines. This is achieved by working the stitches in a different order but without the use of a cable needle. These single stitches are known as travelling stitches rather than cables and are most familiar from Austrian or Bavarian patterns. As well as the stitches changing direction, these designs often incorporate stitches that are worked through the back loop, also known as twisted stitches – but not to be confused with Tw2 stitches described next.

Bavarian Cable. This design, made up of traveling stitches, is frequently used in Aran items and looks good when combined with diamond motifs.

STITCH DICTIONARY 45

Tw2R and Tw2L

These small 2stitch cables can be worked with a cable needle but there are other ways of working them. The simplest are described below.

> **Twist 2 Right – Tw2R**
> - Knit into the back of the second stitch on the left needle, taking the right needle in front of the first stitch, then knit into the back of the first stitch on the left needle before slipping both stitches off the needle.
>
> Here is an alternative way of working the right twist:
> - Knit 2 sts together without taking the stitches off the needle, then knit the first stitch again and slip them both off.
>
> **Twist 2 Left – Tw2L**
> - Insert the right needle behind the first stitch on the left needle into the back of the second stitch on the left needle, behind the first stitch, and knit it without dropping the stitches off the needle. Knit into the front of the first stitch and drop both stitches off the needle.
>
> If these stitches are worked side by side, they form the small chain pattern described later in the Stitch Dictionary.

It should be possible to create 'new' cable patterns of your own once you have become familiar with the way the stitches are moved and crossed. The simplest adaptation is made by working any two cables side by side and crossing in opposite directions. A purl stitch in between them gives the cables greater definition. Groups of cables joined together in this way can be used to make a central panel. The honeycomb stitch is a classic example of this, but I have also used individual honeycombs separated by a few stitches to make an all-over pattern on a design for a beanie.

Celtic Inspiration

Some of the later complex Celtic-inspired interlacings are not part of the traditional Aran oeuvre, but since their introduction by Elsebeth Lavold and Alice Starmore in the 1990s, they have become an accepted addition. I have therefore included some of them here. Most of Lavold's designs are formed through various multiple increases and decreases and often stand alone rather than being worked as vertical panels. Starmore's designs also feature stand-alone motifs, known as interlaced or closed ring cables, but most are based on the traditional Aran technique of moving the crossing stitches to right or left and repeating them vertically.

> **Meanings of Aran Stitches**
>
> Over the years, various meanings have been attributed to the Aran stitches, just as they have to those of the gansey patterns. Some of these meanings are the same, which reinforces the theory that Aran knits stemmed from ganseys.
>
> **Basket Stitch:** Represents the fisherman's basket and the hope of abundant catches.
>
> **Braids:** Are said to denote the intertwining of events in family life.
>
> **Cable Stitch:** Perhaps the stitch most frequently found on so-called fishermens' sweaters and said to represent ropes.
>
> **Diamond Stitch:** Represents the mesh of the fishing net. It is also a traditional symbol of wealth.
>
> **Moss Stitch:** Suggests a good harvest as it is a sign of abundance and growth, like the Carrageen moss that is found all around the islands and used to improve the soil. It is a familiar stitch on ganseys, where it is known in Norfolk as 'hailstones'.
>
> **Honeycomb Stitch:** This stitch is a reminder of the hardworking bee and promises a good catch.
>
> **Tree of Life Stitch:** Another stitch representing the growth of the family. Found on gansey patterns.
>
> **Blackberry Stitch:** Is also known as bramble stitch or trinity stitch, where it is said to represent God the Father, the Son and the Holy Ghost.
>
> **Zigzag Stitch:** Represents the ups and downs of married life, paths down to the sea, or lightning.

A tasselled beanie with separated honeycomb motifs.

The Samples with their Charts

Most of the charts pictured here show one repeat of the pattern with no edge stitches, although the knitted samples sometimes show more than one vertical repeat to give an idea of the appearance of patterns that are linked to one another by repeating from the first row again. These samples are also flanked by reverse stocking stitch and garter stitch borders so that they will lie flat, but these are not shown or counted in the number of stitches in the actual motif in the chart.

The stitches are listed in alphabetical order, but to help you substitute charts in your design, they are listed by number of stitches required to make them in the Appendix.

Arrowheads swatch.

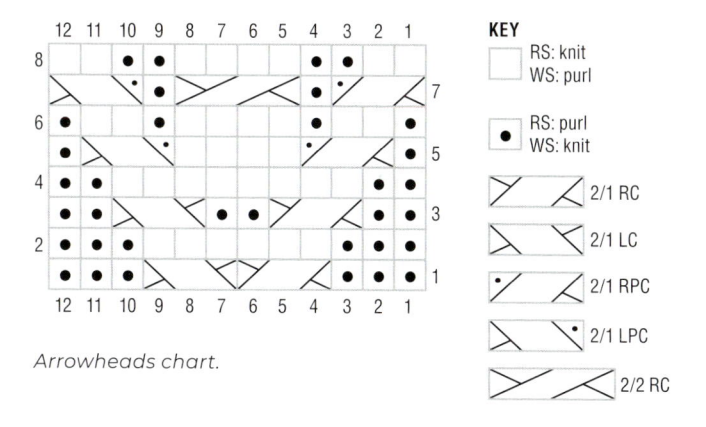

Arrowheads chart.

KEY

- RS: knit / WS: purl
- RS: purl / WS: knit
- 2/1 RC
- 2/1 LC
- 2/1 RPC
- 2/1 LPC
- 2/2 RC

Arrowheads

Row 1 (RS): P3, 2/1RC, 2/1LC, p3 (12 sts).
Row 2 (WS): K3, p6, k3.
Row 3: P2, 2/1RC, p2, 2/1LC, p2.
Row 4: K2, p8, k2.
Row 5: P1, 2/1RPC, k4, 2/1LPC, p1.
Row 6: K1, p2, k1, p4, k1, p2, k1.
Row 7: 2/1RPC, p1, 2/2RC, p1, 2/1LPC.
Row 8: P2, k2, p4, k2, p2.

STITCH DICTIONARY 47

Asymmetrical swatch.

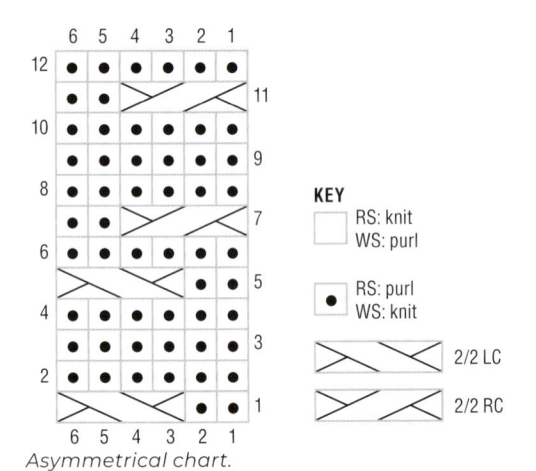

Asymmetrical chart.

Bobbles and diamonds swatch.

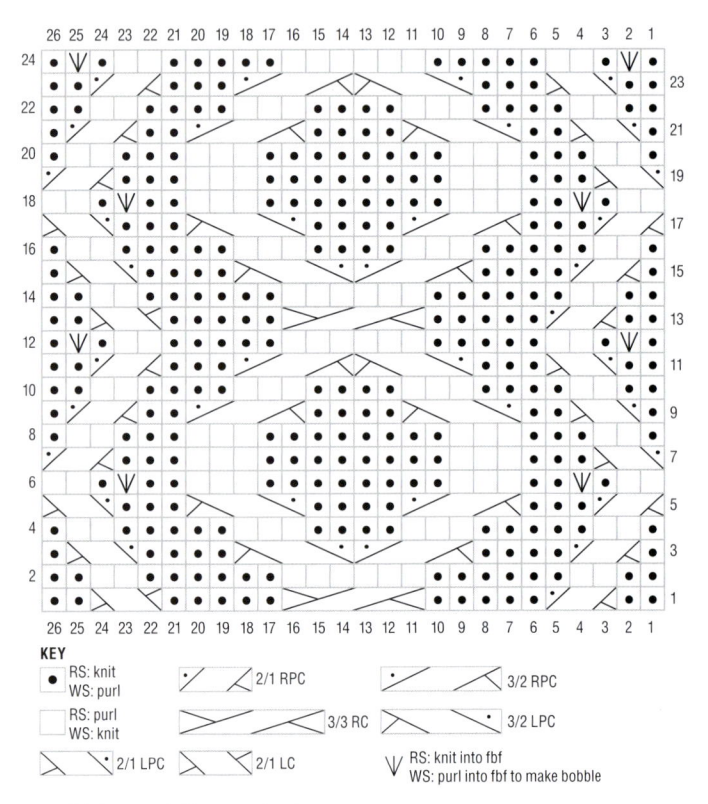

Bobbles and diamonds chart.

Asymmetrical Cable

Row 1 (RS): P2, 2/2LC (6 sts).
Row 2 and all WS rows: Knit.
Row 3: Purl.
Row 5: Repeat row 1.
Row 7: 2/2RC, p2.
Row 9: Purl.
Row 11: Repeat row 7.

Bobbles and Diamond

Row 1 (RS): P2, 2/1RPC, p5, 3/3RC, p5, 2/1LC, p2 (26 sts).
Row 2 (WS): K2, p2, k6, p6, k6, p2, k2.
Row 3: P1, 2/1RPC, p4, 3/2RPC, 3/2LPC, p4, 2/1LPC, p1.
Row 4: K1, p2, k5, p3, k4, p3, k5, p2, k1.
Row 5: 2/1RPC, p3, 3/2RPC, p4, 3/2LPC, p3, 2/1LPC.
Row 6: P2, k1, pfbf, p18, pfbf, p3.
Row 7: 2/1LPC, p3, k3, p8, k3, p3, 2/1RPC (26 sts).
Row 8: K1, p2, k3, p3, k8, p3, k3, p2, k1.
Row 9: P1, 2/1LPC, p2, 3/2LPC, p4, 3/2RPC, p2, 2/1RPC, p1.
Row 10: K2, p2, (k4, p3) twice, k4, p2, k2.
Row 11: P2, 2/1 LPC, p3, 3/2 LPC, 3/2 RPC, p3, 2/1 RPC, p2.
Row 12: K1, pfbf, k1, p2, k5, p6, k5, p2, k1, pfbf, k1 (30 sts).
Rows 13–24: Repeat rows 1–12.

Branches

Row 1 (RS): K1, p2, k1, p3, k2, p4, k2, p3, k1, p2, k1 (22 sts).
Row 2 (WS): P1, k2, p1, k3, p2, k4, p2, k3, p1, k2, p1.
Row 3: 1/1LPC, 1/1RPC, k3, 2/1RPC, p2, 2/1LPC, k3, 1/1LPC, 1/1RPC.
Row 4: K1, 1/1LPT, k5, p2, k2, p2, k5, 1/1LPT, k1.
Row 5: 1/1RPC, 1/1LPC, k4, 2/1LPC, 2/1 RPC, k4, 1/1RPC, 1/1LPC.
Row 6: P1, k2, p1, k5, p4, k5, p1, k2, p1.
Row 7: K1, p2, k1, p5, 2/2RC, p5, k1, p2, k1.
Row 8: Repeat row 6.
Row 9: 1/1LPC, 1/1RPC, p3, 2/2RC, 2/2LC, p3, 1/1LPC, 1/1RPC.
Row 10: K1, 1/1LPT, k4, p8, k4, 1/1LPT, p1.
Row 11: P5, 2/2RPC, p4, 2/2LPC, p5.
Row 12: K5, p2, k2, p4, k2, p2, k5.
Row 13: P3, 2/2RPC, p2, 2/2RC, p2, 2/2LPC, p3.
Row 14: K3, p2, k4, p4, k4, p2, k3.
Row 15: P1, 2/2RPC, p3, 2/1RPC, 2/1LPC, p3, 2/2LPC, p1.
Row 16: K1, p2, k5, p2, k2, p2, k5, p2, k1.
Row 17: 1/1RPC, 1/1LPC, p3, 2/1RPC, p2, 2/1LPC, p3, 1/1RPC, 1/1LPC.
Row 18: Repeat row 2.

Branches swatch.

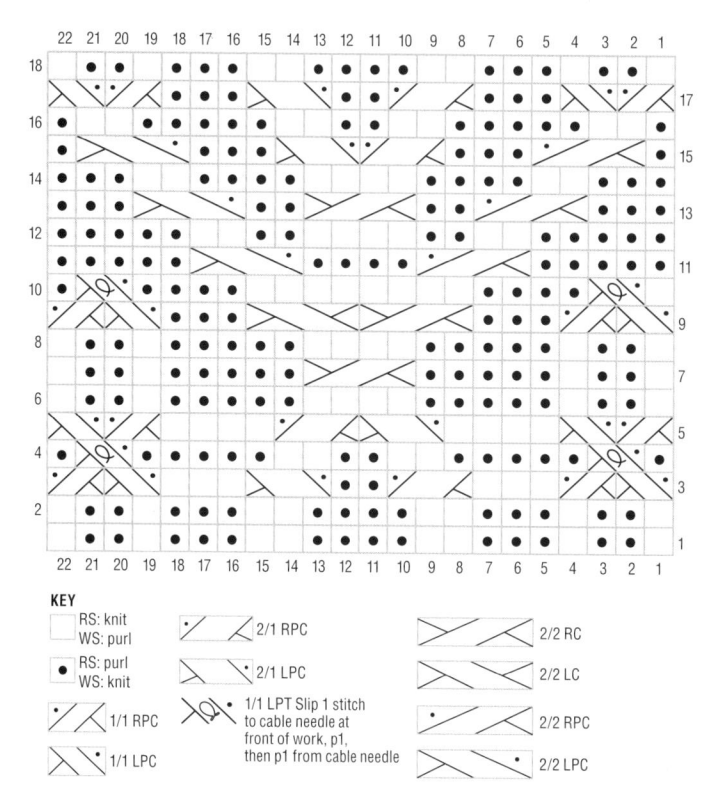

Branches chart.

KEY
- RS: knit / WS: purl
- RS: purl / WS: knit
- 1/1 RPC
- 1/1 LPC
- 2/1 RPC
- 2/1 LPC
- 1/1 LPT Slip 1 stitch to cable needle at front of work, p1, then p1 from cable needle
- 2/2 RC
- 2/2 LC
- 2/2 RPC
- 2/2 LPC

STITCH DICTIONARY 49

Celtic braid swatch.

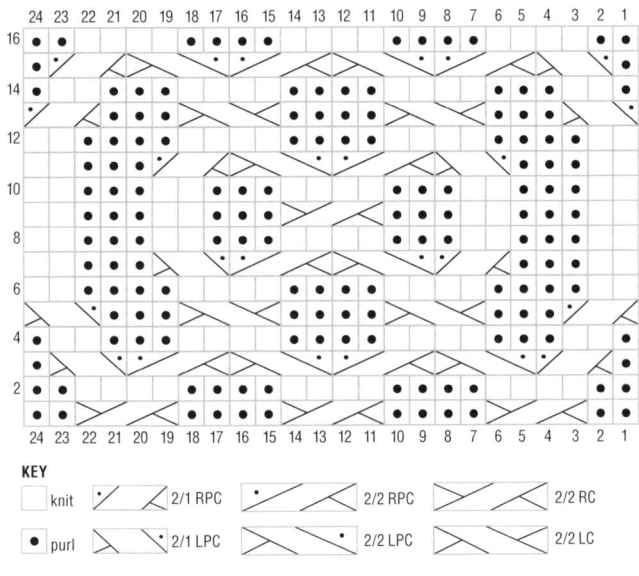

Celtic braid chart.

KEY
- knit
- purl
- 2/1 RPC
- 2/1 LPC
- 2/2 RPC
- 2/2 LPC
- 2/2 RC
- 2/2 LC

Celtic Braid

Row 1 (RS): P2, (2/2 RC, p4) x 2, 2/2 RC, p2. (24 sts)
Row 2 (WS): K2, (p4, k4) x 2, p4, k2.
Row 3: P1, 2/1 RPC, (2/2 LPC, 2/2 RPC) x 2, 2/1 LPC, p1.
Row 4: K1, p2, k3, p4, k4, p4, k3, p2, k1.
Row 5: 2/1 RPC, p3, 2/2 LC, p4, 2/2 LC, p3, 2/1 LPC.
Row 6: P2, (k4, p4) x 2, k4, p2.
Row 7: K2, p3, 2/1 RPC, 2/2 LPC, 2/2 RPC, 2/1 LPC, p3, k2.
Row 8: (P2, k3) x 2, p4, (k3, p2) x 2.
Row 9: (K2, p3) x 2, 2/2 RC, (p3, k2) x 2.
Row 10: Repeat row 8.
Row 11: K2, p3, 2/1 LPC, 2/2 RPC, 2/2 LPC, 2/1 RPC, p3, k2.
Row 12: Repeat row 6.
Row 13: 2/1 LPC, p3, 2/2 LC, p4, 2/2 LC, p3, 2/1 RPC.
Row 14: Repeat row 4.
Row 15: P1, 2/1 LPC, (2/2 RPC, 2/2 LPC) x 2, 2/1 RPC, p1.
Row 16: Repeat row 2.

Celtic Twists

Row 1 (RS): P2, k2, p11, k2, p2 (19 sts).
Row 2 (WS): K2, p2, k11, p2, k2.
Row 3: P2, k2, p3, incto5 tbl, p6, 2/1RPC, p2 (23 sts).
Row 4: K3, p2, k6, (p1, k1) twice, p1, k3, p2, k2.
Row 5: P2, k2, p2, 2/1RPC, p1, 2/2LPC, p3, 2/1RPC, p3.
Row 6: K4, p2, k3, p2, k4, (p2, k2) twice.
Row 7: P2, k2, p2, 2/1LPC, p3, 2/2LPC, 2/1RPC, p4.
Row 8: K5, p4, k5, p2, k3, p2, k2.
Row 9: P2, k2, p3, 2/1LPC, p4, 2/2LC, p5.
Row 10: K5, p4, (k4, p2) twice, k2.
Row 11: P2, 2/1LPC, p3, 2/1LPC, p1, 2/2RPC, 2/1LPC, p4.
Row 12: K4, p2, k3, p2, k1, p2, k4, p2, k3.
Row 13: P3, 2/1LPC, p3, 2/1/2 RPC, p3, 2/1LPC, p3.
Row 14: K3, p2, k4, p2, k1, p2, k3, p2, k4.
Row 15: P4, 2/1LPC, 2/2 RPC, p1, 2/1 LPC, p3, 2/1 LPC, p2.
Row 16: K2, (p2, k4) twice, p4, k5.
Row 17: P5, 2/2LC, p4, 2/1LPC, p3, k2, p2.
Row 18: K2, p2, k3, p2, k5, p4, k5.
Row 19: P4, 2/1RPC, 2/2LPC, p3, 2/1LPC, p2, k2, p2.
Row 20: (K2, p2) twice, k4, p2, k3, p2, k4.
Row 21: P3, 2/1RPC, p3, 2/2LPC, p1, 2/1RPC, p2, k2, p2.
Row 22: K2, p2, k3, p2, k1, p2, k6, p2, k3.
Row 23: P2, 2/1RPC, p6, k5tog, p3, k2, p2 (19 sts).
Row 24: Repeat row 2.

50 STITCH DICTIONARY

Celtic twists swatch.

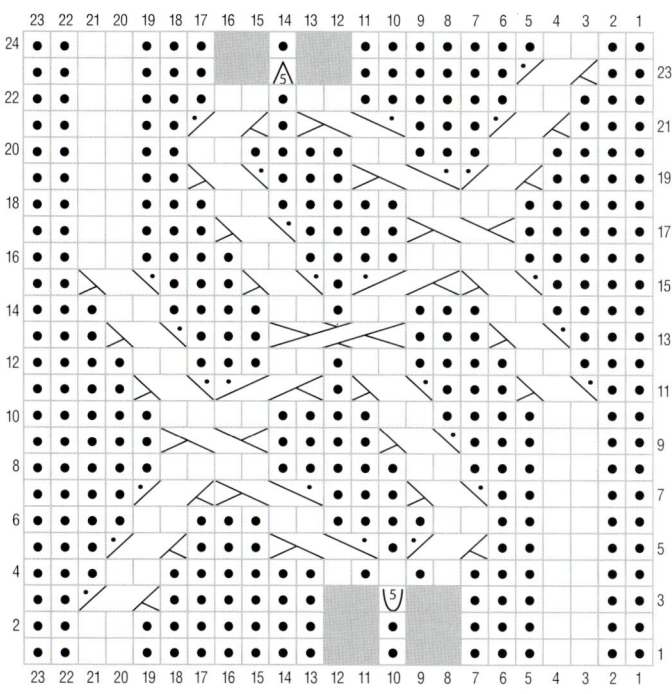

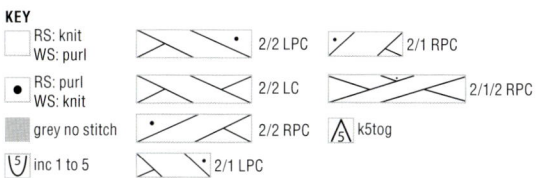

Chain cable swatch.

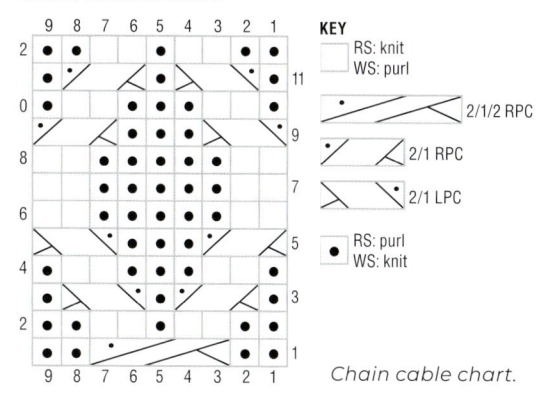

Chain cable chart.

KEY
- RS: knit / WS: purl
- • RS: purl / WS: knit
- 2/1/2 RPC
- 2/1 RPC
- 2/1 LPC

Chain Cable

Row 1 (RS): P2, 2/1/2 RPC, p2 (9 sts).

Row 2 (WS): K2, p2, k, p2, k2.

Row 3: P, 2/1 RPC, p, 2/1 LPC, p.

Row 4: K, p2, k3, p2, k.

Row 5: 2/1 RPC, p3, 2/1 LPC.

Row 6: P2, k5, p2.

Row 7: K2, p5, k2.

Row 8: Repeat row 6.

Row 9: 2/1 LPC, p3, 2/1 RPC.

Row 10: Repeat row 4.

Row 11: P, 2/1 LPC, p, 2/1 RPC, p.

Row 12: Repeat row 2.

KEY
- RS: knit / WS: purl
- • RS: purl / WS: knit
- grey no stitch
- inc 1 to 5
- 2/2 LPC
- 2/2 LC
- 2/2 RPC
- 2/1 LPC
- 2/1 RPC
- 2/1/2 RPC
- k5tog

Celtic twists chart.

STITCH DICTIONARY 51

Claw swatch.

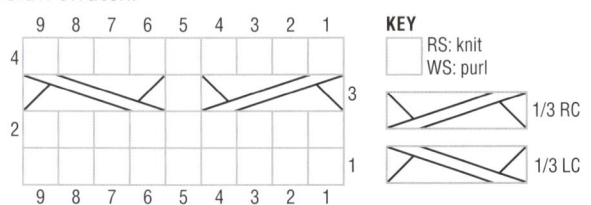

Claw chart.

Claw

Row 1 (RS): Knit (9 sts).
Row 2: Knit.
Row 3: 1/3RC, k, 1/3LC.
Row 4: Knit.

Crossed Ropes

Row 1 (RS): P2, k4, p4, k4, p2 (16 sts).
Row 2 (WS): K2, p4, k4, p4, k2.
Row 3: P2, 2/2LC, p4, 2/2LC, p2.
Row 4: Repeat row 2.
Rows 5–8: Repeat rows 1–4.
Row 9: (2/2RPC, 2/2LPC) twice.
Row 10: Repeat row 1.
Row 11: K2, p4, 2/2LC, p4, k2.
Row 12: Repeat row 1.
Row 13: Repeat row 2.

Crossed ropes swatch.

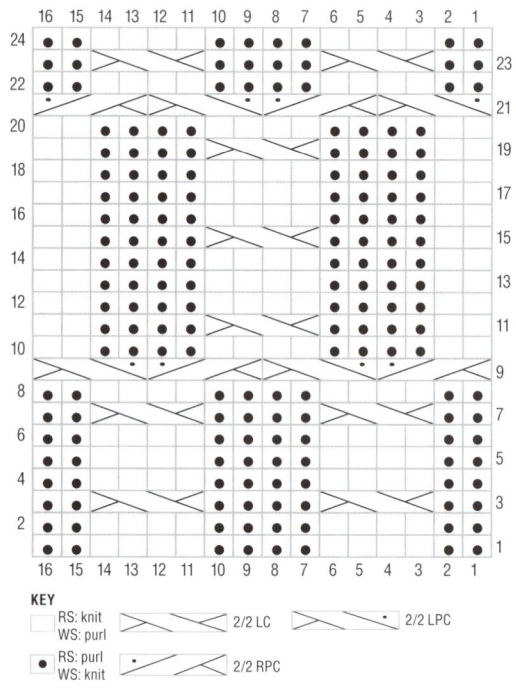

Crossed ropes chart.

Rows 14–17: Repeat rows 10–13.
Row 18: Repeat row 1.
Row 19: Repeat row 11.
Row 20: Repeat row 1.
Row 21: (2/2LPC, 2/2RPC) twice.
Row 22: Repeat row 2.
Row 23: Repeat row 3.
Row 24: Repeat row 2.

Cups swatch.

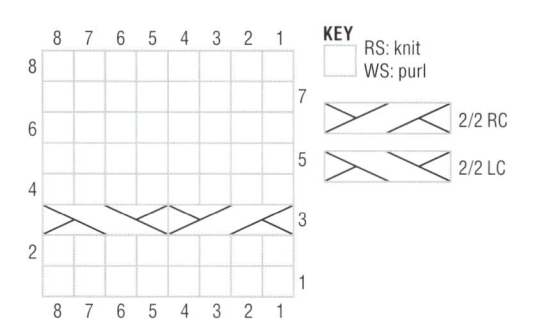

Cups chart.

Cups

Row 1 (RS): Knit (8 sts).
Row 2 and all WS rows: Purl.
Row 3: 2/2RC, 2/2LC.
Row 5: Knit.
Row 7: Knit.

Diamond eight swatch.

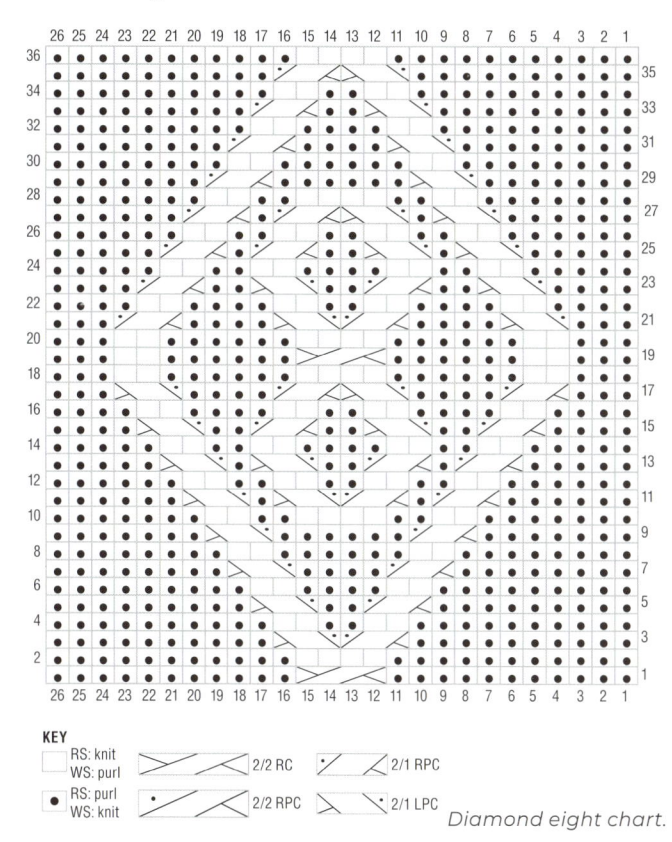

Diamond eight chart.

Diamond Eight

Row 1 (RS): P11, 2/2RC, p11 (26 sts).
Row 2 (WS): K11, p4, k11.
Row 3: P10, 2/1RPC, 2/1LPC, p10.
Row 4: K10, p2, k2, p2, k10.
Row 5: P9, 2/1RPC, p2, 2/1LPC, p9.

STITCH DICTIONARY 53

Row 6: K9, p2, k4, p2, k9.
Row 7: P8, 2/1RPC, p4, 2/1LPC, p8.
Row 8: K8, p2, k6, p2, k8.
Row 9: P7, 2/1RPC, p6, 2/1LPC, p7.
Row 10: K7, p2, k2, p4, k2, p2, k7.
Row 11: P6, 2/1RPC, p1, 2/1RPC, 2/1LPC, p1, 2/1LPC, p6.
Row 12: K6, (p2, k2) 3 times, p2, k6.
Row 13: P5, 2/1RPC, p1, 2/1RPC, p2, 2/1LPC, p1, 2/1LPC, p5.
Row 14: K5, p2, k2, p2, k4, p2, k2, p2, k5.
Row 15: P4, 2/1RPC, p2, 2/1LPC, p2, 2/1RPC, p2, 2/1LPC, p4.
Row 16: (K4, p2) twice, k2, (p2, k4) twice.
Row 17: P3, (2/1RPC, p4, 2/1LPC) twice, p3.
Row 18: K3, p2, k6, p4, k6, p2, k3.
Row 19: P3, k2, p6, 2/2RC, p6, k2, p3.
Row 20: Repeat row 18.
Row 21: P3, (2/1LPC, p4, 2/1RPC) twice, p3.
Row 22: Repeat row 16.
Row 23: P4, 2/1LPC, p2, 2/1RPC, p2, 2/1LPC, p2, 2/1RPC, p4.
Row 24: Repeat row 14.
Row 25: P5, 2/1LPC, p1, 2/1LPC, p2, 2/1RPC, p1, 2/1RPC, p5.
Row 26: Repeat row 12.
Row 27: P6, 2/1LPC, p1, 2/1LPC, 2/1RPC, p1, 2/1RPC, p6.
Row 28: Repeat row 10.
Row 29: P7, 2/1LPC, p6, 2/1RPC, p7.
Row 30: Repeat row 8.
Row 31: P8, 2/1LPC, p4, 2/1RPC, p8.
Row 32: Repeat row 6.
Row 33: P9, 2/1LPC, p2, 2/1RPC, p9.
Row 34: Repeat row 4.
Row 35: P10, 2/1LPC, 2/1RPC, p10.
Row 36: Repeat row 2.

Diamond and Cross

Row 1 (RS): P6, 2/1 RPC, 2/1 LPC, p6 (18 sts).
Row 2 (WS): K6, p2, k2, p2, k6.
Row 3: P5, 2/1RPC, p2, 2/1LPC, p5.
Row 4: K5, p2, k4, p2, k5.
Row 5: P4, 2/1RPC, p4, 2/1LPC, p4.
Row 6: K4, p2, k6, p2, k4.
Row 7: P3, 2/1RPC, p6, 2/1LPC, p3.
Row 8: K3, p2, k8, p2, k3.
Row 9: (P2, 2/1RPC, 2/1LPC) twice, p2.
Row 10: (K2, p2) 4 times, k2.
Row 11: P1, (2/1RPC, p2, 2/1LPC) twice, p1.
Row 12: K1, p2, k4, p4, k4, p2, k1.
Row 13: P1, k2, p4, 2/2RC, p4, k2, p1.
Row 14: Repeat row 12.
Row 15: P1, (2/1LPC, p2, 2/1RPC) twice, p1.
Row 16: Repeat row 10.
Row 17: (P2, 2/1LPC, 2/1RPC) twice, p2.

Diamond and cross swatch.

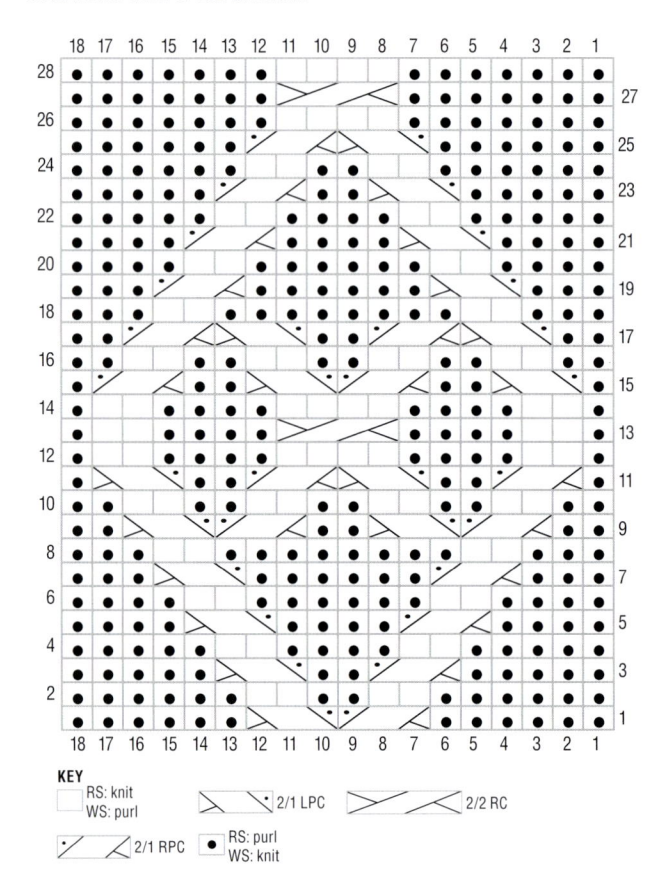

Diamond and cross chart.

54 STITCH DICTIONARY

Row 18: Repeat row 8.
Row 19: P3, 2/1LPC, p6, 2/1RPC, p3.
Row 20: Repeat row 6.
Row 21: P4, 2/1LPC, p4, 2/1RPC, p4.
Row 22: Repeat row 4.
Row 23: P5, 2/1LPC, p2, 2/1RPC, p5.
Row 24: Repeat row 2.
Row 25: P6, 2/1LPC, 2/1RPC, p6.
Row 26: K7, p4, k7.
Row 27: P7, 2/2 RC, p7.
Row 28: Repeat row 26.

Diamond and Moss
(used in the saddle shoulder sweater)

Row 1 (WS): K5, p4, k1, p4, k5 (19 sts).
Row 2 (RS): P5, 3/1RPC, k, 3/1LPC, p5.
Row 3: K5, p3, k1, p1, k1, p3, k5.
Row 4: P4, 3/1RPC, k1, p1, k1, 3/1LPC, p4.
Row 5: K4, p3, (k1, p1) twice, k1, p3, k4.
Row 6: P3, 3/1RPC, (k1, p1) twice, k1, 3/1LPC, p3.
Row 7: K3, p3, (k1, p1) 3 times, k1, p3, k3.
Row 8: P2, 3/1RPC, (k1, p1) 3 times, k1, 3/1LPC, p2.
Row 9: K2, p3, (k1, p1) 4 times, k1, p3, k2.
Row 10: P1, 3/1RPC, (k1, p1) 4 times, k1, 3/1LPC, p1.
Row 11: K1, p3, (k1, p1) 5 times, k1, p3, k1.
Row 12: 3/1RPC, (k1, p1) 5 times, k1, 3/1LPC.
Row 13: P3, (k1, p1) 6 times, k1, p3.
Row 14: 3/1LPC, (p1, k1) 5 times, p1, 3/1RPC.
Row 15: Repeat row 11.
Row 16: P1, 3/1LPC, (p1, k1) 4 times, p1, 3/1RPC, p1.
Row 17: Repeat row 9.
Row 18: P2, 3/1LPC, (p1, k1) 3 times, p1, 3/1RPC, p2.
Row 19: Repeat row 7.
Row 20: P3, 3/1LPC, (p1, k1) twice, p1, 3/1RPC, p3.
Row 21: Repeat row 5.
Row 22: P4, 3/1LPC, p1, k1, p1, 3/1RPC, p4.
Row 23: Repeat row 3.
Row 24: P5, 2/2LC, p1, 2/2RC, p5.
Row 25: Repeat row 1.
Row 26: P5, k4, p1, k4, p5.
Row 27: Repeat row 1.
Row 28: P5, 2/2RC, p1, 2/2LC, p5.
Rows 29–32: Repeat rows 25–28.

Diamond and moss swatch.

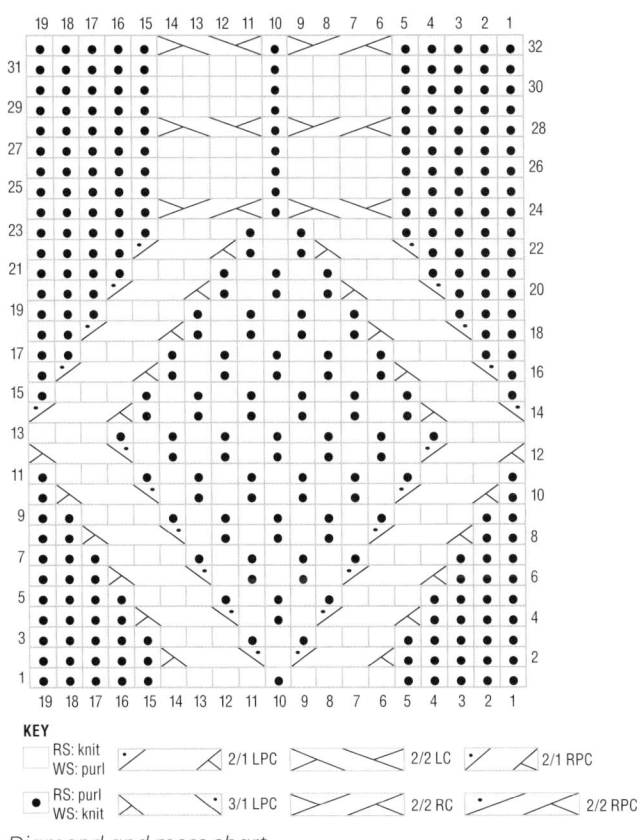

Diamond and moss chart.

STITCH DICTIONARY 55

Diamond (small) swatch.

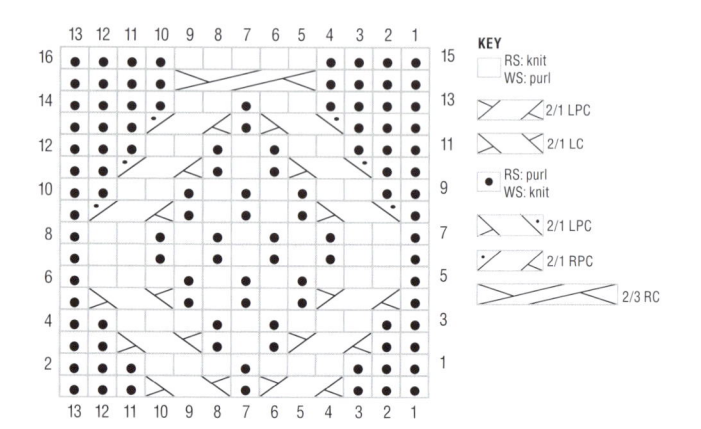

Diamond (small) chart.

Diamond and nosegay swatch.

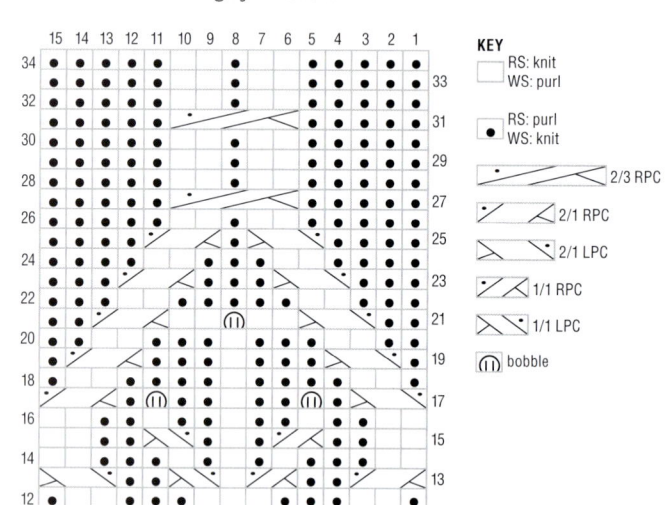

Diamond and nosegay chart.

Diamond (Small)

Row 1 (RS): P3, 2/1RC, p1, 2/1LC, p3 (13 sts).
Row 2 (WS): K3, p3, k1, p3, k3.
Row 3: P2, 2/1RC, p1, k1, p1, 2/1LC, p2.
Row 4: K2, p3, k1, p1, k1, p3, k2.
Row 5: P1, 2/1RC, (p1, k1) twice, p1, 2/1LC, p1.
Row 6: K1, p3, (k1, p1) twice, k1, p3, k1.
Row 7: P1, k2, (p1, k1) 3 times, p1, k2, p1.
Row 8: K1, p2, (k1, p1) 3 times, k1, p2, k1.
Row 9: P1, 2/1LPC, (p1, k1) twice, p1, 2/1RPC, p1.
Row 10: K2, p2, (k1, p1) twice, k1, p2, k2.
Row 11: P2, 2/1LPC, p1, k1, p1, 2/1RPC, p2.
Row 12: K3, p2, k1, p1, k1, p2, k3.
Row 13: P3, 2/1LPC, p1, 2/1RPC, p3.
Row 14: K4, p2, k1, p2, k4.
Row 15: P4, 2/3 RC, p4.
Row 16: K4, p5, k4.

Diamond and Nosegay

Row 1 (RS): P5, k2, p1, k2, p5 (15 sts).
Row 2 (WS): K5, p2, k1, p2, k5.
Row 3: P5, 2/3RPC, p5.
Row 4: Repeat row 2.
Row 5: P4, 2/1RPC, k1, 2/1LPC, p4.

56 STITCH DICTIONARY

Row 6: K4, p7, k4.
Row 7: P3, 2/1RPC, k3, 2/1LPC, p3.
Row 8: K3, p2, k1, p3, k1, p2, k3.
Row 9: P2, 2/1RPC, p1, k3, p1, 2/1LPC, p2.
Row 10: K2, p2, k2, p3, k2, p2, k2.
Row 11: P1, 2/1RPC, p2, k3, p2, 2/1LPC, p1.
Row 12: K1, p2, k3, p3, k3, p2, k1.
Row 13: 2/1RPC, p2, 1/1RPC, k1, 1/1LPC, p2, 2/1LPC.
Row 14: P2, k3, (p1, k1) twice, p1, k3, p2.
Row 15: K2, p2, 1/1RPC, p1, k1, p1, 1/1LPC, p2, k2.
Row 16: P2, (k2, p1) 3 times, k2, p2.
Row 17: 2/1LPC, p1, mb, p2, k1, p2, mb, p1, 2/1RPC.
Row 18: K1, p2, k4, p1, k4, p2, k1.
Row 19: P1, 2/1LPC, p3, k1, p3, 2/1RPC, p1.
Row 20: K2, p2, k3, p1, k3, p2, k2.
Row 21: P2, 2/1LPC, k2, mb, k2, 2/1RPC, p2.
Row 22: K3, p2, k5, p2, k3.
Row 23: P3, 2/1LPC, p3, 2/1RPC, p3.
Row 24: K4, p2, k3, p2, k4.
Row 25: P4, 2/1LPC, p1, 2/1RPC, p4.
Row 26: Repeat row 2.
Row 27: Repeat row 3.
Row 28: Repeat row 2.
Row 29: Repeat row 1.
Rows 30–33: Repeat rows 26–29.
Row 34: Repeat row 2.

Diamond with Cables

Row 1 (RS): P4, 2/2RC, 2/2LC, p4 (16 sts).
Row 2 (WS): K4, p8, k4.
Row 3: P3, 2/2RC, k2, 2/2LC, p3.
Row 4: K3, p10, k3.
Row 5: P2, 2/2RPC, k4, 2/2LPC, p2.
Row 6: K2, p3, k1, p4, k1, p3, k2.
Row 7: P1, 2/2RPC, p1, 2/2RC, p1, 2/2LPC, p1.
Row 8: K1, p3, k2, p4, k2, p3, k1.
Row 9: 2/2RPC, p2, k4, p2, 2/2LPC.
Row 10: P3, k3, p4, k3, p3.
Row 11: K3, p3, 2/2RC, p3, k3.
Row 12: Repeat row 10.
Row 13: 2/2LPC, p2, k4, p2, 2/2RPC.
Row 14: Repeat row 8.
Row 15: P1, 2/2LPC, p1, 2/2RC, p1, 2/2RPC, p1.
Row 16: Repeat row 6.
Row 17: P2, 2/2LPC, k4, 2/2RPC, p2.

Diamond with cables swatch.

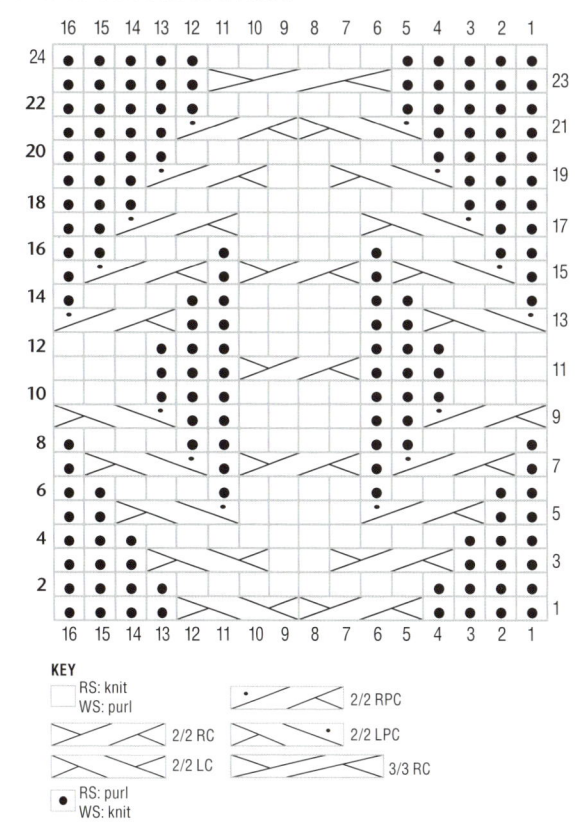

Diamond with cables chart.

Row 18: Repeat row 4.
Row 19: P3, 2/2LPC, k2, 2/2RPC, p3.
Row 20: Repeat row 2.
Row 21: P4, 2/2LPC, 2/2RPC, p4.
Row 22: K5, p6, k5.
Row 23: P5, 3/3RC, p5.
Row 24: Repeat row 22.

Diamond with twisted rib swatch.

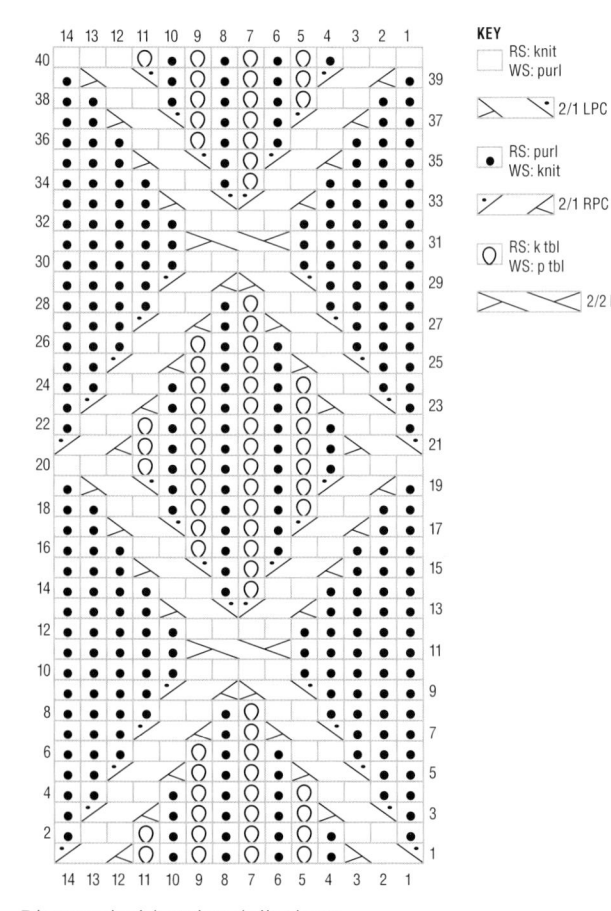

Diamond with twisted rib chart.

Diamond with Twisted Rib

Row 1 (RS): 2/1LPC, (p1, k1 tbl) 4 times, 2/1RPC (14 sts).
Row 2 (WS): K1, p2, (p1 tbl, k1) 4 times, p2, k1.
Row 3: P1, 2/1LPC, (k1 tbl, p1) 4 times, 2/1RPC, p1.
Row 4: K2, p2, (k1, p1 tbl) 3 times, p2, k2.
Row 5: P2, 2/1LPC, (p1, k1 tbl) twice, 2/1RPC, p2.
Row 6: K3, p2, (p1 tbl, k1) twice, p2, k3.
Row 7: P3, 2/1LPC, k1 tbl, p1, 2/1RPC, p3.
Row 8: K4, p2, k1, p1 tbl, p2, k4.
Row 9: P4, 2/1LPC, 2/1RPC, p4.
Row 10: K5, p4, k5.
Row 11: P5, 2/2LC, p5.
Row 12: Repeat row 10.
Row 13: P4, 2/1RPC, 2/1LPC, p4.
Row 14: Repeat row 8.
Row 15: P3, 2/1RPC, k1 tbl, p1, 2/1LPC, p3.
Row 16: Repeat row 6.
Row 17: P2, 2/11RPC, (p1, k1 tbl) twice, 2/1LPC, p2.
Row 18: Repeat row 4.
Row 19: P1, 2/1RPC, (k1 tbl, p1) 3 times, 2/1LPC, p1.
Row 20: P3, (p1 tbl, k1) 4 times, p3.
Rows 21–40: Repeat rows 1–20.

Double Diamonds

Row 1 (RS): P7, 2/2LC, p10, 2/2LC, p7 (32 sts).
Row 2 (WS): K7, p4, k10, p4, k7.
Row 3: P6, 2/1RC, 2/1LC, p8, 2/1RC, 2/1LC, p6.
Row 4: K6, p3, k1, p2, k8, p3, k1, p2, k6.
Row 5: P5, 2/1RC, k1, p1, 2/1LC, p6, 2/1RC, k1, p1, 2/1LC, p5.
Row 6: K5, p3, k1, p1, k1, p2, k6, p3, k1, p1, k1, p2, k5.
Row 7: (P4, 2/1RC, (k1, p1) x 2, 2/1LC) twice, p4.
Row 8: (K4, p3, k1, p1, k1, p1, k1, p2) twice, k4.
Row 9: P3, 2/1RC, (k1, p1) 3 times, 2/1LC, p2, 2/1RC, (k1, p1) 3 times, 2/1LC, p3.
Row 10: K3, p3, (k1, p1) 3 times, k1, p2, k2, p3, (k1, p1) 3 times, k1, p2, k3.
Row 11: P2, (2/1RC, (k1, p1) 4 times, 2/1LC) 4 times, p2.
Row 12: K2, p3, (k1, p1) 4 times, k1, p5, (k1, p1) 4 times, k1, p2, k2.
Row 13: P2, k3, (p1, k1) 4 times, p1, 2/2LC, (k1, p1) 5 times, k2, p2.
Row 14: K2, p2, (k1, p1) 4 times, k1, p5, (k1, p1) 4 times, k1, p3, k2.

58 STITCH DICTIONARY

Row 15: P2, (2/1LPC, (k1, p1) 4 times, 2/1RPC) twice, p2.
Row 16: K3, p2, (k1, p1) 3 times, k1, p3, k2, p2, (k1, p1) 3 times, k1, p3, k3.
Row 17: P3, 2/1LPC, (k1, p1) 3 times, 2/1RPC, p2, 2/1LPC, (k1, p1) 3 times, 2/1RPC, p3.
Row 18: (K4, p2, k1, p1, k1, p1, k1, p3) twice, k4.
Row 19: (P4, 2/1LPC, k1, p1, k1, p1, 2/1RPC) twice, p4.
Row 20: K5, p2, k1, p1, k1, p3, k6, p2, k1, p1, k1, p3, k5.
Row 21: P5, 2/1LPC, k1, p1, 2/1RPC, p6, 2/1LPC, k1, p1, 2/1RPC, p5.
Row 22: K6, p2, k1, p3, k8, p2, k1, p3, k6.
Row 23: P6, 2/1LPC, 2/1RPC, p8, 2/1LPC, 2/1RPC, p6.
Row 24: Repeat row 2.

Double diamonds swatch.

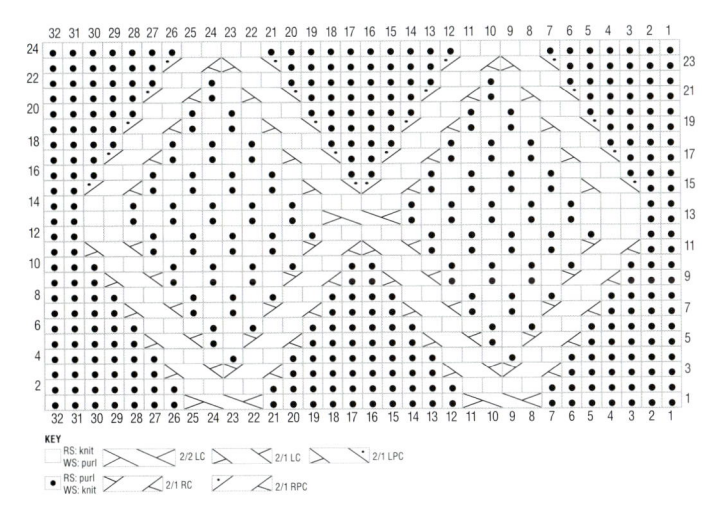

Double cross swatch.

Double diamonds chart.

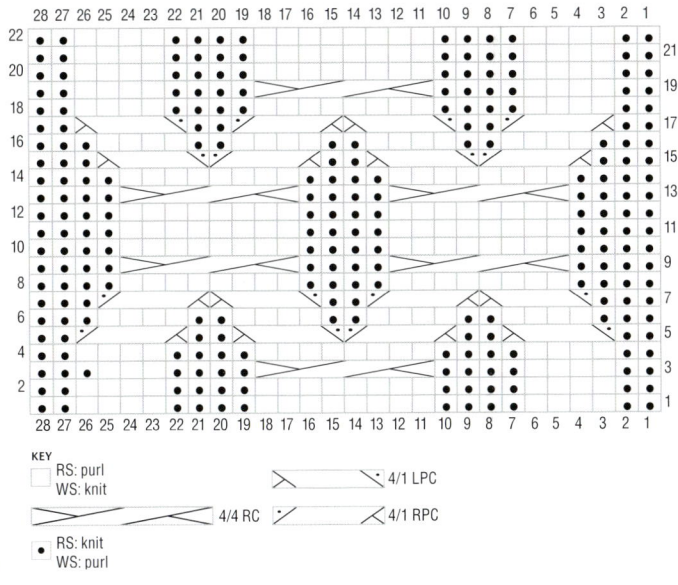

Double cross chart.

Double Cross

Row 1 (RS): P2, k4, p4, k8, p4, k4, p2 (28 sts).
Row 2 (WS): K2, p4, k4, p8, k4, p4, k2.
Row 3: P2, k4, p4, 4/4RC, p4, k3, p3.
Row 4: Repeat row 2.
Row 5: P2, (4/1LPC, p2, 4/1RPC) twice, p2.
Row 6: K3, (p4, k2) 3 times, p4, k3.
Row 7: P3, 4/1LPC, 4/1RPC, p2, 4/1LPC, 4/1RPC, p3.
Row 8: (K4, p8) twice, k4.

STITCH DICTIONARY **59**

Row 9: (P4, 4/4RC) twice, p4.
Row 10: Repeat row 8.
Row 11: (P4, k8) twice, p4.
Row 12: Repeat row 8.
Row 13: Repeat row 9.
Row 14: Repeat row 8.
Row 15: P3, 4/1RPC, 4/1LPC, p2, 4/1RPC, 4/1LPC, p3.
Row 16: Repeat row 6.
Row 17: P2, (4/1RPC, p2, 4/1LPC) twice, p2.
Row 18: Repeat row 2.
Row 19: P2, k4, p4, 4/4RC, p4, k4, p2.
Row 20: Repeat row 2.
Row 21: Repeat row 1.
Row 22: Repeat row 2.

Enclosed rope swatch.

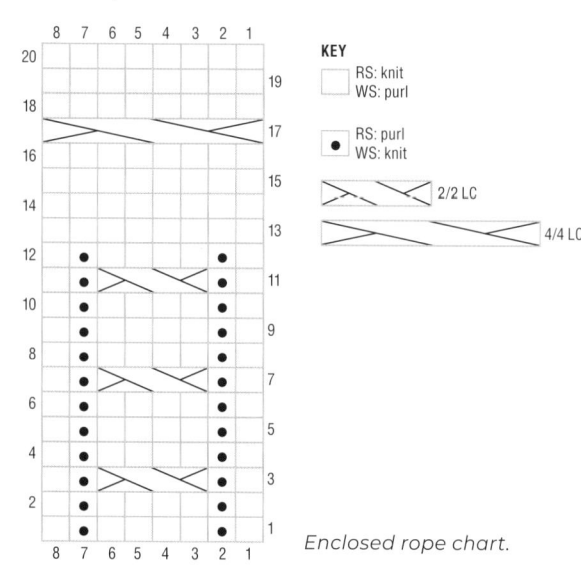

Enclosed rope chart.

Enclosed Rope

Row 1 (RS): K1, p1, k4, p1, k1 (8 sts).
Row 2 (WS): P1, k1, p4, k1, p1.
Row 3: K1, p1, 2/2LC, p1, k1.
Row 4: Repeat row 2.
Rows 5–12: Repeat rows 1–4.
Row 13: Knit.
Row 14: Purl.
Rows 15–16: Repeat rows 13–14.
Row 17: 4/4LC.
Row 18: Purl.
Row 19: Knit.
Row 20: Purl.

Garter Band

Row 1 (RS): P2, k2, p2, k4, p2, k2, p2 (16 sts).
Row 2 (WS): K2, p2, k2, p4, k2, p2, k2.
Rows 3–6: Repeat rows 1–2.
Row 7: P2, 4/2RPC, 4/2LPC, p2.
Row 8: Repeat row 2.
Row 9: Repeat row 1.
Rows 10–11: Repeat rows 8–9.
Row 12–16: Knit.

Goblets

Row 1 (RS): K1, (p2, k2) 3 times, p2, k1 (16 sts).
Row 2 and all WS rows: P1, (k2, p2) 3 times, k2, p1.
Row 3: Slip 4 sts onto cable needle and hold in front, k1, p2, k1, then work k1, p2, k1 on sts on cable needle.
Row 5: Repeat row 1.
Row 7: Repeat row 1.
Row 9: Repeat row 1.
Row 11: Repeat row 1.

60 STITCH DICTIONARY

Garter band swatch.

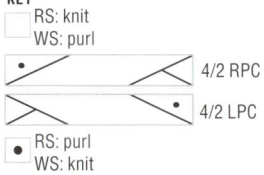

Goblets swatch.

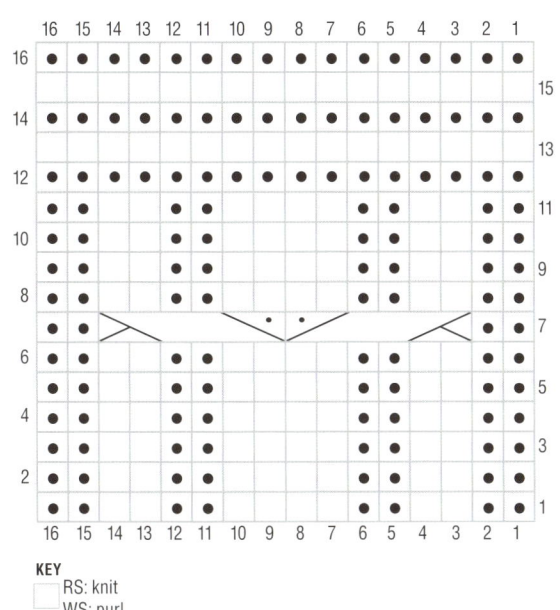

KEY
☐ RS: knit / WS: purl
• RS: purl / WS: knit
⟋⟍ 4/2 RPC
⟍⟋ 4/2 LPC

Garter band chart.

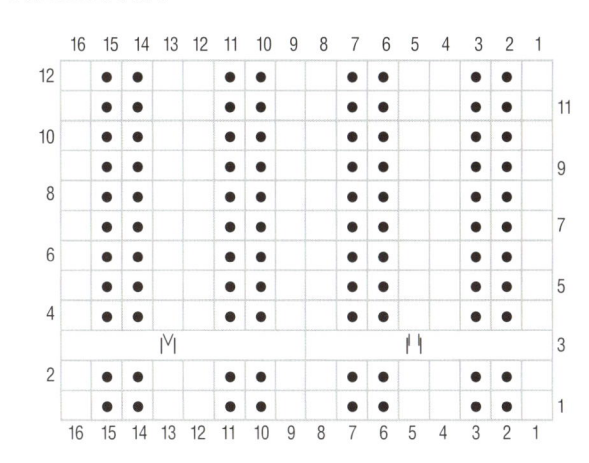

KEY
☐ RS: knit / WS: purl
• RS: purl / WS: knit

| |M| | Rib 8 back, slip 4 to back, k1, p2, k1, then k1, p2, k1 from cable needle |
| ↑↑ | Rib 8 front, slip 4 to back, k1, p2, k1, then k1, p2, k1 from cable needle |

Goblets chart.

STITCH DICTIONARY 61

Gullwing swatch.

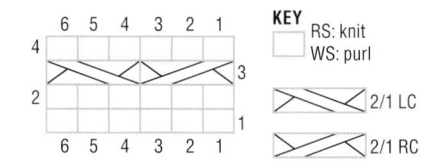

Gullwingchart.

Gullwing

Row 1 (RS): Knit (6 sts).
Row 2 (WS): Purl.
Row 3: 1/2RC, 1/2LC.
Row 4: Purl.

Half Diamond

Row 1 (RS): P7, k2, p1, k2, p7 (19 sts).
Row 2 (WS): K7, p2, k1, p2, k7.
Row 3: P7, 2/3RPC, p7.
Row 4: K7, p5, k7.
Row 5: P6, 2/1RPC, k1, 2/1LPC, p6.
Row 6: K6, p2, k1, p1, k1, p2, k6.
Row 7: P5, 2/1RPC, k1, p1, k1, 2/1LPC, p5.

Half diamond swatch.

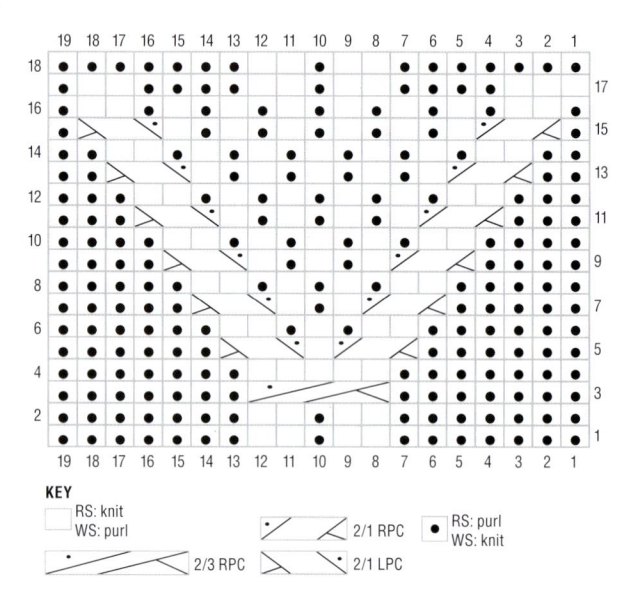

Half diamond chart.

Row 8: K5, p2, (k1, p1) twice, k1, p2, k5.
Row 9: P4, 2/1RPC, (k1, p1) twice, k1, 2/1LPC, p4.
Row 10: K4, p2, (k1, p1) 3 times, k1, p2, k4.
Row 11: P3, 2/1RPC, (k1, p1) 3 times, k1, 2/1LPC, p3.
Row 12: K3, p2, (k1, p1) 4 times, k1, p2, k3.
Row 13: P2, 2/1RPC, (k1, p1) 4 times, k1, 2/1LPC, p2.
Row 14: K2, p2, (k1, p1) 5 times, k1, p2, k2.
Row 15: P1, 2/1RPC, (k1, p1) 5 times, k1, 2/1LPC, p1.
Row 16: K1, p2, (k1, p1) 6 times, k1, p2, k1.
Row 17: (P1, k2, p4, k2) twice, p1.
Row 18: Repeat row 2.

Honeycomb swatch.

Horseshoe swatch.

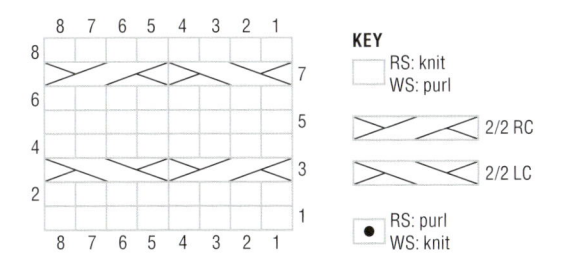

Honeycomb chart.

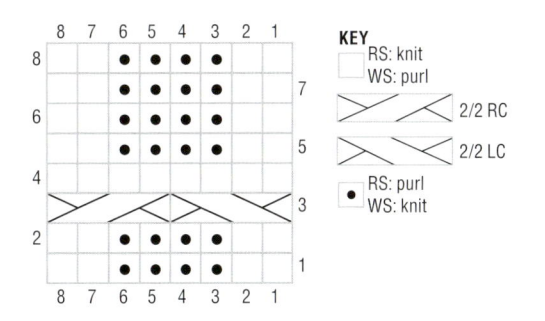

Horseshoe chart.

Honeycomb

Row 1 (RS): Knit (8 sts).
Row 2 and all WS rows: Purl.
Row 3: *2/2RC, 2/2LC; rep from * to end.
Row 5: Knit.
Row 7: *2/2LC, 2/2RC; rep from * to end.

Horseshoes

Row 1 (RS): K2, p4, k2 (8 sts).
Row 2 (WS): P2, k4, p2.
Row 3: 2/2LC, 2/2RC.
Row 4: Purl.
Rows 5–8: Repeat rows 1–2 twice

Medallions swatch.

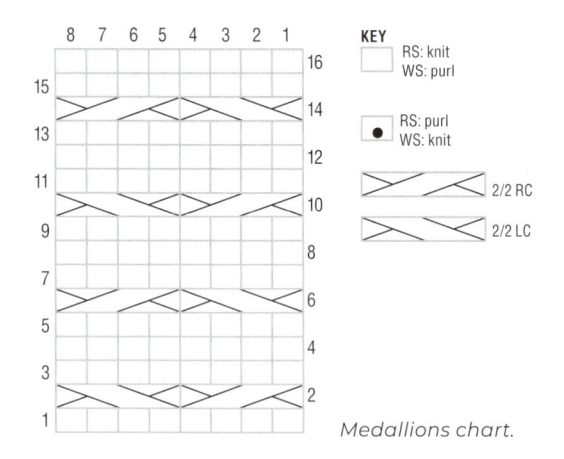

Medallions chart.

Medallion moss swatch.

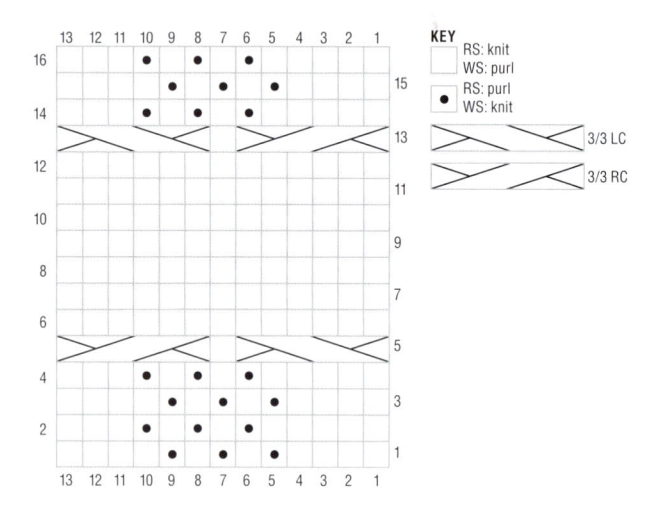

Medallion moss chart.

Medallions

Row 1 and all WS rows: Purl (8 sts).
Row 2 (RS): 2/2RC, 2/2LC.
Row 4: Knit.
Row 6: 2/2LC, 2/2RC.
Row 8: Knit.
Row 10: Repeat row 2.
Row 12: Knit.
Row 14: Repeat row 6.
Row 16: Knit.

Medallion Moss

Row 1 (RS): K4, (p1, k1) twice, p1, k4 (13 sts).
Row 2 (WS): P3, (k1, p1) twice, k1, p5.
Rows 3–4: Repeat rows 1–2.
Row 5: 3/3LC, k1, 3/3RC.
Row 6: Purl.
Row 7: Knit.
Rows 8–11: Repeat rows 6–7 twice.
Row 12: Purl.
Row 13: 3/3RC, k1, 3/3LC.
Row 14: Repeat row 2.
Row 15: Repeat row 1.
Row 16: Repeat row 2.

64 STITCH DICTIONARY

Nautical cable swatch.

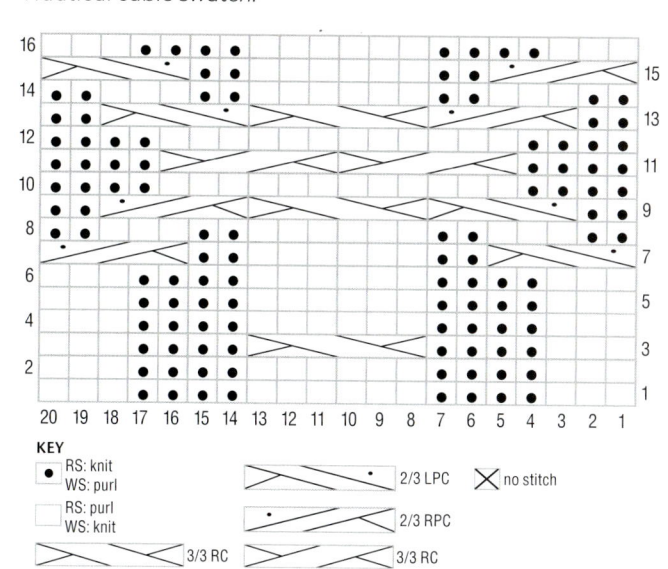

Nautical cable chart.

Row 10: K4, p12, k4.
Row 11: P4, 3/3RC twice, p4.
Row 12: Repeat row 10.
Row 13: P2, 2/3RPC, 3/3LC, 2/3LPC, p2.
Row 14: Repeat row 8.
Row 15: 2/3RPC, p2, k6, p2, 2/3LPC.
Row 16: Repeat row 2.

Nosegay

Row 1 (WS): K6, p2, k6 (14 sts).
Row 2 (RS): P5, 1/1RC, 1/1LC, p5.
Row 3: K4, 1/1LPC, p2, 1/1RPC, k4.
Row 4: P3, 1/1RPC, 1/1RC, 1/1LC, 1/1LPC, p3.
Row 5: K2, 1/1LPC, k1, p4, k1, 1/1RPC, k2.

Nosegay swatch.

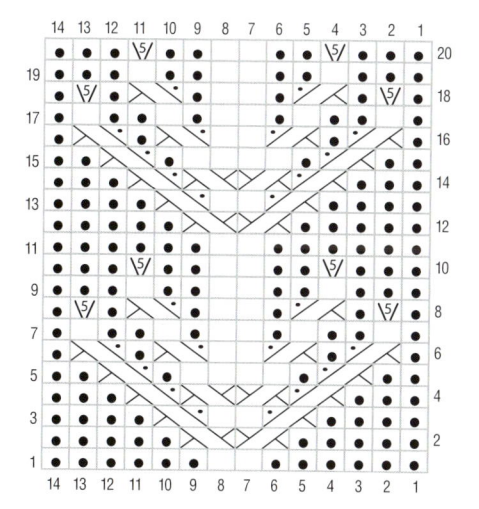

Nautical Cable

Row 1 (RS): K3, p4, k6, p4, k3 (20 sts).
Row 2 (WS): P3, k4, p6, k4, p3.
Row 3: K3, p4, 3/3LC, p4, k3.
Row 4: Repeat row 2.
Row 5: Repeat row 1.
Row 6: Repeat row 2.
Row 7: 2/3LPC, p2, k6, p2, 2/3RPC.
Row 8: K2, p3, k2, p6, k2, p3, k2.
Row 9: P2, 2/3LPC, 3/3LC, 2/3RPC, p2.

Nosegay chart.

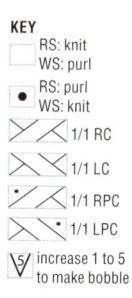

STITCH DICTIONARY 65

Row 6: (P1, 1/1RPC) twice, k2, (1/1LPC, p1) x 2.
Row 7: K1, p1, k2, p1, k1, p2, k1, p1, k2, p1, k1.
Row 8: P1, incto5, p1, 1/1RPC, p1, k2, p1, 1/1LPC, p1, incto5, p1 (22 sts).
Row 9: K3, p1, k2, p2, k2, p1, k3 (14 sts).
Row 10: P3, incto5, p2, k2, p2, incto5, p3 (22 sts).
Rows 11–20: Repeat rows 1–10.

Nutcracker swatch.

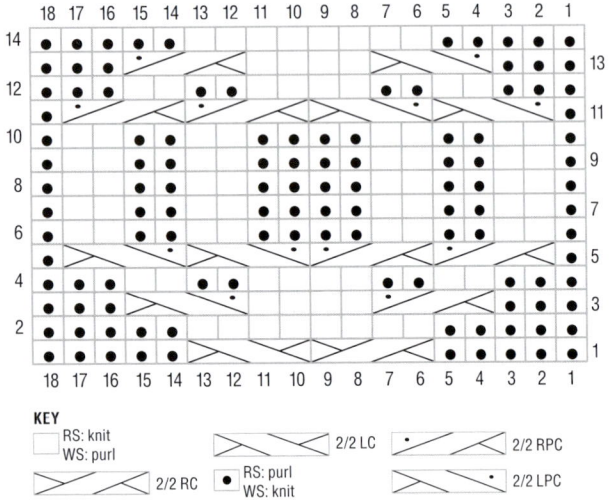

Nutcracker chart.

Nutcracker

Row 1 (RS): P5, 2/2RC, 2/2LC, p5 (18 sts).
Row 2 (WS): K5, p8, k5.
Row 3: P3, 2/2RPC, k4, 2/2LPC, p3.
Row 4: K3, p2, k2, p4, k2, p2, k3.
Row 5: P1, 2/2RPC twice, 2/2LPC twice, p1.
Row 6: K1, p2, k2, p2, k4, p2, k2, p2, k1.
Row 7: P1, k2, p2, k2, p4, k2, p2, k2, p1.
Rows 8–9: Repeat rows 6–7.
Row 10: Repeat row 6.
Row 11: P1, 2/2LPC twice, 2/2RPC twice, p1.
Row 12: Repeat row 4.
Row 13: P3, 2/2LPC, k4, 2/2RPC, p3.
Row 14: Repeat row 2.

Outlined diamonds swatch.

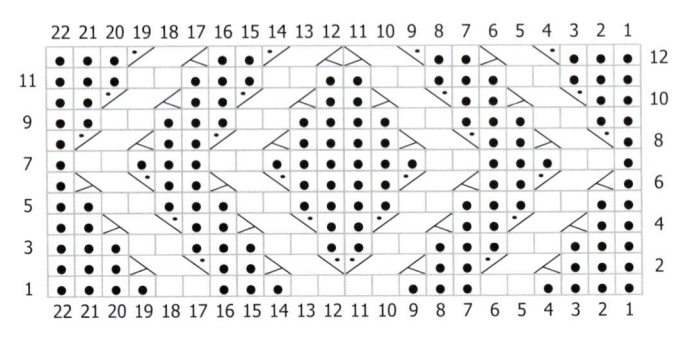

Outlined diamonds chart.

Outlined Diamonds

Row 1 (WS): K4, p2, k3, p4, k3, p2, k4 (22 sts).
Row 2 (RS): P3, 2/1RPC, p2, 2/1RPC, 2/1LPC, p2, 2/1LPC, p3.
Row 3: (K3, p2) twice, k2, (p2, k3) twice.
Row 4: (P2, 2/1 RPC) twice, (p2, 2/1LPC) twice, p2.
Row 5: K2, p2, k3, p2, k4, p2, k3, p2, k2.
Row 6: P1, 2/1RPC, p2, 2/1RPC, p4, 2/1LPC, p2, 2/1LPC, p1.
Row 7: K1, p2, k3, p2, k6, p2, k3, p2, k1.

Row 8: P1, 2/1LPC, p2, 2/1LPC, p4, 2/1RPC, p2, 2/1RPC, p1.
Row 9: Repeat row 5.
Row 10: (P2, 2/1LPC) twice, (p2, 2/1RPC) twice, p2.
Row 11: Repeat row 3.
Row 12: P3, 2/1LPC, p2, 2/1LPC, 2/1RPC, p2, 2/1RPC, p3.

Overlapping Diamonds

Row 1 (WS): K6, p4, k6 (16 sts).
Row 2 (RS): P6, 2/2RC, p6.
Row 3: Repeat row 1.
Row 4: P4, 2/2RPC, 2/2LPC, p4.
Row 5: (K4, p2) twice, k4.
Row 6: P2, 2/2RC, p4, 2/2LC, p2.
Row 7: K2, p4, k4, p4, k2.
Row 8: (2/2RPC, 2/2LPC) twice.
Row 9: P2, k4, p4, k4, p2.
Row 10: K2, p4, 2/2RC, p4, k2.
Row 11: Repeat row 9.
Row 12: 2/2LC, 2/2RPC, 2/2LPC, 2/2RC.
Row 13: P6, k4, p6.
Row 14: K2, 2/2LPC, p4, 2/2RPC, k2.
Row 15: P2, k2, p2, k4, p2, k2, p2.
Row 16: K2, p2, 2/2LPC, 2/2RPC, p2, k2.
Row 17: Repeat row 9.
Row 18: Repeat row 10.
Row 19: Repeat row 9.
Row 20: (2/2LPC, 2/2RPC) twice.
Row 21: Repeat row 7.
Row 22: P2, 2/2LPC, p4, 2/2RPC, p2.
Row 23: Repeat row 5.
Row 24: P4, 2/2LPC, 2/2RPC, p4.
Row 25: Repeat row 1.
Row 26: Repeat row 2.
Row 27: Repeat row 1.
Row 28: Repeat row 4.
Row 29: Repeat row 5.
Row 30: (P4, k2) twice, p4.
Row 31: Repeat row 5.
Rows 32–33: Repeat rows 30–31.
Row 34: Repeat row 24.

Overlapping diamonds swatch.

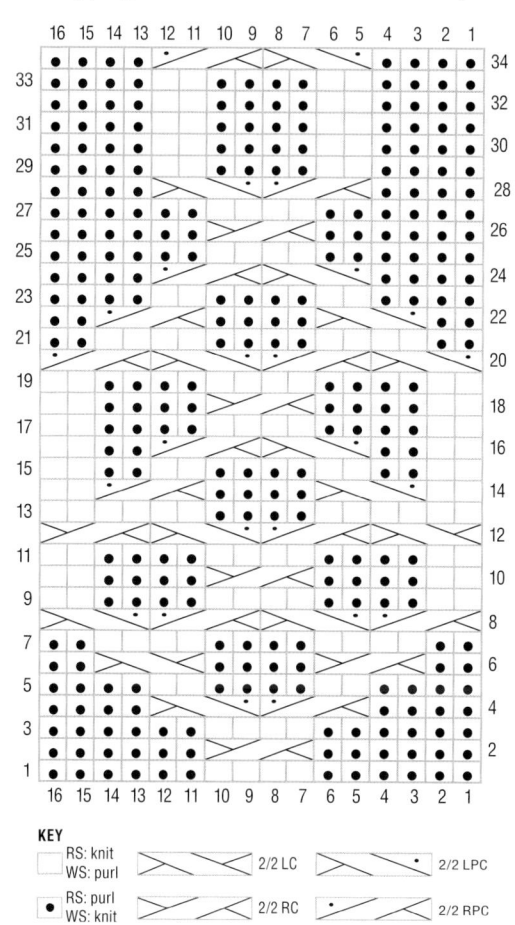

Overlapping diamonds chart.

Oxo swatch.

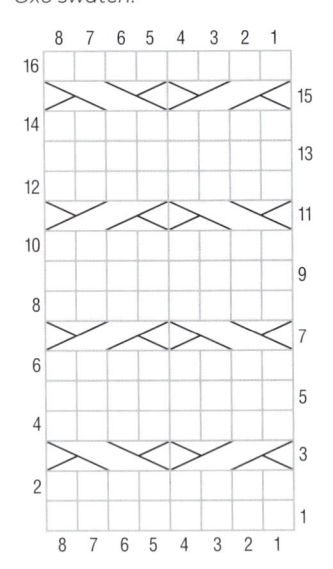

Oxo chart.

Ribbed braid swatch.

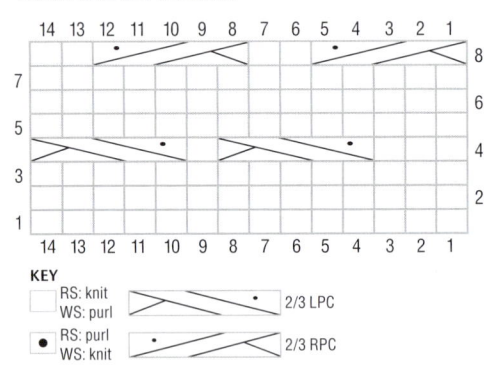

Ribbed braid chart.

Oxo

Row 1 (RS): Knit (8 sts).
Row 2 and all WS rows: Purl.
Row 3: 2/2RC, 2/2LC.
Row 5: Knit.
Row 7: 2/2LC, 2/2RC.
Row 9: Knit.
Row 11: Repeat row 7.
Row 13: Knit.
Row 15: Repeat row 3.

Ribbed Braid

Row 1 and all WS rows: (P2, k1) four times, p2 (14 sts).
Row 2 (RS): (K2, p1) four times, k2.
Row 4: K2, (p1, 2/3LPC) twice.
Row 6: Repeat row 2.
Row 8: (2/3RPC, k2) twice.

Ribbed cable swatch.

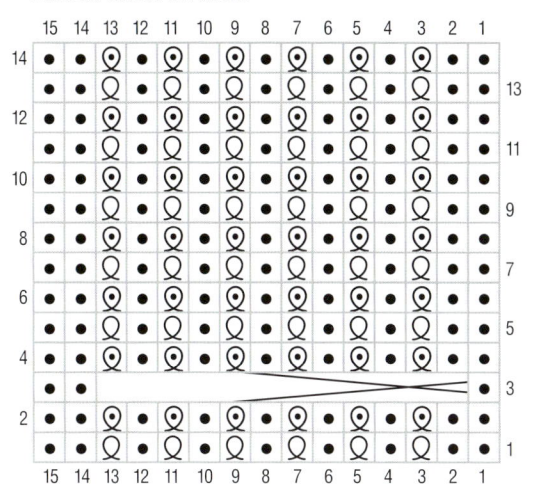

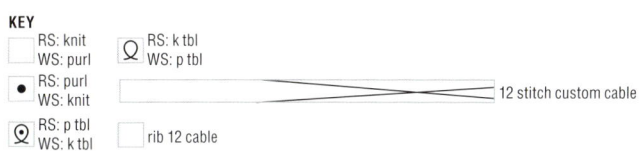

Rope 4-stitch swatch.

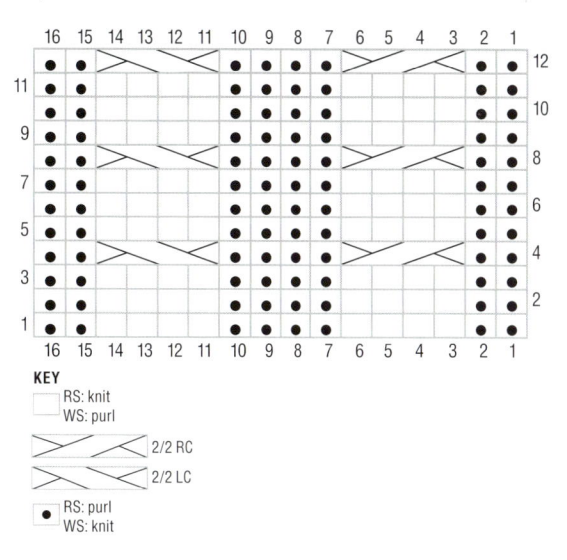

Ribbed cable chart.

Rope 4-stitch chart.

Ribbed Cable

Row 1 (RS): (P1, k1 tbl) 6 times, p1 (13 sts).
Row 2 and all WS rows: (K1, k1 tbl) 6 times, k1.
Row 3: Place next 6 sts on cable needle and leave at back, (k1, p1) 3 times, work (k1, p1) on stitches on cable needle, p1.
Row 5: Repeat row 1.
Row 7: Repeat row 1.
Row 9: Repeat row 1.
Row 11: Repeat row 1.
Row 13: Repeat row 1.

Rope 4-Stitch

Row 1 and all WS rows: K2, p4, k4, p4, k2 (16 sts).
Row 2 (RS): P2, k4, p4, k4, p2.
Row 4: P2, 2/2RC, p4, 2/2LC, p2.

STITCH DICTIONARY 69

Rope 6-stitch crossed every 8th row swatch.

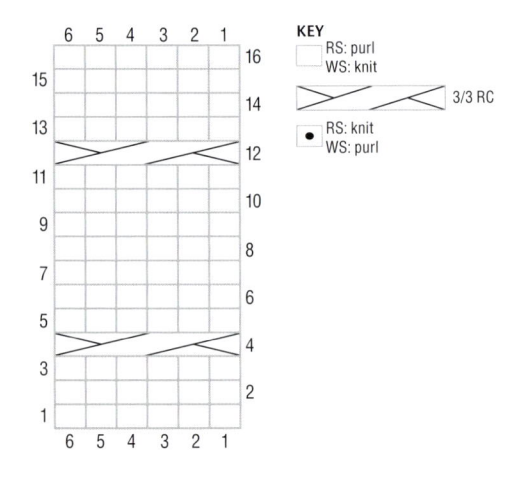

Small chain swatch.

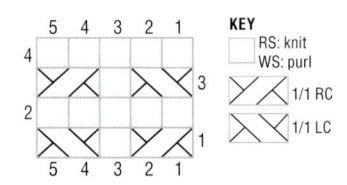

Rope 6-stitch crossed every 8th row chart.

Small chain chart.

Small Chain

Row 1 (RS): 1/1RC, k1, 1/1LC (5 sts).
Row 2 (WS): Purl.
Row 3: 1/1LC, k1, 1/1RC.
Row 4: Purl.

Rope 6-Stitch Crossed Every 8th Row

Row 1 and all WS rows: K2, p6, k2 (10 sts).
Row 2 (RS): P2, k6, p2.
Row 4: P2, 3/3RC, p2.
Row 6: Repeat row 2.
Row 8: Repeat row 2.
Row 10: Repeat row 2.
Row 12: Repeat row 4.
Row 14: Repeat row 2.
Row 16: Repeat row 2.

Snake cables left and right swatch.

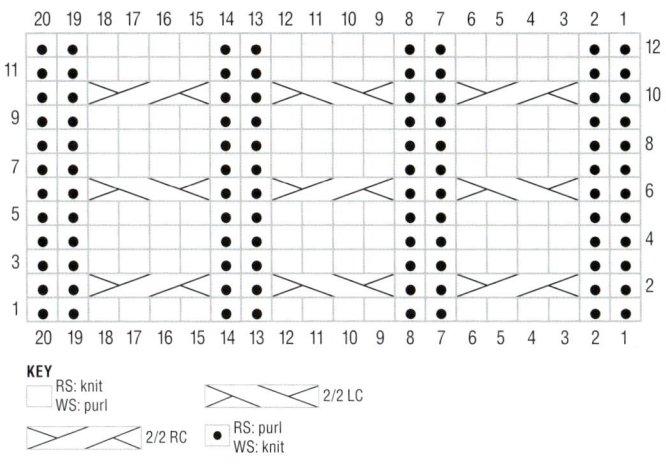

Snake cables left and right chart.

Staghorn swatch.

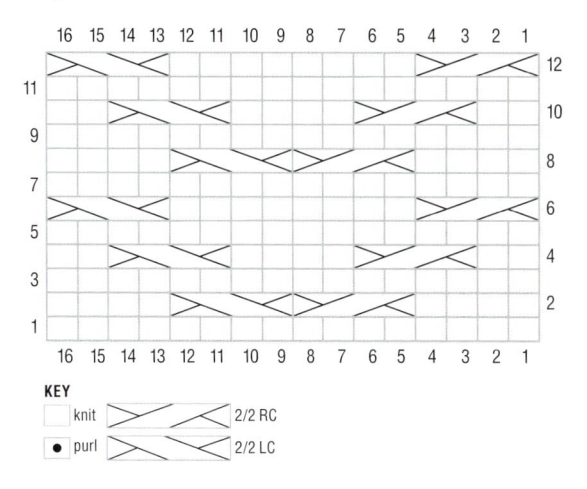

Staghorn chart.

Snake Cables Left and Right

Row 1 and all WS rows: (K2, p4) 3 times, k2 (20 sts).
Row 2 (RS): P2, 2/2RC, p2, 2/2LC, p2, 2/2RC, p2.
Row 4: (P2, k4) 3 times, p2.
Row 6: P2, 2/2LC, p2, 2/2RC, p2, 2/2LC, p2.
Row 8: Repeat row 4.
Row 10: Repeat row 2.
Row 12: Repeat row 4.

Staghorn

Row 1 and all WS rows: Purl (16 sts).
Row 2 (RS): K4, 2/2RC, 2/2LC, k4.
Row 4: K2, 2/2RC, k4, 2/2LC, k2.
Row 6: 2/2RC, k8, 2/2LC.
Row 8: Repeat row 2.
Row 10: Repeat row 4.
Row 12: Repeat row 6.

STITCH DICTIONARY 71

Trellis swatch.

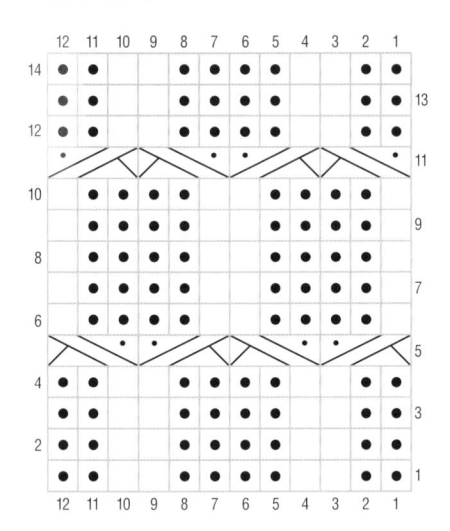

Trellis chart.

Triple cross swatch.

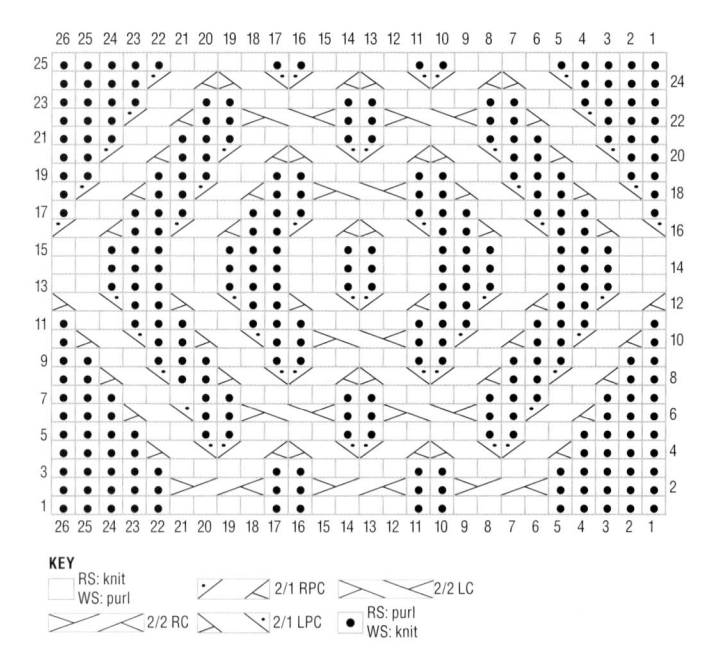

Triple cross chart.

Trellis

Row 1 (RS): P2, k2, p4, k2, p2 (12 sts).
Row 2 (WS): K2, p2, k4, p2, k2.
Rows 3–4: Repeat rows 1–2.
Row 5: (1/2RPC, 1/2LPC) twice.
Row 6: P1, k4, p2, k4, p1.
Row 7: K1, p4, k2, p4, k1.
Rows 8–9: Repeat rows 6–7.
Row 10: Repeat row 6.
Row 11: (1/2LPC, 1/2RPC) twice.
Row 12: Repeat row 2.
Row 13: Repeat row 1.
Row 14: Repeat row 2.

Triple Cross

Row 1 (WS): K5, (p4, k2) twice, p4, k5 (26 sts).
Row 2 (RS): P5, (2/2RC, p2) twice, 2/2RC, p5.
Row 3: Repeat row 1.
Row 4: P4, (2/1RPC, 2/1LPC) 3 times, p4.
Row 5: K4, p2, (k2, p4) twice, k2, p2, k4.
Row 6: P3, 2/1RPC, (p2, 2/2LC) twice, p2, 2/1LPC, p3.
Row 7: K3, p3, (k2, p4) twice, k3, p2, k3.
Row 8: (P2, 2/1RPC) twice, 2/1LPC, 2/1RPC, (2/1LPC, p2) twice.
Row 9: K2, p2, k3, p2, k2, p4, k2, p2, k3, p2, k2.

72 STITCH DICTIONARY

Row 10: P1, (2/1RPC, p2) twice, 2/2 LC, (p2, 2/1LPC) twice, p1.
Row 11: K1, (p2, k3) twice, p4, (k3, p2) twice, k1.
Row 12: (2/1RPC, p2) twice, 2/1RPC, (2/1LPC, p2) twice, 2/1LPC.
Row 13: (P2, k3) twice, p2, k2, (p2, k3) twice, p2.
Row 14: (K2, p3) twice, k2, p2, (k2, p3) twice, k2.
Row 15: Repeat row 13.
Row 16: (2/1LPC, p2) twice, 2/1LPC, (2/1RPC, p2) twice, 2/1RPC.
Row 17: Repeat row 11.
Row 18: P1, (2/1LPC, p2) twice, 2/2LC, (p2, 2/1RPC) twice, p1.
Row 19: Repeat row 9.
Row 20: (P2, 2/1LPC) twice, 2/1RPC, 2/1LPC, (2/1RPC, p2) twice.
Row 21: K3, p2, k3, p4, k2, p4, k3, p2, k3.
Row 22: P3, 2/1LPC, (p2, 2/2LC) twice, p2, 2/1RPC, p3.
Row 23: Repeat row 5.
Row 24: P4, (2/1LPC, 2/1RPC) 3 times, p4.
Row 25: Repeat row 1.

Triple Cable

Row 1 (RS): P9, k4, p9 (22 sts).
Row 2 (WS): K9, p4, k9.
Row 3: P9, 2/2RC, p9.
Row 4: Repeat row 2.
Row 5: P7, 2/2RC, 2/2LC, p7.
Row 6: K7, p8, k7.
Row 7: P5, 2/2RPC, 2/2LC, 2/2LPC, p5.
Row 8: K5, p2, k2, p4, k2, p2, k5.
Row 9: P3, 2/2RPC, p2, k4, p2, 2/2LPC, p3.
Row 10: K3, p2, k4, p4, k3, p3, k3.
Row 11: P2, 2/1RPC, p4, 2/2LC, p4, 2/1LPC, p2.
Row 12: K2, p2, k5, p4, k5, p2, k2.
Row 13: P1, 2/1RPC, p3, 2/2RC, 2/2LC, p3, 2/1LPC, p1.
Row 14: K1, p2, k4, p8, k4, p2, k1.
Row 15: 2/1RPC, p2, 2/2RPC, k4, 2/2LPC, p2, 2/1LPC.
Row 16: P2, k3, p2, k2, p4, k2, p2, k3, p2.
Row 17: K2, p1, 2/2RPC, p2, 2/2RC, p2, 2/2LPC, p1, k2.
Row 18: P2, k1, p2, k4, p4, k4, p2, k1, p2.
Row 19: K2, p1, k2, p4, k4, p4, k2, p1, k2.
Row 20: Repeat row 18.
Row 21: K2, p1, 2/2 LPC, p2, 2/2 RC, p2, 2/2 RPC, p1, k2.
Row 22: Repeat row 16.
Row 23: 2/1LPC, p2, 2/2LPC, k4, 2/2RPC, p2, 2/1RPC.

Triple cable swatch.

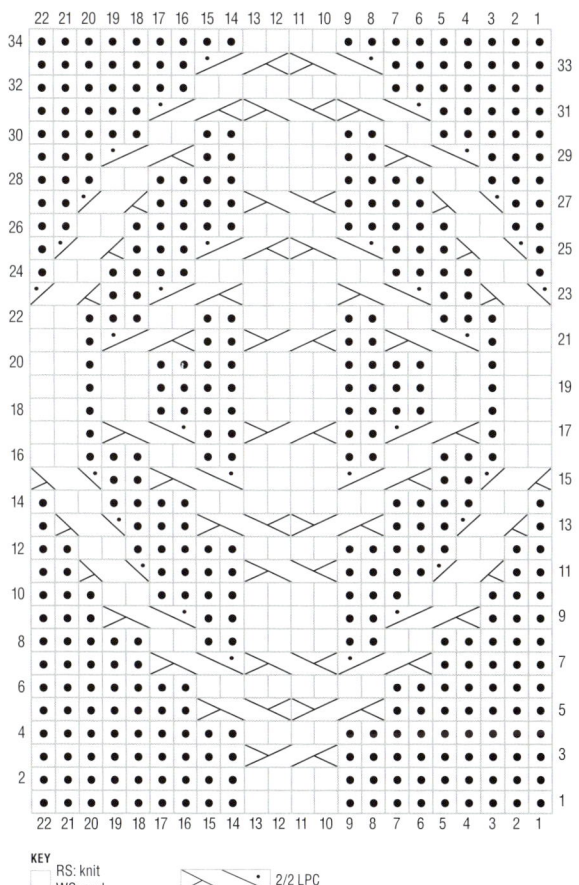

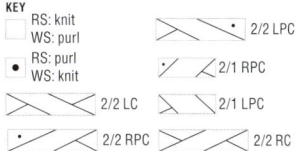

Triple cable chart.

Row 24: Repeat row 14.
Row 25: P1, 2/1LPC, p3, 2/2LPC, 2/2RPC, p3, 2/1RPC, p1.
Row 26: Repeat row 12.
Row 27: P2, 2/1LPC, p4, 2/2LC, p4, 2/1RPC, p2.
Row 28: K3, p2, k4, p4, k4, p2, k3.
Row 29: P3, 2/2LPC, p2, k4, p2, 2/2RPC, p3.
Row 30: Repeat row 8.
Row 31: P5, 2/2LPC, 2/2LC, 2/2RPC, p5.
Row 32: Repeat row 6.
Row 33: P7, 2/2LPC, 2/2RPC, p7.
Row 34: Repeat row 2

Wishbone and Moss

Row 1 (RS): 1/3RPC, 1/3LPC (8 sts).
Row 2 (WS): (P1, k1) 3 times, p2.
Row 3: (K1, p1) 3 times, k2.
Rows 4–7: Repeat rows 2–3 twice.
Row 8: P1, k1, p3, k1, p2.

Wishbone and moss swatch.

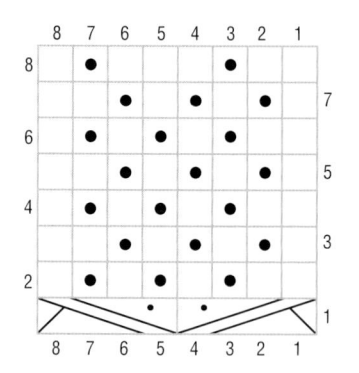

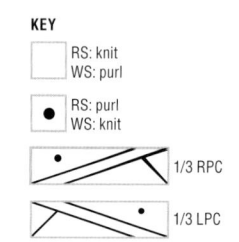

Wishbone and moss chart.

Stitch Modifications

Here are some changes that you can try with some of the stitches described above.

Gullwing can also be worked by slipping the centre stitches on the first two rows and then crossing them on the third. This gives a slightly flatter appearance and does not pull in as much.

Claw is similar to Gullwing but is worked over 9 stitches instead of 6. It is a good alternative if you want the pattern to appear to have more depth, which results from the single stitch being stretched further.

Diamonds are often worked over a purl background and with purl or moss stitches at their centre. To work these stitches without a cable needle, for a 3stitch left purl cross, purl the third stitch through the back loop, then knit the remaining two stitches, one at a time, and slip them all off the needle. For a right purl cross, slip the first stitch from the left needle and pinch it between finger and thumb. Knit 2, then replace the pinched stitch on the left needle and purl it, winding the yarn anticlockwise to avoid creating a loose knit stitch just before it.

Double cross does not have to be as wide as in the sample. It is easy to change the plain columns to two or three stitches instead of four.

Honeycomb is a classic Aran stitch used on many items. Multiples of eight stitches are placed side by side to form a central panel, which looks more complex than it is. It can easily be divided for front-opening garments and only half of one of the groups can be worked if necessary to fit into the required number of stitches.

Rope cable over 4 stitches is the simplest and most useful of all of the cables. It can be crossed every fourth row or, to make a looser, softer cable, on every sixth row. The stitches of rope cables can be made to appear to move to the right or left depending on whether the held stitches are kept at the back or the front of the worked stitches until they too are ready to be worked.

Rope cables can be crossed over any number of stitches, but the wider they are, the more they will distort the fabric. Some of the early Arans would cross over an uneven number of stitches, so that the larger number of stitches passing over the top did not have as far to stretch. I have included different frequencies of crossings in the Stitch Dictionary to show the difference that the number of rows between the crossings makes.

Narrow cables can be used instead of k1, p1 or k2, p2 ribs at the hem or other edges of a garment. A k2, p2 rib could have all of the knit stitches worked as twisted, 1/1 crossed stitches. They could all cross the same way or change direction half way across the hem. You can use 4-stitch rope cables with two purl stitches between them in the same way. Another attractive rib is seen on the copy of the 1936 Aran in Chapter 1. This is made up of three twisted knit stitches followed by a purl stitch and then a small chain cable.

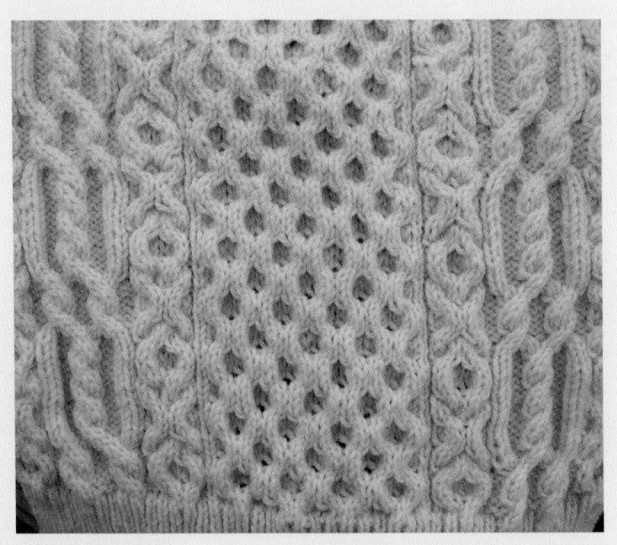

A central panel of honeycomb stitch with other cables alongside.

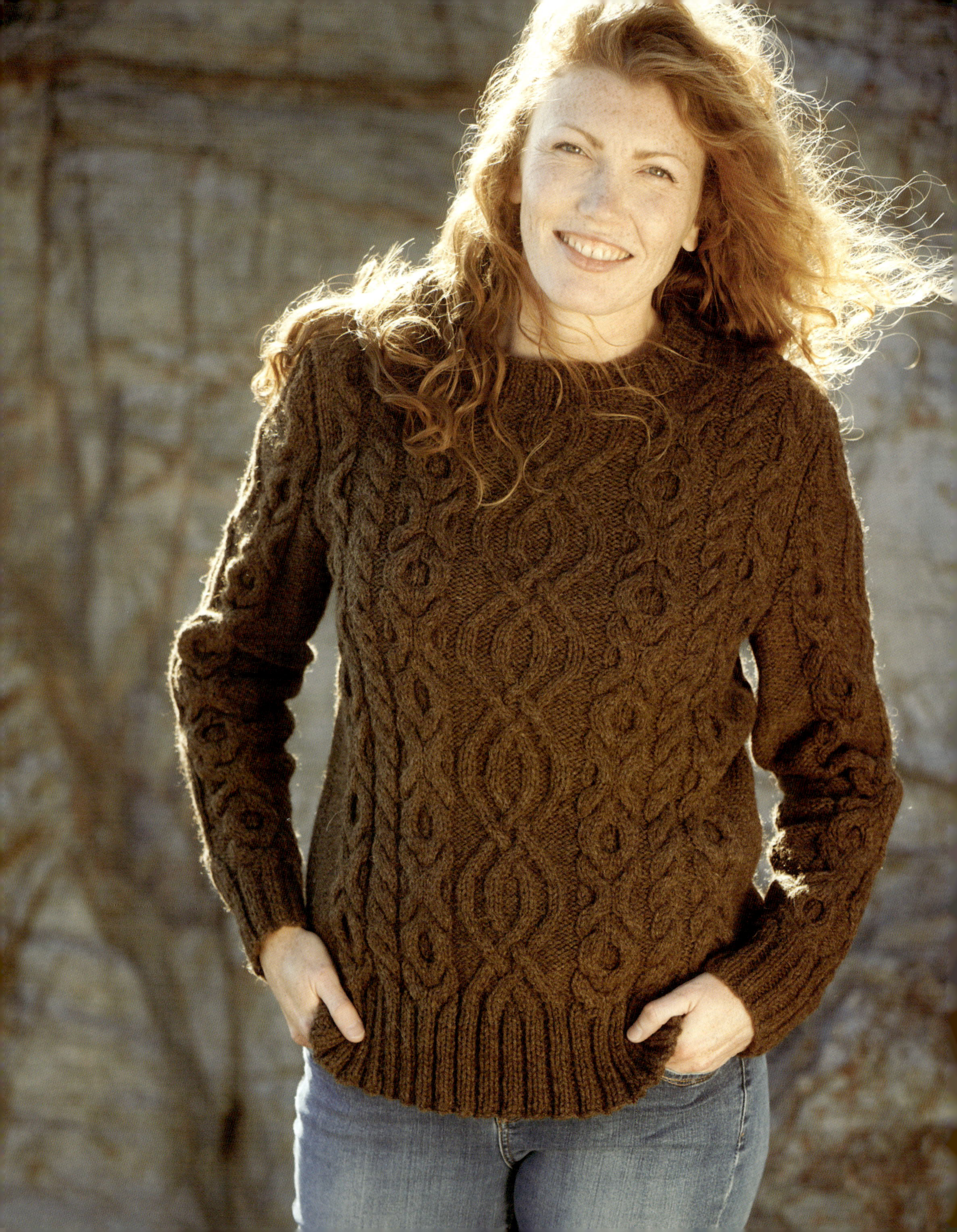

CHAPTER 4

STARTING A PROJECT

Practice Pieces

Now that you have looked through the stitches and have been inspired to start, it is a good idea to work on some practice pieces first.

For a first attempt at Aran knitting, a handy way to practise a mixture of cables is to work a cowl, scarf or wrap. No shaping is involved and tension is not vital. This will give you an idea of how much narrower a piece of cabled knitting is than one that is made over the same number of stitches in stocking stitch.

Working a number of basic cables side by side with panels of reverse stocking stitch between them will make an attractive scarf and help you to familiarize yourself with the technique of working with a cable needle. If you work 4 or 5 stitches in garter stitch or moss stitch at the edges, it will stop the piece from curling.

When you have made your sample swatches, look at the back of them; some of them will look just as good on the wrong side. Garter cable is an example of this, as are any ribbed cables. Where there are at least four stitches of stocking stitch on the wrong side between cables, these panels can also be turned into cables. If you are working a scarf or cowl that turns to the inside when it is wrapped around the neck, you can make use of the stocking stitch sections on the back to create a new pattern.

The back of the garter cable, showing how it is just as interesting on the reverse.

OPPOSITE PAGE: *A pleasing combination of cables.*

When you are comfortable with working rope cables, choose a variety of stitches that will help you to practise the different techniques required and to familiarize yourself with working from charts that look more difficult. For example, a central diamond panel, a pair of twisted stitches and a wider rope cable would look attractive together, and you will gain more experience as each stitch is worked in a slightly different way. Look through the stitch dictionary and choose patterns that you think will look eye-catching together.

Before you start knitting, familiarize yourself with the symbols in the key to the charts. Also note any red or coloured outlines around sections of the stitches on the charts. These lines denote the part of the pattern that is to be repeated. The number of repeats you need will depend on the width of your item; so for a scarf, for instance, you may only need one repeat.

The stitches outside the repeated section will need to be worked at the beginning and end of the row to complete the pattern. Studying the chart before you start knitting will help you to work out how many edge stitches you need and where to start the pattern in your own piece of knitting.

When you are ready, cast on enough stitches to accommodate all of your chosen patterns and work a few rows of rib to stop the piece from curling up. Beginning with row 1 on the chart, work each of your patterns with a few stitches in reverse stocking stitch between them. Again, to prevent the edges from curling, work 3 or 4 stitches in garter stitch at the beginning and end of each row.

Back of cushion.

Another simple project with no shaping is a cushion cover. You can use a cushion cover to practise knitting columns of rope cables of various widths, crossing in different directions and at different frequencies. Make a swatch of three or four of the cables, measure this swatch and calculate how many times to work them and how many extra filler stitches you will need between each one. If you want the back of the cushion in a different stitch – rib or stocking stitch, for example – knit a sample of that too, as the tension will be different to that of the front of the cushion. Work the back and front as separate pieces, or work the whole as a long strip, beginning with the back. Remember to check the difference in tension achieved between the cabled swatches and the stocking stitch swatches to allow for the extra width that the Aran work demands.

The cushion in Chapter 5 starts in the middle of the back with a ribbed edge for buttons, and continues for half the length of the cushion in stocking stitch. A row of increases is worked next before changing to the pattern for the front. These extra stitches are then decreased before the second half of the back is worked in stocking stitch, followed by a ribbed buttonhole edge. There is no shaping to do apart from the increases and decreases.

You can use these simpler projects as the inspiration for a sweater. Measure the width of your piece and work out how many more stitches you need to add to achieve your chest measurement. Any additional stitches can be fitted into the reverse stocking stitch panels, or they can be added at the sides. If you choose to add extra cables, remember to measure them separately, as they can draw the fabric in even more. This method will suffice if you are not too particular about width and length measurements.

To make something with exact dimensions, make swatches of each of your chosen stitches, including the filler stitches and any others at the side edges, and measure them separately. Lay them out side by side to make sure that you are happy with the arrangement before measuring each of the samples. Calculate how many stitches to add between the panels in order to get the size you have in mind.

Taking Measurements

When you are ready to plan a garment, you will need to take a number of measurements to make sure of a perfect fit. Although knitted fabric is more flexible than a woven one, it is still advisable to take accurate measurements. Most commercial patterns base their measurements on the bust or chest; however, it is the torso measurement that will give the best fit, as getting an accurate fit across the shoulders makes a big difference to the success of a knitted garment. The torso measurement is taken above the bust line. Imagine a line down from the outside edge of the shoulder to your armpit at each side of the body and measure between these lines. If a set-in or raglan sleeve top extends beyond the shoulder edge, the garment will not hang properly and will never look right. Ideally, an Aran will fit on the shoulders but have 5–10cm of ease around the body. It isn't a garment that you would normally wear with a tight fit. But once you have a set of accurate measurements, of course, you can design it to fit however you wish.

If the garment is for you, it might be useful to have someone to help you take measurements. The back of the neck is a difficult one to do on your own. If you don't have a helper, then take the measurements from an existing garment that fits well.

Before you start, wear appropriate clothing – something soft and close-fitting, or just your undergarments. Stand up straight (which is why you need someone to help!). Use a soft plastic or cloth tape measure. Don't pull it tight to the body but leave room for a finger behind the tape.

Here are the measurements you need to take.

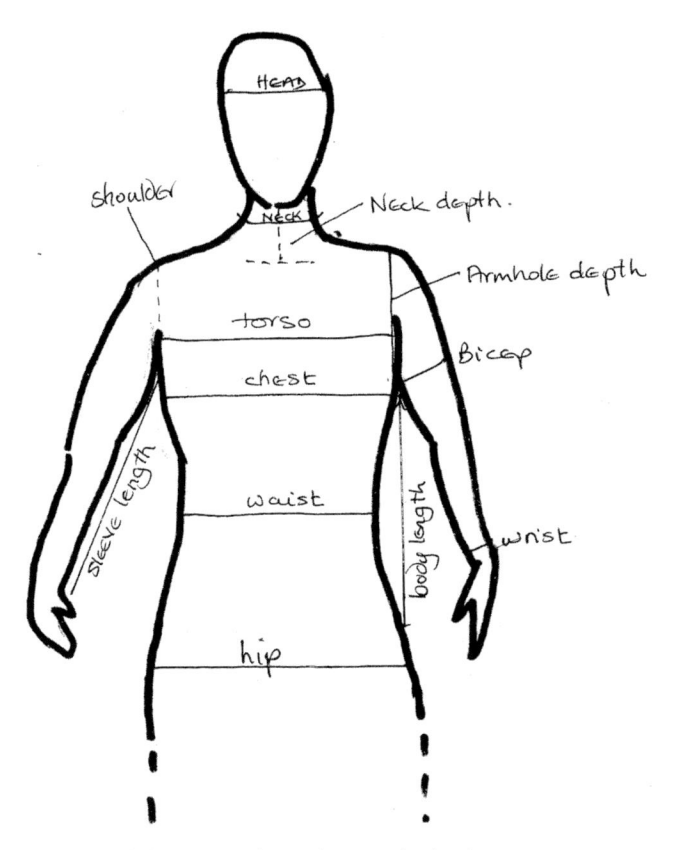

Diagram of the measuring points on the body.

Chest

Measure around the fullest part of your chest, ensuring that the measuring tape is parallel to the floor. The back and front of your sweater will be one half of this width plus however much you decide to add on for comfort.

Torso

Measure around the point where any armhole shaping would end, about midway between the shoulder and chest.

Neck

Measure around the largest part of the neck. If you are creating a circular neckline and would like to make a wider neck, you can add extra room here. However, I would not recommend making the neckline more than 25cm larger than your actual neck.

Neck Depth

For a round neck or V-neck, measure down the front of your neck to where the shaping is to start. Allow no less than 6cm for a crew neck, although it can be less than this for a wide, shallow neckline.

Armhole Depth

Measure from the top outside edge of the shoulder down to the armpit in a perpendicular line.

Body Length

Measure from your underarm to your desired sweater length.

Waist

Measure around the narrowest part of your body. If you are not sure exactly where this is, tip from side and it will be where your body bends.

Back Waist Length

Measure from the most prominent bone at the base of the neck to the natural waist.

Hip

Measure around the widest part of the hip (often about 17 to 18cm) down from the waist. Turn slightly sideways in front of a mirror so that you can see if that is the fullest part of your body.

Waist to Hip

Measure from your natural waist to where you placed the tape measure around your hips.

Sleeve Length

Measure from your armpit to your desired cuff length, bending the arm slightly.

Upper Arm

Measure around the widest part of the upper arm, the bicep.

Wrist

Measure around the wrist where the hand joins the arm.

For a Hat

Measure around the head across the forehead. Then measure the depth from this line to the top of the head.

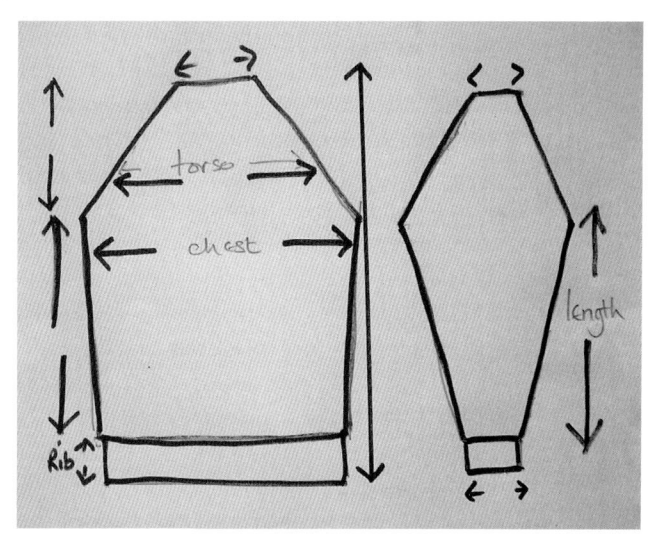

A schematic for a raglan-sleeved jumper with positions of important measuring points shown.

Make yourself a schematic (a diagram) of the shape of the sweater you are planning and mark these measurements on it. Make a photocopy of it (more if you are planning to knit more garments), so that you can also use it to mark the position of the various stitch motifs.

Keep a note of these measurements, and those of anyone else that you are knitting for. You will probably want to add a few extra centimetres for ease depending on how fitted you want the garment to be; 5 to 10cm is the usual amount.

If you are knitting for someone else and you do not have their measurements, then consult an online table of measurements for the average person. An example is given here.

Once you have all the necessary measurements, it is time to decide how much ease allowance needs to be added into the garment in order for it to feel comfortable. Something made in an Aran weight yarn for outerwear would probably need more ease than a garment worn next to the skin. The amount of ease determines how the garment will hang, and in an Aran this can be anything from a few centimetres wider than the chest measurement to almost double the width, depending on current fashion and personal preferences.

Make a diagram of a typical sweater shape and mark on it the actual body measurements. Decide how much ease you require for each piece and make a note of it. The amount of ease you need in the body will not be the same as that for the sleeves. Ease is the amount of extra width, on top of your actual measurments, that you would like in your garment. Remember that something worn next to the skin is likely to need less ease than a garment worn on top of others.

Standard sizes and measurements

Size (cm)	XS	Small	Med	Lge	XL	2X	3X	4X
Bust	71–76	81–86	96–96	101–106	112–117	122–127	132–137	142–147
Waist	58–61	63–67	71–76	81–86	91–96	101–106	112–114	117–119
Hips	83–86	89–91	96–100	106–112	117–122	132–134	137–139	142–144
Sleeve	40–42	43	44	44	44	45	45	45

Finding Inspiration

Now comes the interesting part of the process: designing your own individual Aran sweater. There are hundreds of different cable patterns; only a small portion of them are illustrated here or this book would run into a number of volumes! Choosing your own stitch patterns and combining them to make a unique and pleasing piece of knitting is a rewarding process, and far more satisfying than following someone else's pattern. The patterns illustrated here have been used for many years and will give you a garment that has all the hallmarks of a traditional Aran.

Finding inspiration for the arrangement of cables is a combination of practice and observation. While you are not copying designs exactly, look at as many of them as is practical to get an idea of what it is about that design that makes it so appealing. Which Aran designs have you seen that please you most? And which ones do you dislike? Is it a particular stitch pattern or the combination of the stitches? The more pictures you look at, the more you will begin to understand what is that you like best and how you can use this information to create a design of your own.

You might think that a bold and dramatic cable would work best when flanked by a series of simple rope cables, but many designs that work well have another set of complex stitches each side of the centre cable. In the cardigan design shown here I placed two solid interlocking cables at the centre, followed by a simple rope and then the more open overlapping diamonds pattern. It does seem to work, although you may think differently!

There are many stitch dictionaries available containing images of cable patterns, but apart from *The Harmony Guide to Aran Stitches*, they all show each stitch in isolation. For combinations and the arrangement of shapes, look at commercially available patterns, photographs and sites such as Pinterest. But be wary of copying exactly; there is a fine

Vertical diamond pattern on the wall of a church.

Diamond pattern and interesting motif.

Design for a cardigan featuring interlocking cables, rope and overlapping diamonds.

Wrought iron gate with a star-like pattern that could be used to create a centre panel.

A church kneeler with an embroidery pattern of separated diamonds.

Window with interlinked diamonds.

line between 'copied' and 'inspired by', and copyright rules are strict. Artists of all kinds draw inspiration from various sources, from each other, from nature, other crafts and artefacts. The built environment is very useful for generating ideas; pillars, tiles, windows, wrought iron work, fences, stonework – all of these can all be adapted for the purpose of a design.

And any striped fabric/paper is useful to help with visualizing different widths of patterns together.

Inspiration can be found in many unexpected places, too. The farm gate shown here turned sideways might well have inspired the diamond panel with its twisted ribs.

As well as working from stitch dictionaries, it is also possible to create unique cables of your own. As Elsebeth Lavold and Alice Starmore have found, Viking and Celtic knotwork are ideal sources of inspiration for intricately twisted cable patterns. Take photographs of anything that appears interesting to you and use them as a starting point for creating a new stitch. The invention of software for creating charts has made this process much simpler, but plotting them out on graph paper works just as well, if at a slower pace.

These newer motifs, inspired by the intricate interwindings of lines found in works such as the Book of Kells or on carved stones are termed 'open' or 'infinite' cables. To work them, a number of stitches need to be increased at the beginning and decreased at the end. There are various ways of creating the extra stitches that are needed to begin one of these motifs. My preferred method is to work to one stitch before the stitch on which the cable is to be centred. Work that stitch, then insert the left needle into the left leg of the stitch in the row below and knit into it. In the centre stitch of the cable, work into the back and front, then into the left leg at the base of the stitch you have just created, making three stitches from one. Then work into the right leg of the stitch below the next stitch on the left needle. You will have five stitches where there were previously three.

There are several books of illustrations which give instructions for creating your own 'Celtic knotwork' in calligraphy. These can be a great source of inspiration for knitted cables.

Once you have chosen your preferred cable panels, using mathematical sequences and ratios is a useful way of judging whether a design will work and look pleasing to the eye. A

A design that could be repeated vertically.

A section of wallpaper showing stripes of different proportions.

central cable flanked by others gradually decreasing in width always works well and is the traditional way of working an Aran sweater. When planning your design, remember that the eye sees shape, value and texture, in that order. So we are attracted to the overall shape of the cable, the shadow it creates and the way it stands out from the background, plus its relationship to the other shapes around it. This is why Aran knits are best worked in a smooth, light-coloured yarn for the best definition of the motifs.

A typical traditional sweater design has about five different stitch patterns in vertical columns with the widest panel, often a diamond or honeycomb, at the centre flanked by others that become progressively narrower towards the edges. But while this is a traditional sequence, it is not a rule set in stone. There is no reason why you could not have an asymmetrical design with the widest panel at one side and other cables placed across the rest of the body

A piece of fabric as inspiration for varying widths of stripes.

The pattern on this farm gate turned sideways as inspiration for a diamond cable.

Diamond with twisted rib.

STARTING A PROJECT 83

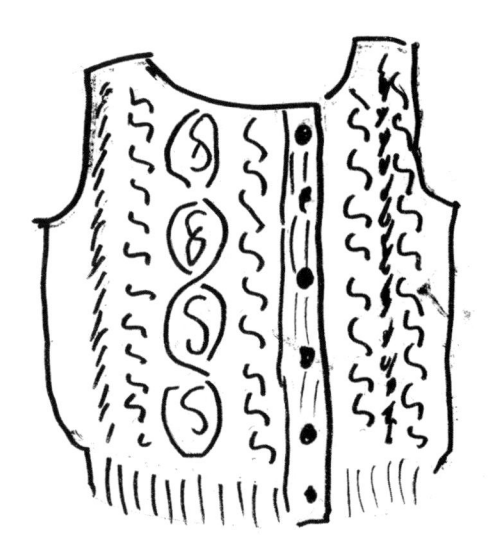

Sketch for an asymmetrical cardigan.

> **Fibonacci Sequence**
>
> The first number is 1, the next number is also 1, which is added to the first number, making 2. The next number is 2 + 1 making 3, then 2 + 3 and so on, with each of the previous 2 numbers added together.

as you please. Perhaps a wide Celtic panel could feature prominently on the right front of a cardigan, with narrower cables each side of it and a less ornate panel and rope cables on the left side. This could look especially striking if the cardigan shape was also asymmetric.

If choosing a symmetrical design, consider arranging the cables according to the Fibonacci sequence. Use, perhaps, an 8cm cable at the centre with the others gradually decreasing in size outwards towards the edge. The cable next to the centre would be 5cm, followed by one of 3cm. To isolate each panel and to make it stand out more, work at least one single purl stitch between each one.

The Aran sweater with underarm gussets on page 24, probably dating from the 1950s, repeats the diamond panel, but each one is divided by a cable of a different width. Incidentally, note the saddle shoulder straps and the underarm gussets – the traditional method of constructing a gansey. This sweater was probably knitted in the round.

All or part of the pattern is usually repeated on the sleeves, but sometimes the sleeves are worked all-over in one of the filler stitches, especially where the main motif is very wide.

The Design Process

Arranging the Stitches

Now that you have your inspiration and have chosen the stitches that will make up the different panels in your project, it would be a good idea to see how the patterns look side by side. From a stitch dictionary, take photocopies of the individual stitches that you like, then lay these out in the order you plan for your design. Choose your main central cable first, then some of the smaller ones. The central cable is often flanked by narrow rope cables before a second motif is introduced, usually a narrower one than the centre cable and frequently less intricate so as not to detract from the central feature. To give your garment a balanced and harmonious appearance, introduce a filler stitch that you have used in the central stitch in other parts of the design. For instance, where you have a moss stitch-filled diamond at the centre, use moss stitch elsewhere as a filler stitch or inside a medallion, for example. This will give your garment a balanced and harmonious appearance.

These days the cables on the left side of the body are often twisted in the opposite direction to those on the right, although most of the early Arans would have them all crossed in the same direction. Reverse stocking stitch is frequently used between the cables, but rib, moss stitch, rice stitch, garter stitch and occasionally blackberry stitch can also be used.

The sweater shown at the beginning of the introduction (An Currach) uses garter stitch at the side edges, but instead of a group of filler stitches, there is a single twisted knit stitch between each of the panels.

The sleeves can carry any of the cables used in the body or a selection of the smaller ones. Try to maintain a sense of harmony throughout the garment; however, if the cables are too similar to one another, the pattern could end up looking bland – more like a cricket pullover than an authentic Aran garment. Conversely, motifs with very different characteristics – sharp angles set next to more rounded cables, for example – could look too fussy and uneven.

If using sharply angled motifs such as diamonds and zigzags alongside one another, try to use those patterns where the change of direction takes place on the same row so as not to disrupt the arrangement of the shapes. If necessary, alter the number of stitches and rows in one of the stitch patterns.

One pattern repeated across body and sleeves.

Beware! Different frequencies of crossings could spoil the symmetry of the design. One traditional method used was to cross the cables at the same interval as the number of stitches in the cable. For example, an 8-stitch rope cable would be crossed on every 8th row. But if your central panel contains an 8-stitch cable crossed on every 6th row, the design would

The garter stitch panels used at the sides of An Curragh instead of underarm gussets.

Showing a modified pattern on the sleeve.

STARTING A PROJECT **85**

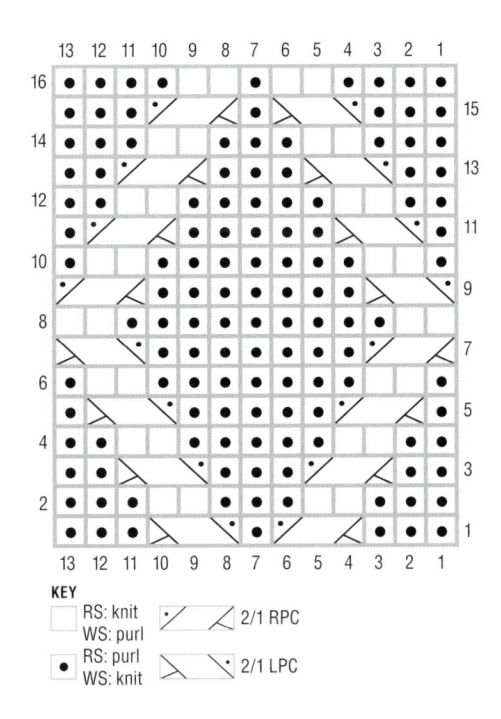

An Aran diamond with zigzag panels that repeat out of sequence with the main motif.

13-stitch diamond chart.

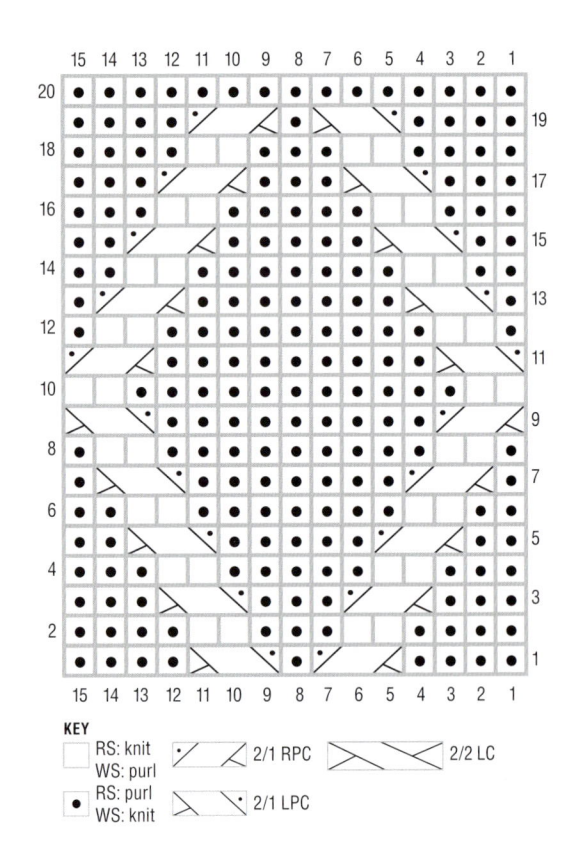

KEY
- RS: knit / WS: purl
- RS: purl / WS: knit
- 2/1 RPC
- 2/1 LPC

20-stitch diamond chart.

KEY
- RS: knit / WS: purl
- RS: purl / WS: knit
- 2/1 RPC
- 2/1 LPC
- 2/2 LC

look more harmonious if the crossings in all the stitches used took place on the same row. The simplest way to achieve this is to make the 8-stitch cable also cross on every 6th row. If an extra row was added between crossings of the central panel, it could disrupt the flow of any other stitch patterns within it, especially so in a panel that contains a braided section.

Diamonds are formed by moving groups of stitches over a number of background stitches, then moving them back again at the same rate to their original starting positions. They are made more interesting by filling them with a variety of filler stitches, such as moss stitch, rather than reverse stocking stitch. To give even more variety, they can contain short cables or other smaller diamonds. Some examples of filled diamonds are shown in the stitch dictionary. Diamonds can be worked in a single column or they can be joined together horizontally to form a trellis pattern. Where they join, they can just touch or they can cross each other, as in the motif on the cushion pattern in Chapter 5. Try out a few diamonds for yourself and fill them with other stitches and motifs to create your own patterns.

Altering the number of stitches in a diamond panel also changes the width and the length of the panel. It will mean that the change of stitch direction will occur on a different row to that in the original chart. Bear this in mind when placing it alongside cables if you prefer all of the crossings to occur at well-matched intervals, or if you have a zigzag panel alongside it. The patterns look better if the sideways movements of diamonds and zigzags occur at the same point.

The large diamond shown in the 20-stitch diamond chart is only two stitches wider than the smaller 13-stitch chart, but it is four rows longer. Virtually all diamond motifs cross the stitches on alternate rows, so any other cables that cross on an even row will be well matched.

It is also important to consider the row counts of motifs when balancing a design top to bottom. It can look tidier if a diamond or similar pattern is split to start halfway through at the beginning of a piece and also end halfway through, rather than starting with a complete pattern repeat and then finding it ends part way through at the top. This is especially noticeable at the front neck of a sweater or cardigan.

Making Samples

When you are pleased with the arrangement of your photocopied stitches, make knitted samples of each of the stitches. Working them singly in this way you will be able to familiarize yourself with how they are formed. You may find that some of them are awkward or time-consuming to work, so you may be happier choosing a different stitch. Better to do this now than to be put off knitting a sweater because of it.

These knitted samples will give you a more accurate view of how the stitches will look when placed alongside one another on your garment. Some may knit up to a different width than can be judged from a photograph. If you are choosing pictures of stitches from different sources, they will most likely all be printed at a different scale.

If your sample looks too stiff, change to larger needles and work it again; if it is too loose, change to smaller ones and work it again. If you like the look and feel of your sample, take a photograph of it as a reminder. Note the type of yarn and the needle sized used, so that when you collect your swatches together, you will have a record of how you intended your sweater to look.

The knitting of samples may seem tedious, but it is a great way to understand the construction of the stitch patterns and to familiarize yourself with the way of working them. It can also generate ideas for completely new stitches.

When you have knitted all of your samples, lay them out in the order of half of a back piece. Unless you want to knit two samples in each stitch, you will have to imagine the other half! You may find that some samples might look better in a different position, even though you liked the arrangement in the initial photocopied version. In the samples shown here, to me, the second arrangement (orange, turquoise and gold) looks more harmonious than the first.

The texture of the actual stitches will be different to the photographs taken from a book. The angle of light and the colour selected by the printer will probably be different to yours. Making individual samples means that, if you choose to alter the sequence, it is an easier matter to do this with separate pieces rather than to knit across a whole panel again with the stitches in a different order. Be prepared to move your samples around as often as you like, or even to choose different stitches altogether. Which arrangement do you prefer? There is no right or wrong answer, it is just a matter of which one pleases you most.

Working different filler stitches can also have an effect on the cables and the way in which they stand out from the background. Don't let the filler stitches detract from the cables by being too elaborate themselves. Make swatches of two of your cables with a few different filler stitches between them to see which one works best.

An arrangement of swatches for planning an Aran sweater.

My preferred arrangement with a more balanced blend of stitch patterns.

Designing the Garment Shape

The next step is to choose the shape that you would like for your garment. Decide if you would like it to be fitted or a more loose and casual style. How long do you want it to be? What shape would you like the neck: round or V-shaped, deep or shallow, or perhaps a U-shaped or square neckline? Choose the length and shape of the sleeves: T-shape, raglan or set-in sleeve. It is unlikely that you would want short sleeves in an Aran garment, but you might want a sleeveless one.

Unless you are really intent on having a set-in or raglan sleeve, I would recommend that you begin your design process with a basic T-shape so that you are not distracted by having to work out where to place armhole and neck decreasings. A square neckline is an alternative option if you prefer not to have one going straight across.

Sketching

When you have made your final decision on the shape of your sweater, it is time to make a sketch. If you are making a sweater with a simple square shape with dropped shoulders, this does not need to be an accurate diagram with the precise measurements – just a rough sketch. For a more shaped garment – with a set-in sleeve and round neck, for example – plot it on knitters' graph paper, using one square for each stitch. This specially designed paper, which shows cells at the same ratio as knitted stitches, will give you a better idea of the proportions of your garment. It will also show where neck and armhole shaping will occur and how increasing or decreasing will affect the cables.

Make the sketch large enough to include information on the different cables to be used. Note the position and the width of each of the cables and the filler stitches and mark these on your diagram in the order that they will appear. Unless you are intent on making a garment with an asymmetrical pattern, you will only need to plot half of the cables as far as the centre. Remember to include the middle stitch if the central panel has an odd number of stitches. Draw the central cable first and then the position of the ones at the sides. Finally, work out how many stitches you will probably have left over after you have added together the numbers of stitches in each of the cables. These will be your filler stitches and side stitches where necessary. Give each cable a name or a letter, and mark this on your sketch. Also note the number of stitches in each cable and how many stitches are in each of the filler sections. This will be helpful if you want to make the item again in a different size.

Positioning the cables on this sketch will help you to see whether your design is compatible with the shape of the garment – whether some of the cables will look unattractive when they are cut through by any decreasing. You may decide to change the sleeves to drop or modified drop rather than changing the cable patterns. Or you might want to leave out the side cables and use filler stitches there instead. It is much better to make this decision at this point than when you are part way through the knitting.

Plot the cable stitches for the sleeves in the same way, deciding whether to incorporate all of the patterns used on the body or only some of the less complex ones.

Sleeveless Aran waistcoat.

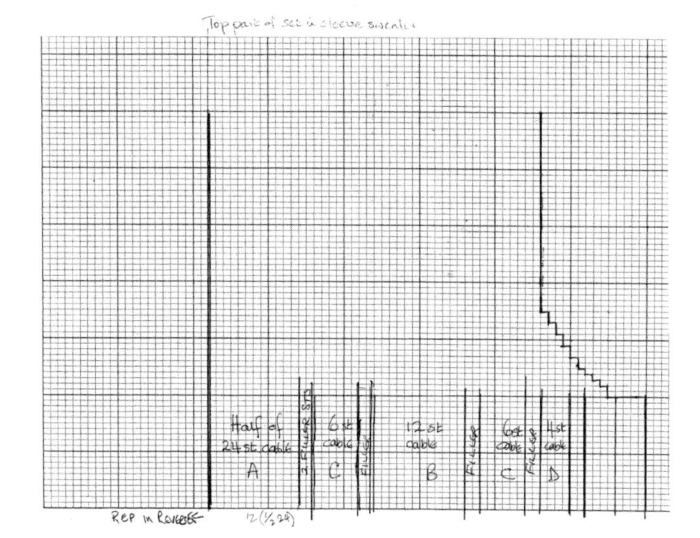

A schematic for a set-in sleeve sweater with the positions and widths of the cables marked.

The schematic diagram shows the top part of a sweater with set-in sleeves. The curve of the armhole has been worked out according to the tension to be used and the cables are plotted in position to calculate how many stitches are left at the side edges. There are 10 stitches in this case, so they could take two more filler stitches and another 4stitch cable, followed by 4 filler stitches, or all of the side edge could be made up of filler stitches. Because the armhole shaping would not disrupt a complex cable, either choice would work.

Calculating the Number of Stitches for a Simple Rib

Now that you have a plan of the number of stitches in each cable, and remembering that cables pull in much more than ribbing or moss stitch, and more again than garter stitch or stocking stitch, work out how many stitches you will need to cast on for the hem of your garment. As a general rule, the ribbing is about 10 per cent narrower than the body of a cabled garment, which gives a fairly close-fitting rib. If you are working a simple knit/purl rib, you can calculate this easily enough. If the body requires 120 stitches, 10 per cent of 120 is 12, so you would need 108 stitches for the rib. For every 4 stitches of a crossing cable, you need to increase one stitch from a ribbed or moss stitch hem, and 2 stitches from a garter stitch hem, to accommodate the narrowing effect of cables.

Example

Supposing we are working a k1, p1 rib and have two 4-stitch cables, three 8-stitch cables and two 6-stitch cables in the body: that makes 11 stitches that need to be increased after the ribbing is done, in this case 119 stitches, which can be rounded up to 120.

Calculating the Number of Stitches for a Rib that 'Grows' into the Cables of the Body

If you would like to work a patterned rib and want the cables to continue seamlessly into those on the body of your garment, the increases will need to be placed more appropriately. The best way to do this is to plot the arrangement of the cable panels on paper before working out where the cables in the rib will go. The pattern for the saddle-shouldered Aran in Chapter 5 has a rib with k1, p1 panels alternated with 4-stitch cables and one central 6-stitch cable. In order to integrate these with the cables on the body of the sweater, I made a detailed sketch of both the ribbing and the cables on the body, then calculated where best to place the increases. Use the same method to plan the placement of cables in the ribs on the sleeves – you should take into account their relationship to the cables on the body when you do this.

Alternatively, begin the body with a provisional cast-on; then, when it is finished, pick up the stitches from the cast-on row. Decrease the appropriate number of stitches, depending on the width of the cable, each time that you reach one of them. Work the rib downwards in whichever pattern you choose, remembering that you might need to reverse the direction of any crossings in order to match those in the body.

> If all of this seems too daunting for a first attempt, look at a pattern that you like the style of, but perhaps not the actual stitches used. Take the pattern as your starting point and replace the stitches that don't appeal to you with others of the same width. Make sure that you can achieve the same tension as that in the pattern, then fill in the directions for your chosen stitches in place of the printed ones.

Blocking

When you are happy with your design, the next stage is to work out the overall tension so that you can begin knitting according to the dimensions in your schematic. Before calculating the tension for the full-sized item, the samples need to be blocked in the same way that you are going to be blocking the final piece. Blocking methods are explained in Chapter 6.

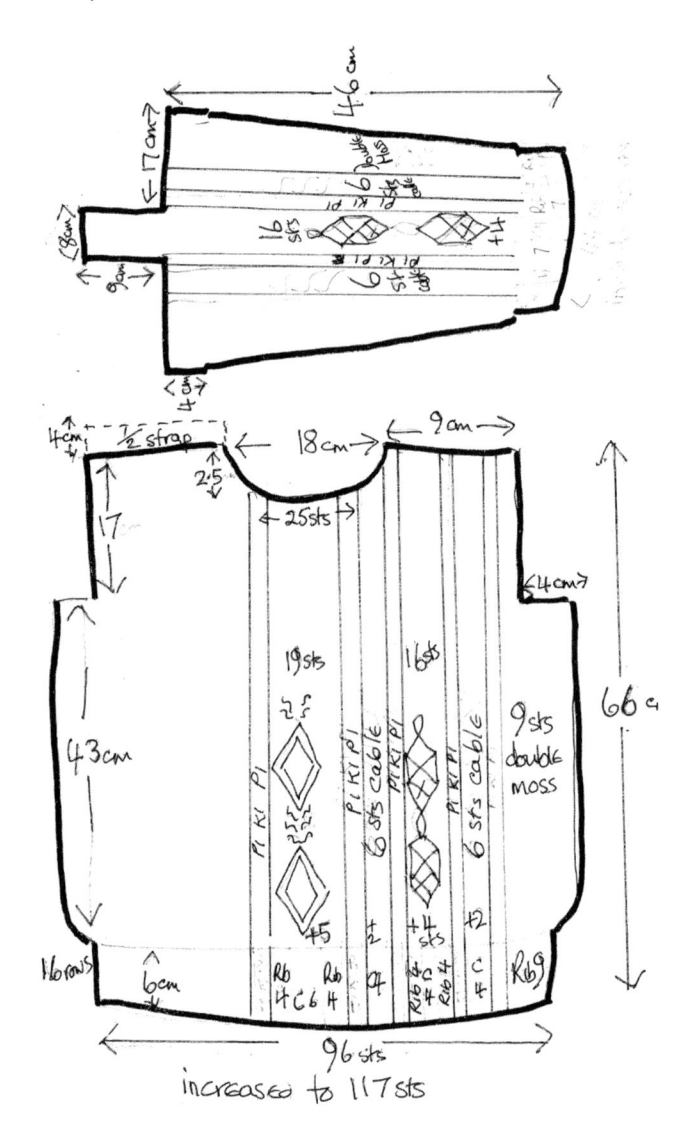

Sketch for Saddle-Shouldered Sweater.

Tension

Working out the tension is a critical part of the process for designing any pieces of knitting. Unless you use an accurate count of stitches and rows, your item will not achieve the measurements that you require. Even half a centimetre out can make a big difference to the finished width, especially if it is over a wide piece of knitting such as a man's Aran garment. Your count may be 17 stitches to 10cm, which would give you 170 sts for a 100cm chest. But supposing the actual count was 17½ stitches to 10cm; this would mean that you need 175 sts for a 100cm chest. Those 5 extra stitches measure about 4cm, which would mean your garment would be 8cm smaller than required.

> **Tip**
>
> If you are knitting in the round, for example a cabled hat or mittens, then knit your sample in the round too. Flat knitting and circular knitting don't always produce the same tension.

A rough guide to the finished size of the garment can be worked out by measuring the largest of the panels plus two or three of the filler stitches. If your sample has 22 stitches – 18 stitches in the panel and 2 stitches each side – and measures 10cm, a rough calculation would give you 220 stitches to 100cm. If you are making a loose-fitting garment, this number will probably suffice. The back and front of the garment would have 110 stitches each and you can plan your design and filler panels accordingly.

Because the different panels may all produce a different tension, it is not possible to use only one of them to work out the tension for the whole garment. For the most accurate result, measure the individual swatches of all the different patterns that you intend to use (assuming that you made them with the same yarn and needles); include the dividing stitches between the panels and any filler stitches from the edges. Remember that if you use a stitch more than once, you need to include those measurements more than once in your calculations. Add all of these measurements together to give a more precise width for the finished piece. If the measurements don't agree with those in your schematic, add or subtract filler stitches and stitches at the side edges, or insert more rope cables for a wider garment.

Measuring a Piece of Cabled Knitting

It can be difficult to measure the tension of a piece of cabled knitting. When making a sample of a complex stitch, run a length of contrast yarn through a few stitches of the first and last rows of the pattern and place stitch markers at the first and last stitches. Measure the dimensions of the marked points, counting the number of stitches and rows between them. Divide the number of stitches between the markers by the measurement. If you have 16 stitches in a panel of 5cm, this gives you a tension of just over 3 stitches per centimetre. Do the same for the rows. If a panel of cables containing 24 rows measures 10cm, this means that 2.4 rows will measure 1cm.

If you are not happy about calculating the measurements of all of the separate swatches and filler panels, you will need to knit a whole width of all of the stitches, just as though you were working the back of the sweater. Make it large enough so that you can measure the length too. This will enable you to work out the best point to start shaping for the neck or the shoulder line.

Example:
Let's assume the main pattern repeat is over 16 rows measuring 8cm long, that is 2 rows to 1cm.
The body, minus the ribbing, needs to measure 50cm, or 100 rows.
The round neckline is 6cm deep.
50 – 8 = 42cm, that is 84 rows

Divide 84 by 16 to give the number of times that the pattern will repeat in 84 rows. This comes to 5.25, meaning that you will be one quarter of the way through the last pattern before starting the neck shaping. This might be an appropriate place to end, but if not, make the body a little longer or shorter, or start the pattern part way through. A diamond shape often looks better when started and finished at its widest point. If you choose to start the pattern at a different point to that on the chart, try it out on a swatch first to make sure that it still looks good.

Measuring

Lay your swatches out flat on a solid base. For best accuracy, measure with a ruler or a specially designed accessory rather than a tape measure, as fabric tape measures can stretch over time. There are various tools that have 10cm slots in them, and these can be useful as they hold your work still and flat. If you are using a ruler, pin your work down and then insert a dressmaker's pin at the 10cm point and another one at the 0cm point. Count the stitches between the markers, including any half stitches. Do the same for the rows. Now you are ready to work out the number of stitches and rows required to obtain the measurements you want for your finished item.

Front of the ladies' cardigan showing the pattern on the cuffs.

Marking and measuring a tension square.

Working Out the Numbers – Set-in Sleeve Sweater

Body

If you are knitting flat pieces to be joined together with seams, the back and front will each be half of your bust/chest measurement. A medium size will need to be around 46cm across. You may want to add another 5–10cm for ease. For our example we will add 10cm. If your swatch gives you a tension of 25sts to 10cm, that equals 2.5sts to 1cm. You require the back and front to measure 56cm each:
56 x 2.5 =140sts.

If this is the same number that you got when adding the number of stitches in your panels together, well done! However, it is probably out by a few stitches. You can either add or subtract these in the side panels or change the number of stitches between the panels. If it is out by a much greater number of stitches, then you will need to rethink your design and either choose a different centre panel or alter the number of cables on each side.

You will probably want the ribbed hem to have approximately 10 per cent fewer stitches than the main body. In our example, that would be 126 stitches. For a k2, p2 rib, beginning and ending on the same pair of stitches, this needs to be a number divisible by 4, with 2 extra stitches added. This does not fit exactly into our example, so you would need to cast on 124 or 128 stitches. A single rib needs an uneven number of stitches, so in this case 125 or 127. If you are working a complex rib with various cables, then you will need to calculate the number of stitches to cast on, as shown in the pattern for the saddle-shouldered sweater in Chapter 5.

When you have finished the hem and the body as far as the armholes, calculate the shaping required there.

Armholes

For a set-in sleeve, the shaping takes place over approximately 5cm. If there are 3 rows to 1cm in the tension used, that makes 15 rows. Before working out how many stitches to decrease for the armhole, first calculate how many stitches need to be left for the torso after the armhole shaping is completed. Let's suppose the torso measurement is 40cm and the stitch tension, as before, is 2.5 stitches to 1cm; multiply 40 by 2.5, which equals 100 stitches. There are currently 140 stitches on the needles, so 40 stitches need to be decreased for the armholes over approximately 15 rows. At least 2cm should be taken off on the first row, which equates to 5 stitches for each armhole here. The rest of the stitches should be decreased at each end of the following rows. In this case, where there are 30 stitches left to be decreased, that will be 1 stitch at each end of the next 15 rows, leaving 60 sts for the rest of the back.

Shoulders

Continue to work straight as far as the shoulders, then work out how many stitches are needed for the back neck. The average measurement here is about 15cm, which is 37.5 stitches at a tension of 2.5 stitches to 1cm. Round this up or down depending on whether your stitch pattern will fit best into an odd or even number of stitches. Because we are left with 60 stitches in this example, it is best to use an even number, so I would suggest putting 36 stitches on a holder for the back neck, leaving 24 stitches after the shoulder decreasing is done – 12 stitches for each shoulder.

For a gentle slope, about 2cm deep, cast off 3 times for each shoulder, that is cast off 4 stitches at the beginning of each of the next 6 rows.

Front Neck Shaping

The front is worked the same as the back as far as the point where the armhole shaping needs to start. You then need to work out how deep to make the neck, so that you can then plan the vertical placement of your cables. Let's assume that the neck will be 8cm deep. Deduct that number from the number of rows on the back between the start of the armhole shaping and the last row of stitches for the back neck. Assuming that the depth of the armhole is 20cm (the average for a medium-sized sweater), that gives 12cm to the start of the front neck shaping. There are 60 stitches on the needles after the armhole shaping and usually about one third of the number of stitches cast off for the centre back neck are left on a holder for the front. We left 36 stitches for the back neck, so that would make 12 stitches left at the centre front with 24 stitches at each side. Of these, 12 need to be decreased at the front neck edge so that it will match the width of the back neck, and the number of stitches in the shoulders will then match those cast off for the back shoulders.

You have 8cm left in which to decrease these 12 stitches. Again, 3 rows measure 1cm, so that gives 24 rows in which to lose these extra stitches. To make a rounded curve, half the stitches should be decreased at the neck edge of every row, and then decrease on alternate rows to lose the rest. This takes 18 rows and leaves 6 more rows to be worked straight before starting the shoulder shaping as for the back.

Sleeves

Estimate the depth you would like the cuff, then measure the width of the sleeve, both above this cuff and at the bicep, as you did for the body. Let us say these measurements are 20cm above the wrist and 36cm at the bicep. This would give you 40 stitches and 90 stitches respectively. Add on any stitches for ease here depending on how loose you would like your sleeve. Subtract your wrist measurement from your bicep measurement, which in this case is 50 stitches. In the tension we are using (30 rows to 10cm), there are 3 rows to 1cm. Work out how many rows you require for the length of your sleeve from above the cuff to your underarm. For a medium size, which would be approximately 38cm, the calculation would be 38 x 3, which is 114 rows. This means that you need to increase 50 stitches over 114 rows. Because you increase one stitch at each end of a row, therefore 2 stitches per row, there need to be 25 increase rows. Dividing 114 rows by 25 gives a figure of 4.56; round this down to increase on every fourth row. This leaves 14 rows worked straight before you need to start the armhole shaping. If you prefer to always increase on a right side row, work the increases at each end of every sixth row and work a few more rows straight before shaping the sleeve head.

Back view of a set-in sleeve Aran sweater knitted in wool from Manx sheep.

Sleeve Head

The first two cast-off rows of the sleeve head should match those of the back and front, which means that 5 stitches need to be cast off at the beginning of each of them. For the sleeve head to fit neatly into the armhole, without being stretched or gathered, the last row of the sleeve head should be between 5cm and 8cm wide. The curve between these two points should be gently rounded, often quite sharply at the beginning, then becoming more gentle until, finally, the slope levels off before the last straight row.

The distance around the head of the sleeve should be the same or just very slightly larger than the distance around the armhole. A convenient way to measure this is to place a piece of string or yarn around the armhole curve from the first stitch cast off for the armhole shaping to the first cast-off stitches of

Front view of the sweater showing the round neck shaping and srt-in sleeve.

the shoulder. Holding the string carefully at these two points, carefully straighten it out and measure the distance between the points with a ruler.

The height of the sleeve head should be approximately two-thirds of the depth of the armhole, so about 14cm where the armhole depth is 20cm. Using the calculations of the sleeve width above, there are 72 stitches measuring roughly 29cm across the sleeve before starting the shaping. Casting off 5 stitches at the beginning of the first 2 rows leaves us with 62 stitches, or 25cm. If the last row has 16 stitches measuring 6cm, we need to lose 62 – 16 stitches, which equals 46 stitches in total, or 23 stitches at each side of the sleeve. These stitches need to be decreased within the 14cm of the sleeve head. At a tension of 3 rows to 1cm, that gives us 14 x 3 = 42 rows. To make a well-shaped curve, decrease on every row at first. Let's say we decrease 1 stitch at each end of the next 5 rows, which leaves us with 36 stitches to decrease in 32 rows. Next, decrease 1 stitch at each end of alternate rows 12 times, which takes up 24 rows and leaves 12 stitches. There are 6 rows left in which to decrease down to the 16 stitches for the sleeve head. In order to gradually level out the top of the sleeve, cast off 2 stitches at the beginning of the next 6 rows. Then cast off the remaining 16 stitches.

If you are unsure how the shape of the curve should look, take a set-in sleeve sweater with a nicely shaped sleeve head. Draw this shape as accurately as you can, then cut around the shape and plot it on your knitters' graph paper. You can see where the slope needs to be sharper in some places than in others and this will help you to work out how frequently to decrease.

Round Neckband

After joining one of the shoulder seams (or both of them if you are working it in the round), work out how many stitches to pick up for the neckband.

In our example there are 36 stitches in the back neck and 12 stitches on the holder for the front. The number of rows that were worked for the neck before the shoulder shaping is 24. To give a smooth curve to the neckband, not too tight or too loose, pick up stitches from about 20 per cent of the rows worked after leaving the stitches at the centre front. Twenty per cent of 24 is 4.8, which would mean picking up approximately 19 stitches from the front neck edges. Either divide this edge into three equal sections and pick up 7 stitches from the first one and 6 from each of the other two, or pick up 5 stitches for every 6 row ends, with 4 stitches picked up for the first section.

V Neckband

Pick up approximately 20 per cent of stitches to the number of rows and, depending on the method of working the rib, mark either 1 or 2 stitches at the centre front. Decrease at each side of this marked stitch on every row, including the cast-off row.

Shawl Collar

If you would like a shawl collar on your sweater or cardigan, work it in one of the reversible cable patterns instead of rib, so that when it folds over, it will still show the right side of the pattern. This applies to any pattern on a high polo neck collar too. A k2, p2 rib with alternate knit panels of twisted stitches, as seen on the cuffs of the ladies cardigan in Chapter 5, works well.

Working Out the Numbers – Raglan Sleeve Sweater

Body

The calculations for the body are the same as for a set-in sleeve garment until you get to the starting point for the armholes.

Armhole

Let's say that we have 100 stitches for the back of the sweater. Using a tension of 2 stitches per centimetre, this makes the back measurement 50cm. Armhole depths are usually slightly deeper in a raglan sweater than in a set-in sleeve sweater, so if the tension is 3 rows per centimetre and the armhole is 22cm deep, that will mean there are 66 rows in which to lose 100 stitches minus however many stitches we need for the back neck. For a back neck width of 12cm, this would be 36 stitches, 100 – 36 = 64, so 64 stitches need to be decreased over 66 rows. The raglan edge should be as even as possible and should end at the back neck without having to work any straight rows. Cast off between 2cm and 3cm of stitches on the first 2 rows, that is 5 stitches each side, which leaves 56 stitches. Then decrease 2 stitches at a time, one at each end of the row, meaning that 28 decreases have to be made over 64 rows (remember that 2 rows have already been used for the first set of cast-off stitches). If the decreases start on the fifth row and are then made every alternate row, this will use 61 rows and the armhole will measure 21cm deep instead of 22cm. Decreasing once more would leave 34 stitches for the back of the neck. Sometimes it is necessary to 'fudge' the measurements a bit.

Sleeves

The calculations for the sleeve are the same as for a set-in sleeve garment until you get to the point where you need to start decreasing to form the sleeve head.

Sleeve Head

To work out how to shape the sleeve, use the same frequency of decreasing as used for the armhole shaping: in this case

Side view of a sweater showing the raglan sleeve shaping.

56 stitches to be decreased. Start at the top of the sleeve and imagine you are working in reverse: calculate the stitches as if they are to be increased as you work down the sleeve, rather than decreased as you work up. To fill in the extra stitches that were lost at the back of the neck, decide to leave 4 stitches at the top of the sleeve. Add this to the 56 stitches decreased, making 60 stitches. Add on the two sets of 5 stitches cast off at the underarm, making 70 stitches. This is the number of stitches that are needed before starting to shape the raglan sleeve head.

If we take the same sleeve head length as for the set-in sleeve sweater, this means there needs to be 114 rows over which to increase 35 times: 1 stitch at each end of the row, making 2 stitches increased per row. Increasing at each end of every third row will give a total length of 105 rows, which will measure 35cm. Work a few more rows before starting the sleeve head shaping if you want the sleeve to be longer.

To make a neat join between body and sleeve, have the same cable panels at the sides of each. When the decreases are worked, the cables will fit against one another more neatly. Alternatively, work the decreases on the inside edge of the cable so that it carries on unbroken along the raglan seam.

V Neckband in a Raglan Sweater

Half of the stitches used for the back neck need to be lost. Depending on how deep the neck is to be, divide the number of rows by the number of stitches to lose at each side. The edge should be a smooth straight line with a few rows worked straight at the top edge to help the neckline to lie flat. The decreases do not need to be at the same frequency as those for the raglan edges, which is where pencil and paper and row counters come in handy. Work as for the set-in sleeve sweater neckband.

> When decreasing in a raglan-sleeved garment, an attractive finish is achieved if the raglan shapings are worked inside a cable, or if a small cable is worked along the edge.

Top-Down Raglan

To date, I have never seen an Aran garment worked in the round top-down. There are instances of yoked sweaters and cardigans where the cabled section is worked first sideways on, then the stitches for the body and sleeves are picked up from the side edge of this piece and continued downwards. There are also a few patterns with cables at the yoke only, but none with cables that continue down through the body and sleeves, as far as I am aware. A top-down cabled raglan might work with a diamond pattern, starting quite small and then gradually increasing in width and length as it moves down the body. It might be fun to try this for yourself.

Calculating Yarn Requirements

Quick Method

Work a row or two over about 20 stitches. Tie a piece of sewing cotton or other yarn in a good contrast colour

Tip

Once you have all the details marked on your graph paper, note down the critical numbers; when to cross the cables, where to cast off and where to place the increases and decreases. These notes can then be kept beside you as you are working, so that you don't need to have your large piece of graph paper on the armchair.

tightly onto the yarn close to the ball after the last stitch you have just worked. Measure a metre more of the yarn from the ball and tie on another piece of cotton. Knit that metre, going beyond the second piece of cotton. Count the number of stitches that you have just made with that metre. Check how many metres are in one ball on the ball band and work out, from your tension square, roughly how many stitches will be in the finished piece. If you have worked 20 stitches with your metre of yarn, and the ball band claims 160 metres per ball, one ball will produce 3,200 stitches. Estimate how many stitches there will be in your garment by thinking of it as four rectangles and using your stitch and row tension to calculate the overall number. If there are 18,000 stitches in your garment, you will need 18,000 divided by 3,200, which totals about five and a half balls. For use in your swatches and just to be on the safe side, buy an extra one or two balls.

Slower but Slightly More Accurate Method

Knit a 10cm square in your chosen yarn, unravel it and measure how many metres it has used. Again, thinking of the garment as rectangles, calculate how many of these 10cm squares will fit into it. Multiply that number by the number of metres you used for the square.

> **Example:**
> 20 squares in the garment at 60 metres per square = 1,200 metres.

Check how many metres are in each ball of the yarn you intend using. For example, Rico Essentials Aran has 100 metres per ball, so an easy calculation for this yarn is that you will need 12 x 50gm balls.

Further Inspiration

I have written here as though you were always designing for a basic sweater or cardigan, but there are many other garments that can be knitted in the Aran style. An Aran coat can look very dramatic. While it could be made in the same way as a cardigan but longer, it could also be an A-line shape. This will need more stitches at the hem that gradually decrease to the width of the chest measurement. The simplest way to do this is to have wider panels of a filler stitch at the hem that will still look attractive when the stitches are decreased within them. The ladies cardigan in Chapter 5 is worked in this way with reverse stocking stitch between the panels.

Waistcoats and gilets are useful Aran garments and look most stylish with shaped armholes. If you are adapting a set-in sleeve cardigan to use for a waistcoat pattern, remember to cast off a few more stitches at the underarm to accommodate the armbands that need to be added.

Aran garments for small children can look cumbersome with a multitude of solid-looking cables. For a lighter look, choose stitches that are more open, or leave a number of plain stocking stitch panels between each motif.

A 1960s Aran with a shawl collar.

Child's Aran cardigan with Moss stitch filler stitches at the sleeve edges.

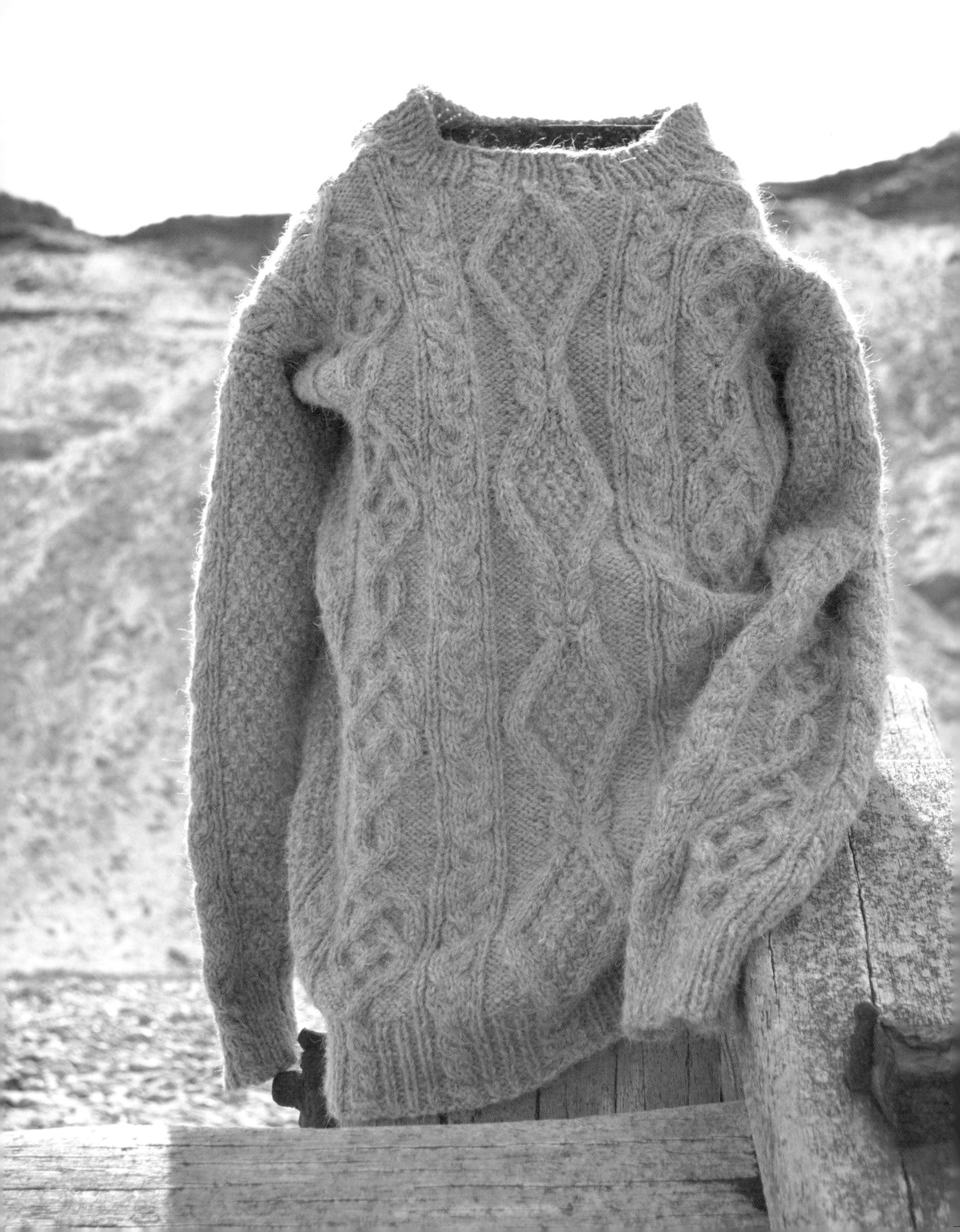

CHAPTER 5

ARAN KNITTING PATTERNS

The patterns shown here can be worked exactly as they are written, or they can be used as starting points for designs of your own. For the easiest design adaptation, replace some of the cables with others that have similar stitch counts. Or, if you want to be more adventurous, substitute all of the cables in a different sequence to make a totally new design.

Refer back to Chapter 4 if you would like to retain the suggested cables but make the garment in a different size.

Front view of Saddle Shouldered Sweater.

Diamond Patterned Cushion Cover

If you feel a bit daunted at the thought of making your first project with increases and decreases and precise measurements, try making a cushion cover. Cushion covers are ideal first projects as there is no shaping to affect the flow of the cables. You don't even have to make a tension swatch if you don't want to, although you will need to if you want your cover to fit a particular size cushion pad. Besides, you might not like your chosen cables once they are knitted, or they might feel awkward to work, in which case a cushion cover is less daunting to unravel than a whole garment.

The central pattern used in this cushion cover may look complicated, but it is just basic diamonds joined together with rope cables. It shows what can be done by combining cable patterns horizontally. The back is in stocking stitch, but could be worked in a series of rope cables. If you choose to do a cabled back, then work with the same size needles as for the front, rather than switching to larger needles as instructed below, as the tension of the two sections will be closer than if the back were worked in stocking stitch.

Size

30cm square

Materials

300g Aran weight yarn. I used Drops Big Fabel (75% wool, 25% nylon; 150m/100g).

Needles

1 pair 4mm, 1 pair 4.5mm, 1 pair 5mm needles
3 buttons approx 3.5cm in diameter
1 cushion pad 30cm square

Tension

17 sts x 24 rows = 10 x 10cm over st st using 5mm needles

Pattern

Row 1 (RS): K3, p2, 2/2 LC, p2, 3/3 LC, p2, k3, (p, k) x 3, 3/3 RC, (p, k) x 3, 3/3 LC, (p, k) x 2, p, k4, p2, 3/3 LC, p2, 2/2 LC, p2, k3. (74 sts)

Row 2 (WS): P3, k2, p4, k2, p6, k2, p3, ((k, p) x 2, k, p7) x 2, (k, p) x 2, k, p4, k2, p6, k2, p4, k2, p3.

Row 3: K3, p2, k4, p2, k6, p2, k3, ((p, k) x 2, p, k7) x 2, (p, k) x 2, p, k4, p2, k6, p2, k4, p2, k3.

Row 4: Repeat row 2.

Row 5: Repeat row 1.

Rows 6–9: Repeat rows 2–5.

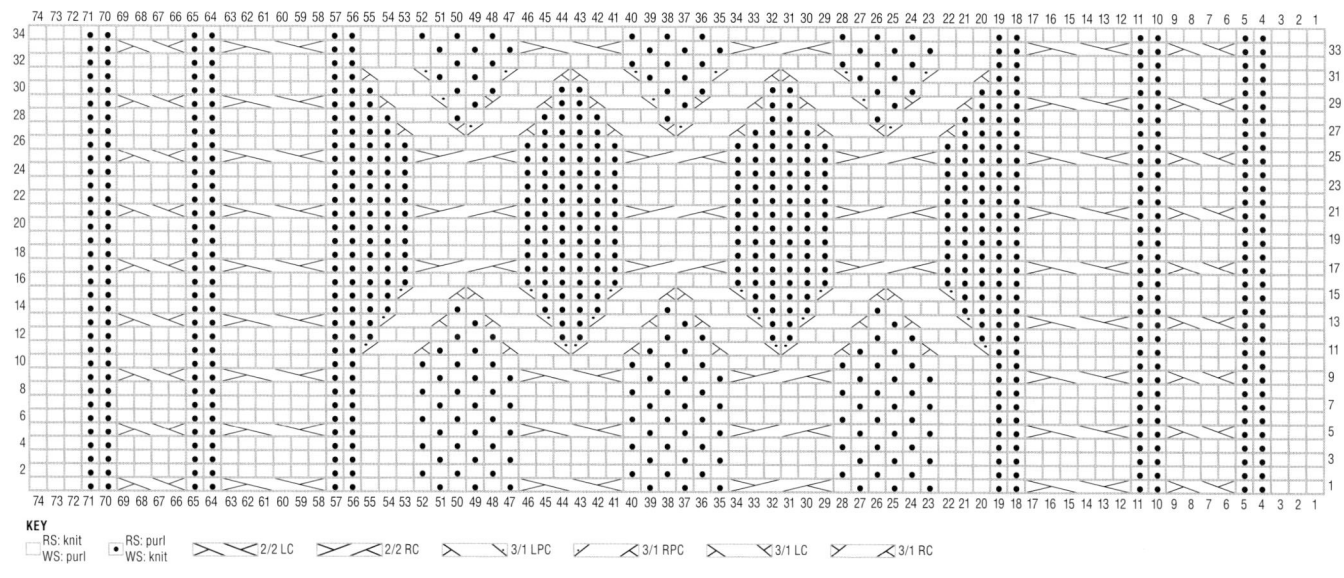

Chart for cushion cover.

Close-up of the diamonds on the cushion cover.

Row 10: Repeat row 2.
Row 11: K3, p2, k4, p2, k6, p2, (3/1 LPC, (k, p) x 2, 3/1 RPC) x 3, p2, k6, p2, k4, p2, k3.
Row 12: P3, k2, p4, k2, p6, k3, (p4, k, p, k, p3, k2) x 2, p4, k, p, k, p3, k3, p6, k2, p4, k2, p3.
Row 13: K3, p2, 2/2 LC, p2, 3/3 LC, p3, (3/1 LPC, p, k, 3/1 RPC, p2) x 2, 3/1 LPC, p, k, 3/1 RPC, p3, 3/3 LC, p2, 2/2 LC, p2, k3.
Row 14: P3, k2, p4, k2, p6, (k4, p3, k, p4) x 3, k4, p6, k2, p4, k2, p3.
Row 15: K3, p2, k4, p2, k6, (p4, 3/1 LPC, 3/1 RPC) x 3, p4, k6, p2, k4, p2, k3.
Row 16: P3, k2, p4, k2, p6, k5, (p6, k6) x 2, p6, k5, p6, k2, p4, k2, p3.
Row 17: K3, p2, 2/2 LC, p2, 3/3 LC, p5, (3/3 RC, p6) x 2, 3/3 RC, p5, 3/3 LC, p2, 2/2 LC, p2, k3.
Row 18: Repeat row 16.
Row 19: K3, p2, k4, p2, k6, p5, (k6, p6) x 2, k6, p5, k6, p2, k4, p2, k3.
Rows 20–23: Repeat rows 16–19.
Row 24: Repeat row 16.
Row 25: Repeat row 17.
Row 26: Repeat row 16.
Row 27: K3, p2, k4, p2, k6, (p4, 3/1 RPC, 3/1 LC) x 3, p4, k6, p2, k4, p2, k3.
Row 28: Repeat row 14.
Row 29: K3, p2, 2/2 LC, p2, 3/3 LC, p3, (3/1 RC, p, k, 3/1 LPC, p2) x 2, 3/1 RC, p, k, 3/1 LPC, p3, 3/3 LC, p2, 2/2 LC, p2, k3.
Row 30: Repeat row 12.
Row 31: K3, p2, k4, p2, k6, p2, (3/1 RPC, (k, p) x 2, 3/1 LPC) x 3, p2, k6, p2, k4, p2, k3.
Row 32: P3, k2, p4, k2, p6, k2, p5, (k, p, k, p7, k, p) x 2, k, p, k, p4, k2, p6, k2, p4, k2, p3.
Row 33: Repeat row 1.
Row 34: Repeat row 2.

Instructions

Begin with lower half of back.
Using 4mm needles cast on 67 sts.
Work 6 rows of k1, p1 rib.
Change to 4.5mm needles and st st. Cont until work measures 18cm ending with RS facing.

Next row (RS, increase row): K3, p2, k1, kfb, k1, p2, k2, kfb, k2, p2, k3 *(p1, k1) three times, k2, kfb, k2; rep from * once more, (p1, k1) three times, k3, p2, k2, kfb, k2, p2, k1, kfb, k1, p2, k1, kfb (74 sts).
Change to 5mm needles and work 1 row knitting and purling sts as they appear.
Now work the 34 rows of the pattern from the chart or the written instructions above.
Repeat the chart once more. The work should measure approx 30cm ending with RS facing.
Change to 4.5mm needles.

Next row (RS, decrease row): K3, p2, k1, k2tog, k1, p2, k2, k2tog, k2, p2, k3, *(p1, k1) three times, k2, k2tog, k2; rep from * once more, (p1, k1) three times, k3, p2, k2, k2tog, k2, p2, k1, k2tog, k1, p2, k1, k2tog (67 sts).
Work 12cm in st st.
Change to 4mm needles and work 3 rows k1, p1 rib.

Make buttonholes: *Rib 13, cast off 5; rep from * twice more, rib to end.
Work another three rows of k1, p1 rib, then cast off loosely.

Finishing

With RS together, fold bottom st st section up and fold top section over it so that the ribbed bands overlap. Stitch side seams using a firm back stitch.
Sew on buttons, darn in any ends.

Arans can sometimes make a person look a little bit bulky, so this design is given a more fitted shape by decreasing within the purl fillers and changing to a smaller needle size at the waist.

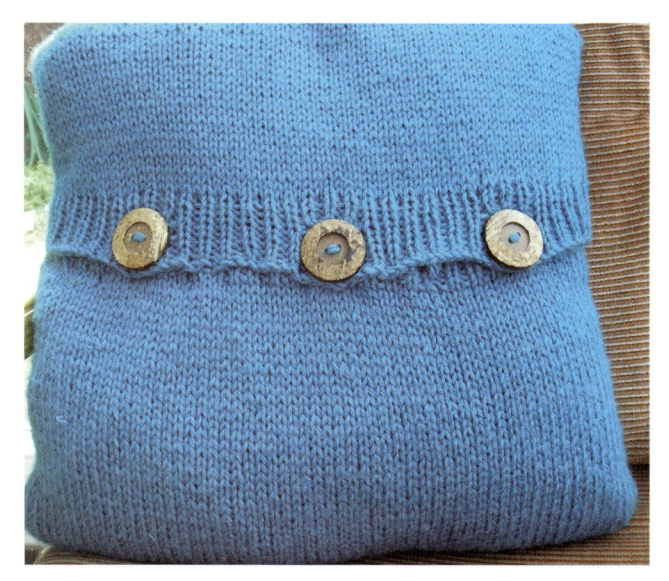

Back of cushion.

This chart can be used in various ways to make other lovely pieces.

Blanket

The 40 stitches in the central portion of the chart would make a wonderful blanket. The square shape of the pattern is symmetrical, so several cables could be arranged in different directions to create a new pattern. Alternatively, repeat the diamond pattern with one of the cables vertically in strips.

Wrap

To make a striking wrap, use either the central 40 stitches, adding other cables or panels of stocking stitch each side, or use all 74 stitches of the chart. Edge the wrap with groups of moss stitch at each side to stop it from curling. Begin and end the wrap with a few rows of moss stitch too.

Cowl

Use the whole panel for a cowl. Depending on your tension, work the panel two or three times with button and buttonhole bands at the beginning and end, as for the cushion.

Have a look through the stitch dictionary to see which other patterns can be joined together in the same way as these to make a wider panel.

Ladies' Set-in Sleeve Cardigan

Size

Actual chest measurement: 96cm
Length: 58cm
Sleeve length: 48cm

Materials

900g Blacker Classic Aran (100% wool; 69m/50g)
Blacker Classic Aran is slightly heavier than most other Arans, so if you are substituting for another brand, you might need to use more filler stitches.

Needles

Sizes 4mm, 4.5mm, 5mm and 5.5mm

Tension

20 sts x 25 rows = 10 x 10cm over rev st st on 5mm needles.

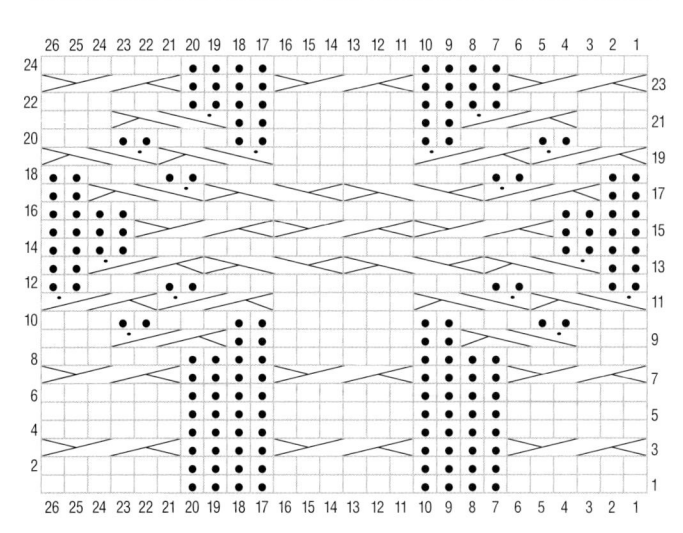

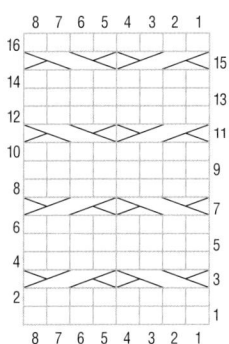

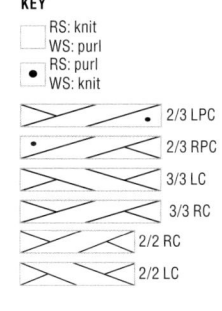

Braid and Rope

Row 1 (RS): (K6, p4) twice, k6.
Row 2 (WS): (P6, k4) twice, p6.
Row 3: (3/3RC, p4) twice, 3/3RC.
Row 4: Repeat row 2.
Rows 5–8: Repeat rows 1–4.
Row 9: K3, 2/3LPC, p2, k6, p2, 2/3RPC, k3.
Row 10: (P3, k2) twice, p6, (k2, p3) twice.
Row 11: (2/3LPC) twice, k6, (2/3RPC) twice.
Row 12: K2, p3, k2, p12, k2, p3, k2.
Row 13: P2, 2/3LPC, (3/3LC) twice, 2/3RPC, p2.
Row 14: K4, p18, k4.
Row 15: P4, (3/3RC) three times, p4.
Row 16: Repeat row 14.
Row 17: P2, 2/3RPC, (3/3LC) twice, 2/3LPC, p2.
Row 18: Repeat row 12.
Row 19: (2/3RPC) twice, k6, (2/3LPC) twice.
Row 20: Repeat row 10.
Row 21: K3, 2/3RPC, p2, k6, p2, 2/3LPC, k3.
Row 22: Repeat row 2.
Row 23: Repeat row 3.
Row 24: Repeat row 2.

Gullwing

Row 1 (RS): Knit.
Row 2 (WS): Purl.
Row 3: 1/2RC, 1/2LC.
Row 4: Purl.

Oxo

Row 1 (RS): Knit.
Row 2 and all WS rows: Purl.
Row 3: 2/2RC, 2/2LC.
Row 5: Knit.
Row 7: 2/2LC, 2/2RC.
Row 9: Knit.
Row 11: Repeat row 7.
Row 13: Knit.
Row 15: Repeat row 3.

Lots of wooden buttons.

Left Rope

Row 1 (RS): Knit.
Row 2 and all WS rows: Purl.
Row 3: 3/3LC.
Row 5: Knit.
Row 7: Knit.
Row 9: 3/3LC.
Row 11: Knit.

Right Rope

Row 1 (RS): Knit.
Row 2 and all WS rows: Purl.
Row 3: 3/3RC.
Row 5: Knit.
Row 7: Knit.
Row 9: 3/3RC.
Row 11: Knit.

Back

Using 5.5mm needles, cast on 130 sts and work set-up stitch pattern as follows and from the first rows of the charts as directed:

Row 1 (RS): P2, k2, p2, Right Rope Cable, p6, Braid and Rope Cable, p6, Oxo Cable, p4, Gullwing Cable, p4, Oxo Cable, p6, Braid and Rope Cable, p6, Left Rope Cable, p2, k2, p2.
Row 2 and all WS rows: Knit and purl stitches as they present themselves.
Row 3: P2, tw2R, p2, Right Rope Cable, p6, Braid and Rope Cable, p6, Oxo Cable, p4, Gullwing Cable, p4, Oxo Cable, p6, Braid and Rope Cable, p6, Left Rope Cable, p2, tw2R, p2.
Row 4: As Row 2.
This sets the position of the various panels. Repeat these four rows, working though the charts.

Row 17 (RS, decrease): P2, k2, p2, Right Rope Cable, p2, p2tog, p2, Braid and Rope Cable, p2, p2tog, p2, Oxo Cable, p4, Gullwing Cable, p4, Oxo Cable, p2, p2tog, p2, Braid and Rope Cable, p2, p2tog, p2, Left Rope Cable, p2, k2, p2 (126 sts).
Work a further 15 rows, then change to 4.5mm needles.

Row 33 (RS, decrease): P2, k2, p2, Right Rope Cable, p1, p2tog, p1, Braid and Rope Cable, p1, p2tog, p1, Oxo Cable, p4, Gullwing Cable, p4, Oxo Cable, p1, p2tog, p1, Braid and Rope Cable, p1, p2tog, p1, Left Rope Cable, p2, k2, p2 (122 sts).
Work 6 rows then change to 4mm needles.
Work 6 rows then change to 4.5mm needles.
Work 6 rows then change to 5mm needles.
Cont until work measures 40cm.

Shape Armhole

Cast off 5 sts at beg next 2 rows (112 sts).
Dec 1 at each end of next and every alt row to 98 sts.
Cont until work measures 20cm.

Shape shoulder

Cast off 8 sts at beg of next 8 rows. Leave rem 34 sts on holder.

Left Front

Using 5.5mm needles, cast on 64 sts.
Row 1 (RS): P2, k2, p2, Left Rope Cable, p6, Braid and Rope Cable, p6, Oxo Cable, p2, k2, p2.
Row 2 (WS): K2, p2, k2, Oxo Cable, k6, Braid and Rope Cable, k6, Left Rope Cable, k2, p2, k2.
Row 3: P2, tw2R, p2, Left Rope Cable, p6, Braid and Rope Cable, p6, Oxo Cable, p2, tw2R, p2.
Row 4: As Row 2.
This sets the position of the various panels. Repeat these four rows, working though the charts.

Row 17 (RS, decrease): P2, k2, p2, Left Rope Cable, p2, p2tog, p2, Braid and Rope Cable, p2, p2tog, p2, Oxo Cable, p2, k2, p2 (62 sts).
Work 15 rows then change to 4.5mm needles.

Row 33 (RS, decrease): P2, k2, p2, Left Rope Cable, p1, p2tog, p1, Braid and Rope Cable, p1, p2tog, p1, Oxo Cable, p2, k2, p2 (60 sts).
Work 6 rows then change to 4mm needles.
Work 6 rows then change to 4.5mm needles.
Work 6 rows then change to 5mm needles.
Cont until work measures 40cm.

Shape armhole
Cast off 5 sts at beg next RS row (55 sts).
Work 1 row.
Dec 1 st at beg of next and every foll alt row 6 times (49 sts).
Cont until armhole measures 11cm.

Shape neck
With RS facing, work 43 sts, leave rem 6 sts on holder.
Dec 1 st at neck edge of every row to 34 sts and then on alt rows to 32 sts.
Work straight until armhole measures 20cm.

Shape shoulder
Cast off 8 sts at beg of next and foll alt rows 4 times.

Right Front

Using 5.5mm needles, cast on 64 sts.
Row 1 (RS): P2, k2, p2, Oxo Cable, p6, Braid and Rope Cable, p6, Right Rope Cable, p2, k2, p2.

You could insert pockets behind this wide cable.

Row 2 (WS): K2, p2, k2, Right Rope Cable, k6, Braid and Rope Cable, k6, Oxo Cable, k2, p2, k2.
Row 3: P2, tw2R, p2, Oxo Cable, p6, Braid and Rope Cable, p6, Right Rope Cable, p2, tw2R, p2.
Row 4: As Row 2.
This sets the position of the various panels. Repeat these four rows, working though the charts.
Row 17 (RS, decrease): P2, k2, p2, Oxo Cable, p2, p2tog, p2, Braid and Rope Cable, p2, p2tog, p2, Right Rope Cable, p2, k2, p2 (62 sts).
Work a further 15 rows then change to 4.5mm needles.
Row 33 (RS, decrease): P2, k2, p2, Oxo Cable, p1, p2tog, p1, Braid and Rope Cable, p1, p2tog, p1, Right Rope Cable, p2, k2, p2 (60 sts).
Work 6 rows then change to 4mm needles.
Work 6 rows then change to 4.5mm needles.
Work 6 rows then change to 5mm needles.
Cont until work measures 40cm.

Shape armhole
Cast off 5 at beg of next WS row (55 sts).
Work 1 row.

ARAN KNITTING PATTERNS

Dec 1 st at beg of next and every foll alt row 6 times (49 sts).
Cont until armhole measures 11cm.

Shape neck
With WS facing, work 43 sts, leave rem 6 sts on holder.
Dec 1 st at neck edge of every row to 34 sts and then alt rows to 32 sts.
Work straight until armhole measures 20cm.

Shape shoulder
Cast off 8 sts at beg of next and foll alt rows 4 times.

Sleeves

Using 4.5mm needles, cast on 50 sts and work twisted cable rib as follows:
Row 1 (RS): (P2, k2) to last 2 stitches, p2.
Row 2: (K2, p2) to last 2 stitches, k2.
Row 3: (P2, tw2r) to last 2 stitches, p2.
Row 4: As row 2.
Rep these 4 rows for 7cm, ending after a row 1.
Change to 5mm needles.

Next Row (WS): K2, p2, k2, p6, k2, p6, k2, p1, p twice in next st, p2, p twice in next st, p1, k2, p6, k2, p6, k2, p2, k2 (52 sts).
Row 1 (RS): P2, tw2r, p2, Right Rope Cable, p2, Gullwing Cable, p2, Oxo Cable, p2, Gullwing Cable, p2, Left Rope Cable, p2, tw2r, p2.
Row 2 (WS): K2, p2, k2, Left Rope Cable, k2, Gullwing Cable, k2, Oxo Cable, k2, Gullwing Cable, k2, Right Rope Cable, k2, p2, k2.
Row 3: P2, k2, p2, Right Rope Cable, p2, Gullwing Cable, p2, Oxo Cable, p2, Gullwing Cable, p2, Left Rope Cable, p2, k2, p2.
Row 4: As row 2.
Cont in patt as set, increasing 1 st at each end of 5th and every foll 6th row to 78 sts, working increased sts in rev st st.
Work straight until sleeve measures 48cm.

Shape cap
Cast off 5 sts at beg of next 2 rows (68 sts).
Dec 1 st at each end of every row 5 times (58 sts).
Work 8 rows straight.
Dec 1 st at each end of every row to 28 sts.
Cast off loosely.

Detail of sleeve pattern.

Detail showing the twisted rib button bands.

Front Bands

Button band
Using 4.5mm needles, cast on 8 sts and work in twisted rib as for sleeve cuff.
Row 1 (RS): P1, k2, p2, k2, p1.
Rows 2 and 4: K1, p2, k2, p2, k1.
Row 3: P1, tw2r, p2, tw2r, p1.
Continue until band fits along left front edge. Leave stitches on a holder.
Mark positions of buttons, noting that the last one will be on the neckband.

Buttonhole band
Work as for button band, making buttonholes at marked positions as follows:
Row 1 (RS): P1, k2tog, yo, k2tog, p1.
Row 2: K1, p2, kfb, p2, k1
Leave stitches on a holder.
Sew shoulder seems and then sew Bands to Fronts before working Neckband.

Neckband

Using 4.5mm needles, work in patt across 7 sts of Buttonhole Band, p next st together with first st of the Right Front, pick up and knit the rem 4 cast-off sts from the Right Front neck edge, pick up and knit 21 sts from Right Front neck edge, knit 34 sts from Back neck, pick up and knit 21 sts down Left Front neck edge, pick up and knit across next 4 cast-off sts, p together last st from Left Front and first st of Button Band, patt 7sts from Button Band (100 sts).
Work 3 rows in twisted rib pattern as for sleeve cuff.
Next row: Make buttonhole as directed above.
Work 4 more rows.
Cast off.

Finishing

Join remaining seams and sew on buttons. Weave in all ends.

It should be fairly easy to change this design to a crew neck sweater.

Work the Back and Sleeves as for the Cardigan, then work the Front as for the Back until the armhole measures 10cm and you have 98 sts on the needles.

Shape neck
With RS facing, work 40 sts, leaving rem 58 sts on holder. Dec 1 st at neck edge of every row to 34 sts, then on every alt row to 32 sts.
Work straight until armhole measures 20cm.

Shape shoulder
Cast off 8 sts at beg of next and foll alt rows 4 times. Return to sts on holder, slip 18 sts onto another holder for front neck and work on rem 40 sts as for first side. Join right shoulder.

Neckband
Using 4.5mm needles pick up and knit 22 sts from right front neck edge, 18 sts from front neck holder, 22 sts up left front neck and 34 sts from back neck (96 sts).
Work 8 rows in twisted rib pattern as for sleeve cuff. Cast off loosely.

This version of the cardigan with different patterns and using another yarn shows how the same pattern can be used with a number of different stitch motifs.

ARAN KNITTING PATTERNS

Child's Round Neck Cardigan

This pattern is designed for a 3 to 4-year-old child. If you want to make a different size, there are several options. At this tension, you would need to add or subtract 9 stitches for every 5 centimetres of difference. If you wanted to make this for an eight-year-old with a chest measurement of 70 centimetres instead of the 60 centimetres used here, you would need another 9 stitches all around. As 9 is an odd number and you don't want a different number of stitches at each side, add 2 more moss stitches at each side edge of the back, fronts and sleeves. And don't forget to add a bit more to the length of the body and sleeves too, and perhaps make the neck a bit wider. Alternatively, you could place the extra stitches in the purl section between the cable panels. Remember to buy extra yarn if you are making a larger size.

Back view of child's Aran cardigan.

Size
Child aged 3–4.
Chest: 60cm
Body Length: 33cm
Sleeve Length: 30cm

Materials
300g Rico Essentials Merino Aran (100% merino; 100 metres/50g)
Shade: Blackberry

Needles
4mm and 5mm needles
6 buttons approx 2cm in diameter

Tension
24 sts x 25 rows = 10 x 10cm, over patt using 5mm needles

Ropes and Medallion

Row 1 (RS): P1, k1, *p2, k6, p2, k12, p2, k6*, p3, k1.
Row 2 and all WS rows: K1, p1, k2, *p6, k2, p12, k2, p6, k2*, k1, p1.
Row 3: P1, k1, *(p2, 3/3RC) twice, 3/3LC, p2, 3/3LC*, p3, k1.
Row 5: Repeat row 1.
Row 7: Repeat row 1.
Row 9: P1, k1, *p2, (3/3RC, p2, 3/3LC) twice*, p3, k1.
Row 11: Repeat row 1.

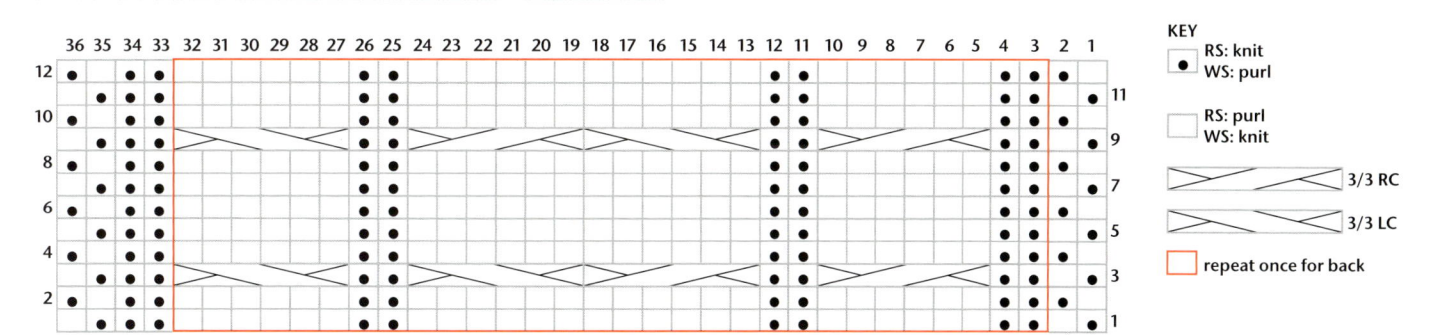

KEY
- RS: knit / WS: purl
- RS: purl / WS: knit
- 3/3 RC
- 3/3 LC
- repeat once for back

Just three different cable patterns, so it is not too fussy for a small child.

Back

Using 4mm needles, cast on 66 sts. Work in k1, p1 rib for 5cm.
Change to 5mm needles and work Ropes and Medallion cable pattern, working repeat section outlined in red on chart and indicated by asterisks (*) in the text version twice.
Work straight until piece measures 20cm.

Armhole shaping

Cast off 3 sts at beginning of next 2 rows (60 sts).
Dec 1 st at each end of every alternate row three times until 54 sts remain.
Work straight until armhole measures 16cm.

Shoulder shaping

Cast off 7 sts at beginning of next 4 rows.
Place rem 26 sts for back of neck on a holder.

Right Front

Using 4mm needles, cast on 36 sts. Work in k1, p1 rib for 5cm.
Change to 5mm needles and work Ropes and Medallion cable as per chart
Work straight until piece measures 20cm.

Armhole shaping

Ending with WS facing, cast off 3 sts at beg of row.
Dec 1 st at armhole on next and foll 2 alt rows (30 sts).
Work straight until armhole measures 11cm.

Neck shaping

With WS of work facing, work 20 sts. Slip last 10 sts onto a holder.
Dec 1 st at neck edge every row 6 times, until 14 sts rem.
Work straight until armhole measures 16cm ending with WS facing.

Shoulder shaping

Cast off 7 sts at beg of next and foll alt row.

Left Front

Using 4mm needles, cast on 36 sts. Work in k1, p1 rib for 5cm.
Change to 5mm needles and work Ropes and Medallion cable as per chart.
Work straight until piece measures 20cm.

Armhole shaping

Ending with RS facing, cast off 3 sts at beg of row.
Dec 1 st at armhole on next and foll 2 alt rows (30 sts).
Work straight until armhole measures 11cm.

Neck shaping

With RS facing, work 20 sts. Slip last 10 sts onto a holder.
Dec 1 st at neck edge every row 6 times, until 14 sts rem.
Work straight until armhole measures 16cm, ending with RS facing.

Shoulder shaping

Cast off 7 sts at beg of next and foll alt row.

Side view of a child's cardigan showing the same patterns used on the sleeves.

Sleeves

Using 4mm needles, cast on 36 sts. Work in k1, p1 rib for 4cm. Change to 5mm needles and work Ropes and Medallion cable as per chart.
Inc 1 st at each end of 7th row and every following 6th row until there are 50 sts, working these sts in the moss stitch patt.
Work straight until sleeve measures 29cm.

Shape cap
Cast off 3 sts at beg of next two rows (44 sts).
Dec 1 st at each end of every alt row thee times (38 sts).
Dec 1 st at each end of every row three times (32 sts).
Work 12 rows without shaping.
Dec 1 st at each end of every alt row three times (26 sts).
Dec 1 st at each end of every row four times (18 sts).
Cast off loosely.

Neckband

Sew Fronts to Back along shoulder seams.
With RS of work facing, pick up and work 10 sts for Right Front neck from holder, 13 sts from Right Front neck edge, 26 sts for Back neck from holder, 13 sts from Left Front neck edge and 10 sts for Left Front neck from holder (72 sts).
Work 2cm in k1, p1 rib.
Cast off loosely.

Button Band

Using 4mm needles, cast on 7 sts. Work in k1, p1 rib until band will fit along cardigan front, from bottom of front hem to top of collar band, when slightly stretched.
Cast off.
Sew button band to Left Front for girls, Right Front for boys. Mark positions for 6 buttons, the first one 1cm above the bottom edge, the last one 1cm below the top edge. The rest should be evenly spaced between these two, approximately 7cm apart.

Buttonhole Band

Work Buttonhole Band as for Button Band, working buttonholes on right side at the marked positions as follows:
Next Row: Rib 3, cast off 2 sts, rib 2.
Next Row: Rib 2, cast on 2 sts, rib 3.
Cast off. Sew band to rem Front.

Finishing

Sew remaining seams and sew on buttons. Darn in any ends.

> It is not difficult to make this cardigan into a sweater, remembering that you will have 6 sts fewer on the front when you get to the neck shaping. Work out how wide you would like the neck to be, remembering that small children have proportionately larger heads than adults. You could alter the shoulders so that one or both of them fasten with buttons, as the knitters of the Aran Islands did for their small children.

Raglan Sleeved Round Neck Sweater

This sweater also uses basic rope cables, but the difference between this sweater and the child's cardigan is that the crossings are not made on the same row. It is a unisex sweater and looks just as good on a man.

Size
Actual chest measurement: 94cm
Length: 58cm
Sleeve length: 44cm

Materials
800g Aran weight yarn. I used Wendy Aran (100% wool; 146m/100g).

Needles
4mm and 4.5mm needles

Tension
19 sts x 24 rows = 10 x 10cm over st st using 4.5mm needles
21 sts x 21 rows = 8cm over pattern using 4.5mm needles

West Runton beach on a bright and windy morning..

Combining Basic Cables

Simple rope cables like those used here can be arranged in a variety of ways to create what look like complex stitches. Patterns such as this are also easy to adapt to different sizes by working more or fewer stitches between each set of cables. For example, the pattern here could have p1, k2, p1 between the pairs of 4-stitch rope cables, which would give 12 extra stitches, giving another 7cm in width. To make it smaller, leave out the repeat of Chart A at the sides. This will give a width of 62cm, small enough for a child's sweater.

The two columns of cables at the centre also make an ideal splitting point for converting this sweater to a cardigan, and adding an extra stitch or two at the front edges.

Raglan designs need a little more careful planning as the shaping can often cause an unattractive disruption of the side cables. There are two ways of overcoming this.

The simplest way is to work a wide panel of a filler stitch at the side edges but a more attractive way is to draw attention to the raglan shaping by working the decreases inside a group of stitches, which could be another narrow cable, or, as in this case, a few rib stitches.

This pattern is one that could easily be knitted top-down in the round. The chart for the cables can easily be reversed, or they can look equally good upside down. See Chapter 6 for ways of working a top-down sweater in the round.

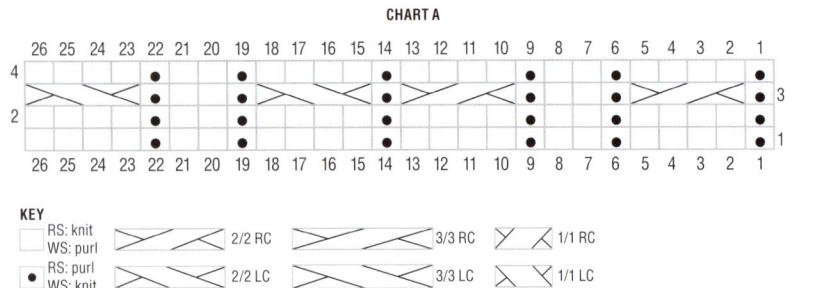

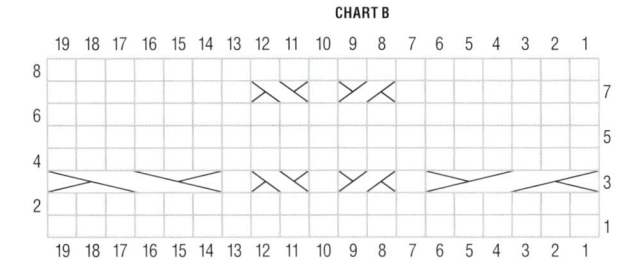

Charts for raglan sweater.

Front of the raglan sleeved round neck sweater on West Runton beach.

Chart A

Row 1 (RS): P1, k4, p1, k2, p1, k4, p2, k4, p1, k2, p1, k4.
Row 2 (WS): P4, k1, p2, k1, p4, k2, p4, k1, p2, k1, p4, k1.
Row 3: P1, 2/2RC, p1, k2, p1, 2/2RC, p2, 2/2LC, p1, k2, p1, 2/2LC.
Row 4: Repeat row 2.

Chart B

Row 1 (RS): K6, (p1, k2) twice, p1, k6.
Row 2 and all WS rows: P6, (k1, p2) twice, k1, p6.
Row 3: 3/3RC, p1, 1/1RC, p1, 1/1LC, p1, 3/3LC.
Row 5: Repeat row 1.
Row 7: K6, p1, 1/1RC, p1, 1/1LC, p1, k6.

Back

Using 4mm needles, cast on 99 sts and work 4cm k1, p1 rib, ending with a RS row.
Next row (RS, inc): K1, p1, k1, p2, k1, p1, k1, kfb, k1, p1, k2, p1, k4, p2, k1, kfb, k1, p1, k2, p1, k4, p2, k2, kfb, k2, p1, k2 p1, k2 p1, k2, kfb, k2, p2, k2, kfb, k2, p1, k2, p1, k2, p1, k2, kfb, k2, p2, k4, p1, k2, p1, k1, kfb, k1, p2, k4 p1, k2, p1, k1, kfb, k1, p1, k1, p2, k1, p1, k1 (110 sts).
Change to 4.5mm needles and work in patt, beginning from row 2 of the charts and setting them out as follows.

Next row (RS): K1, p1, k1, p2, k1, Chart A, p2, Chart B, p2, Chart B, p2, Chart A, k1, p2, k1, p1, k1.
Continue until work measures 38cm or length required to underarm.

116 ARAN KNITTING PATTERNS

A clear view of the arrangement of the cables.

Showing the patterns on the sleeves.

Shape armholes

Cast off 3 sts at beg of next two rows.
Next row (RS): (K1, p1) twice, ssk, patt to last 6 sts, k2tog, (p1, k1) twice.
Decrease on every alt row to 48 sts.
Leave sts on a holder.

Front

Work as for Back until there are 60 sts left.

Shape neck

[K1, p1] twice, ssk, patt 15, turn and work on these 20 sts, dec at neck edge of every row and cont to decrease at armhole edge of alt rows.
When 5 sts rem, dec at neck edge and armhole edge of alt rows to 3 sts, work 3 tog and fasten off.
Return to rem sts, leave 18 sts on holder and work other side to match.

Sleeves

Using 4mm needles, cast on 40 sts and work 6cm k1, p1 rib, ending with WS facing.
Next row (WS): Rib 1, *rib 2, inc in next st; rep from * ending rib 3 (52 sts).
Change to 4.5mm needles.

Row 1 (RS): (K1, p2) twice, Chart B, p2, Chart B, (p2, k1) twice.
Cont in patt, inc 1 st each end of 5th and every foll 6th row to 76 sts, keeping increased sts in rib pattern.

Shape Raglan

Cast off 3 sts at beg of next 2 rows. Dec as on Back to 10 sts. Leave sts on a holder.

ARAN KNITTING PATTERNS 117

Neckband

Join Sleeves to Body using mattress stitch (see Chapter 6), leaving left back seam open.

Using 4mm needles, knit 10 sts from Left Sleeve, 12 sts down Left Front, 18 sts from Front Neck, 12 sts up Right Front, 10 sts from Right Sleeve and 48 sts from Back Neck (110 sts).

Next row (dec): (P1, k1) 3 times, p2tog, (k1, p1) 5 times, k2tog, (p1, k1) 3 times, p1, k2tog, (p1, k1) five times, p1, k2tog, (p1, k1) 16 times, p2tog, (k1, p1) 3 times, k1, p2tog, (k1, p1) 13 times (104 sts).
Work 7 rows k1, p1 rib. Cast off loosely.

Finishing

Join left back sleeve seam and edges of neckband. Join side and sleeve seams. Weave in any loose ends.

Close-up of centre cables of the round neck sweater, showing an ideal position for dividing up two fronts.

To Turn this Design into a Cardigan

Work the Back and Sleeves as for the sweater.

Left front
Using 4mm needles, cast on 49 sts and work 4cm k1, p1 rib, ending with a RS row
Next row: K1, p1, k1, p2, k1, p1, k1, kfb, k1, p1, k2, p1, k1, kfb, k1, p1, k1, kfb, k1, p1, k2, p1, k1, kfb, k1, p2, k2, kfb, k2, p1, tw2r, p1, tw2l, p1, k2, kfb, k2, p1, k1.
Continue in pattern following chart and decreasing for raglan until there are 31 sts left

Shape neck
(K1, p1) twice, ssk, patt 15, turn and work on these 20 sts, leaving 10 sts at neck edge. Decrease at neck edge of every row and cont to decrease at armhole edge of alt rows.
When 5 sts rem, dec at neck edge and armhole edge on alt rows to 2 sts, work 2 tog and fasten off.

Work Right Front to match, reversing shapings.

Neckband
Using 4mm needles, with right side facing, knit 10 sts from sts left on holder at neck, 14 sts from Right Front, 10 sts from Right Sleeve, 48 sts from Back Neck, 10 sts from Left Sleeve, 14 sts from Left Front and 10 sts from holder (116 sts).

Decrease row: K1, p1, k1, p2tog, (k1, p1) 20 times, p1, k2tog, (k1, p1) 5 times, k2tog, (k1, p1) twice, k1, p2tog, (k1, p1) 20 times, p1, k2tog, k1, p1, k1 (108 sts).
Work 7 rows k1, p1 rib.
Cast off loosely.

Button band
Using 4mm needles, pick up and knit 90 sts along front edge.
Work 7 rows k1, p1 rib.
Cast off.

Buttonhole band (with 8 buttonholes)
Using 4mm needles, pick up and knit 90 sts along front edge.
Work 3 rows k1, p1 rib.
Next row: Rib 5, *cast off 3, rib 8; rep from * 6 times, cast off 3, rib 5.
Work 3 rows k1, p1 rib, casting on 3 sts over buttonholes in the next row.
Cast off.

If you would like to add pockets, see Chapter 6 for two ways to do this without disrupting the cable pattern.

Traditional Saddle Shoulder Aran

Moss stitch filler at the sides.

Some saddle shoulder Arans begin with the saddle and work from the top downwards. But bear in mind if working this way that the cables either have to be worked upside down, or a cable that looks the same in both directions, such as the Medallion or Oxo cable, has to be chosen for that section.

Planning a Design of Your Own

If you want to make a similar shaped garment but of your own design and to your own measurements, begin by drawing a diagram of your chosen shape and mark on it which cables you would like to use. Next mark your measurements on the diagram and work out how these cables will fit in and how many filler stitches you will need.

In a squared armhole such as this design has, it is a good idea to have enough filler stitches at the sides to accommodate the number of cast-off stitches at the underarm while leaving enough edge stitches to be able to make a neat join between the sleeve and the armhole edge.

At this point you can either plot your stitch patterns on graph paper or, when you know the number of stitches in each of your panels, mark them on your diagram.

Because this design has a ribbed hem with cables that will carry up into the body, the positions of the increases are not evenly spread across the rib but are fitted in to the cabled portion. Chapter 4 has instructions for how to work this out according to your own design. I worked it out by plotting the position of the body and the rib's cables on a diagram.

Size
Actual chest measurement: 108cm
Length: 65cm
Sleeve length: 52cm

Materials
750g Blacker Yarns Boreray (100% wool; 70m/50g)
This is the natural fleece colour of this rare breed sheep.

Needles
4mm, 4.5mm and 5mm needles

Tension
19 sts x 22 rows = 10 x 10cm over double moss stitch using 4.5mm needles.

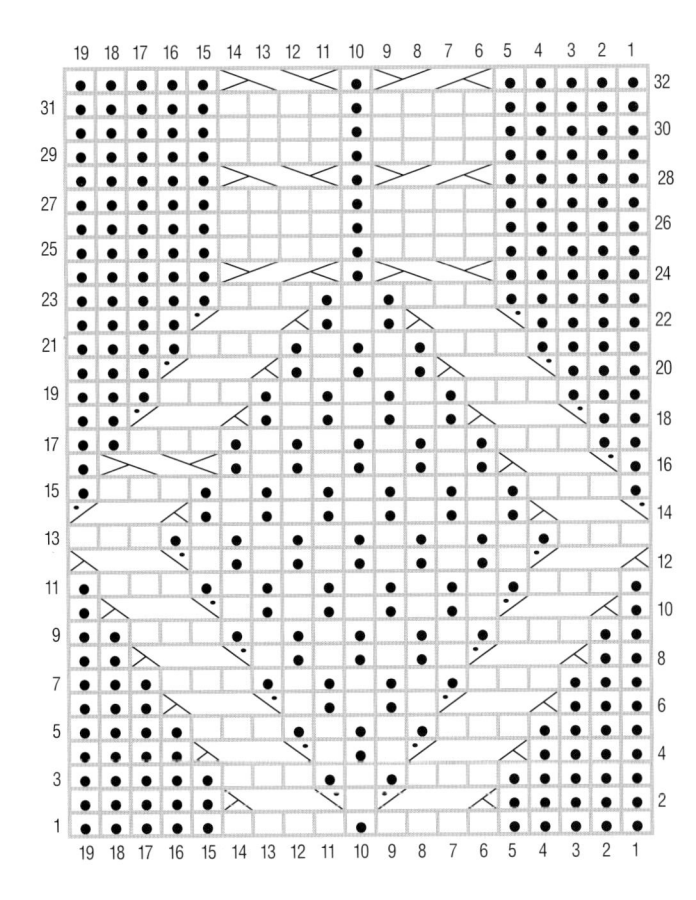

Diamond and moss chart.

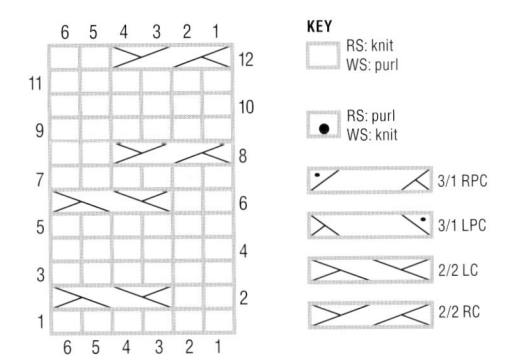

Asymmetric rope chart.

KEY
- RS: knit / WS: purl (blank)
- RS: purl / WS: knit (●)
- 3/1 RPC
- 3/1 LPC
- 2/2 LC
- 2/2 RC

Diamond and Moss

Row 1 (WS): K5, p4, k1, p4, k5.
Row 2 (RS): P5, 3/1RPC, k1, 3/1LPC, p5.
Row 3: K5, p3, k1, p1, k1, p3, k5.
Row 4: P4, 3/1RPC, k1, p1, k1, 3/1LPC, p4.
Row 5: K4, p3, [k1, p1] twice, k1, p3, k4.
Row 6: P3, 3/1RPC, (k1, p1) twice, k1, 3/1LPC, p3.
Row 7: K3, p3, (k1, p1) three times, k1, p3, k3.
Row 8: P2, 3/1RPC, (k1, p1) three times, k1, 3/1LPC, p2.
Row 9: K2, p3, (k1, p1) four times, k1, p3, k2.
Row 10: P1, 3/1RPC, (k1, p1) four times, k1, 3/1LPC, p1.
Row 11: K1, p3, (k1, p1) five times, k1, p3, k1.
Row 12: 3/1RPC, (k1, p1) five times, k1, 3/1LPC.
Row 13: P3, (k1, p1) six times, k1, p3.
Row 14: 3/1LPC, (p1, k1) five times, p1, 3/1RPC.
Row 15: Repeat row 11.
Row 16: P1, 3/1LPC, (p1, k1) four times, p1, 2/2LC, p1.
Row 17: Repeat row 9.
Row 18: P2, 3/1LPC, (p1, k1) three times, p1, 3/1RPC, p2.
Row 19: Repeat row 7.
Row 20: P3, 3/1LPC, (p1, k1) twice, p1, 3/1RPC, p3.
Row 21: Repeat row 5.
Row 22: P4, 3/1LPC, p1, k1, p1, 3/1RPC, p4.
Row 23: Repeat row 3.
Row 24: P5, 2/2LC, p1, 2/2RC, p5.
Row 25: Repeat row 1.
Row 26: P5, k4, p1, k4, p5.
Row 27: Repeat row 1.
Row 28: P5, 2/2RC, p1, 2/2LC, p5.
Rows 29–32: Repeat rows 25–28.

Asymmetric Rope

Row 1 and all WS rows: Purl.
Row 2 (RS): K2, 2/2LC.
Row 4: Knit.
Row 6: Repeat row 2.
Row 8: 2/2RC, k2.
Row 10: Knit.
Row 12: Repeat row 8.

ARAN KNITTING PATTERNS

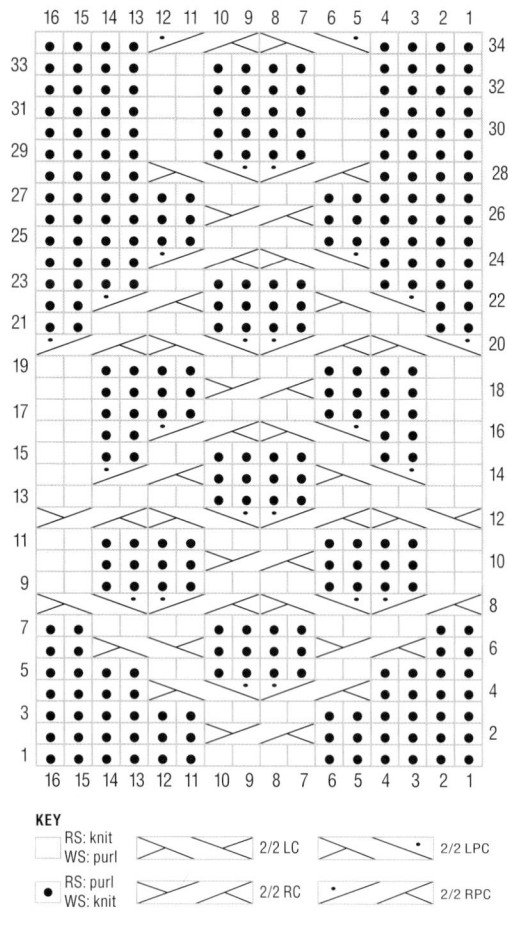

Overlapping diamonds chart.

Asymmetric rope outlining the diamond and moss.

Overlapping Diamonds

Row 1 (WS): K6, p4, k6.
Row 2 (RS): P6, 2/2RC, p6.
Row 3: Repeat row 1.
Row 4: P4, 2/2RPC, 2/2LPC, p4.
Row 5: (K4, p2) twice, k4.
Row 6: P2, 2/2RC, p4, 2/2LC, p2.
Row 7: K2, p4, k4, p4, k2.
Row 8: (2/2RPC, 2/2LPC) twice.
Row 9: P2, k4, p4, k4, p2.
Row 10: K2, p4, 2/2 RC, p4, k2.
Row 11: Repeat row 9.
Row 12: 2/2LC, 2/2RPC, 2/2LPC, 2/2RC.
Row 13: P6, k4, p6.
Row 14: K2, 2/2LPC, p4, 2/2RPC, k2.
Row 15: P2, k2, p2, k4, p2, k2, p2.
Row 16: K2, p2, 2/2LPC, 2/2RPC, p2, k2.
Row 17: Repeat row 9.
Row 18: Repeat row 10.
Row 19: Repeat row 9.
Row 20: (2/2LPC, 2/2RPC) twice.
Row 21: Repeat row 7.
Row 22: P2, 2/2LPC, p4, 2/2RPC, p2.
Row 23: Repeat row 5.
Row 24: P4, 2/2LPC, 2/2RPC, p4.
Row 25: Repeat row 1.
Row 26: Repeat row 2.
Row 27: Repeat row 1.
Row 28: Repeat row 4.
Row 29: Repeat row 5.
Row 30: (P4, k2) twice, p4.
Row 31: Repeat row 5.
Rows 32–33: Repeat Rows 30–31.
Row 34: Repeat row 24.

Back

Using 4mm needles, cast on 96 sts and work rib pattern as follows:

Row 1: (K1, p1) six times (k4, p1, k1, p1, k1, p1, k1, p1) three times, k6, (p1, k1, p1, k1, p1, k1, p1, k4) three times, (p1, k1) to end.

Row 2: (P1, k1) six times, (p4, k1, p1, k1, p1, k1, p1, k1) three times, p6, (k1, p1, k1, p1, k1, p1, k1, p4) three times, (k1, p1) to end.

Row 3: (K1, p1) six times (2/2RC, p1, k1, p1, k1, p1, k1, p1) three times, 1/2RC, 1/2LC, (p1, k1, p1, k1, p1, k1, p1, 2/2LC) three times, (p1, k1) to end.

Row 4: As row 2.

Rep these 4 rows until work measures 6cm, ending with RS facing.

Change to 4.5mm needles and work foundation row as follows, with the [|] symbol marking the dividing point between each panel.

Next row (RS): (P1, k1) four times, p1 | p1, k1, p1 | k1, m1, k2, m1, k1 | p1, k1, p1 | p2, m1, p2, m1, k4, m1, p2, m1, p2 | p1, k1, p1 | k1, m1, k2, m1, k1 | p1, k1, p1 | p2, m1, p2, k1, m1, k2, m1, k2, m1, k1, p2, m1, p2 | p1, k1, p1 | k1, m1, k2, m1, k1 | p1, k1, p1 | p2, m1, p2, m1, k4, m1, p2, m1, p2 | p1, k1, p1 | k1, m1, k2, m1, k1 | p1, k1, p1 | [p1, k1] four times, p1 (117 sts).

Cont in pattern, following charts or written instructions for cables and placing them as follows:

Row 1 (WS): Moss st 9 | k1, p1, k1 | Asymmetric Rope | k1, p1, k1 | Overlapping Diamonds | k1, p1, k1 | Asymmetric Rope | k1, p1, k1 | Diamond and Moss | k1, p1, k1 | Asymmetric Rope | k1, p1, k1 | Overlapping Diamonds | k1, p1, k1 | Asymmetric Rope | k1, p1, k1 | Moss st 9.

Row 2 (RS): Moss st 9 | p1, k1, p1 | Asymmetric Rope | p1, k1, p1 | Overlapping Diamonds | p1, k1, p1 | Asymmetric Rope | p1, k1, p1 | Diamond and Moss | p1, k1, p1 | Asymmetric Rope | p1, k1, p1 | Overlapping Diamonds | p1, k1, p1 | Asymmetric Rope | p1, k1, p1 | Moss st 9.

Cont in pattern until work measures 44cm.

Armhole shaping

Cast off 7 sts at beginning of next 2 rows (103 sts).
Work straight until armhole measures 17cm.
Place sts on holder.

A warm sweater for relaxing by the sea.

Front

Work as for Back until armhole measures 13cm.

Neck shaping

Left shoulder worked first:
Work 41 sts, slip next 21 sts onto a holder. Turn.
Dec 1 st at neck edge of every row four times (17 sts).
Work to same length as Back.
Leave sts on holder.

Right shoulder

Leave 21 sts at centre on holder and working on rem 41 sts, complete second side to match. Leave sts on a holder.

A close-up of the pattern on the Saddle Shoulder Sweater.

Asymmetric Rope | p1, k1, p1 | (k1, p1) three times.
Increase 1 st at each end of 3rd and every following 4th row four times (58 sts), then every 6th row to 84 sts, taking extra sts into double moss stitch at the edge.
Work until Sleeve measures 52cm or required length, if possible ending at a point where it looks like a complete pattern has been worked.

Next row: Cast off 32 sts at beg next 2 rows, leaving 20 sts for saddle strap.
Continue in pattern on sts for saddle strap, joining it to the 'live' sts of shoulder edge of the body by working the first and last stitches of the saddle strap together with the next stitch of the shoulder on every row as follows:
Row 1 (RS): Pattern to last stitch of saddle strap, work this stitch and first live stitch of shoulder as ssk.
Row 2 (WS): Purl tog tbl live stitch of shoulder and first st of saddle strap, work to last st of saddle strap and purl it tog with live st from shoulder.
Row 3 (RS): Knit tog live stitch of shoulder with first st of saddle strap, patt to last stitch of saddle strap, work this stitch and first live stitch of shoulder as ssk.
Rep rows 2 and 3 until all live sts are worked off.
Do not break off yarn.

Sleeves

Using 4mm needles, cast on 44 sts and work rib and cable pattern as follows:
Row 1 (RS): (P1, k1) four times, p1, (k4, p1, k1, p1, k1, p1, k1, p1) three times, k1, p1.
Row 2 (WS): (K1, p1) four times, k1 (p4, p1, k1, p1, k1, p1, k1) three times, p1, k1.
Row 3: (P1, k1) four times, p1, (2/2LC, p1, k1, p1, k1, p1, k1, p1) three times, k1, p1.
Row 4: As row 2.
Work these four rows three times more, then row 1 again.

Next row (WS): (K1, p1) four times, k1, p4, (k1, p1) three times, k1, (kfb) four times, (k1, p1) three times, k1, p4, (k1, p1) four times, k1 (48 sts).

Change to 5mm needles and RS facing, work in patt following charts and placing them as follows:
Row 1 (RS): (K1, p1) three times, p1, k1, p1 | Asymmetric Rope | p1, k1, p1 | Interlocking Diamonds | p1, k1, p1 |

Neckband

Using 4mm circular needle, pick up 7 sts down Left Front; from the Front Neck holder knit 9, sk2p, knit 9 sts from holder; pick up and knit 7 sts up Right Front; across the Saddle Strap knit 7 sts, ssk, k2, k2tog, knit 7 sts; across the Back Neck knit 14 sts, sk2p, knit 14 sts from Back Neck; across the Saddle Strap knit 7, ssk, k2, k2tog, knit 7 sts from Saddle Strap (98 sts).

Round 1: (P1, k1) 4 times, p1, 2/2RC, (p1, k1) 3 times, p1, 2/2RC, rib to end.
Round 2: (P1, k1) 4 times, p1, k4, (p1, k1) 3 times, p1, k4, rib to end.
Rep round 2 once more.
Rep last 3 rounds once more.
Rep rounds 1 and 2 once more.
Cast off loosely.

To Turn this Design into a Cardigan

Work the Back and the Sleeves as for the sweater.

Left front
Using 4mm needles, cast on 49 sts.
Row 1: (P1, k1) 4 times, p1, *k4, (p1, k1) 3 times, p1; rep from * 3 times, k4.
Row 2: K1, p3, *(k1, p1) 3 times, k1, p4; rep from * 3 times, (k1, p1) 4 times, k1.
Row 3: (P1, k1) 4 times, p1, *2/2RC, (p1, k1) 3 times, p1; rep from * 3 times, k4.
Row 4: As row 2.
Work to same length as rib on back.
Change to 4.5mm needles.

Row 1: (P1, k1) 4 times, p1 | p1, k1, p1 | m1, k2, m1 | p1, k1, p1 | p4, (kfb) 4 times, p4 | p1, k1, p1 | m1, k2, m1 | p1, k1, p1 | p4, (kfb) 4 times, k1 (58 sts).
Cont in pattern as set as for back until armhole measures 13cm.

Shape neck
Cast off 12 sts, work to end.
Dec 1 st at neck edge of every row to 32 sts.
Work to same length as back.
Leave sts on holder.

Right front
Work as for Left Front, reversing position of cables and shaping.

Neckband
Using 4mm needles and starting at neck edge of Right Front, rib across 12 cast-off sts, pick up and knit 7 sts from Right Front; knit 7 sts from Saddle Strap, ssk, k2, k2tog, knit 7 sts from Saddle Strap; knit 14 sts from Back Neck, sk2p, knit 14 sts from Back Neck; knit 7 sts from Saddle Strap, ssk, k2, k2tog, knit 7 sts from Saddle Strap; knit 7 sts from Left Front and rib across 12 cast-off sts (103 sts).
Work in k1, p1 rib for 9 rows.
Cast off.

Button band/Buttonhole band
Using 4mm needles, cast on 9 sts and work k1, p1 rib until band will fit along front edge from hem to top of neckband. Mark positions for however many buttons you require and make buttonhole band to match, casting off however many stitches you need for the size of buttons you are using.

If you would prefer not to have a saddle strap at the shoulder, work the sleeves as in the pattern but cast off all stitches on the last row. Because the neck will not be as deep at the back as it is with a saddle strap, the front neck will need to be wider and deeper to compensate. For the back, work the armhole to 20cm, then cast off 7 sts at the beginning of each of the next 6 rows. This will leave 40 stitches for the back neck.

Work the front as for the back but to 4cm less.

Shape neck
Work 41 sts, turn.
Cast off 2 sts, work to end.
Dec 1 st at neck edge of every row to 21 sts.
Work to same length as back.
Cast off 7 sts at the armhole edge of next and following 2 alternate rows.

The First 'Discovered' Aran

The replica of the 'first' Aran created from my hand drawn chart.

Finishing

Join remaining seams. Weave in all ends.
This is the pattern for the sweater that I recreated for the Knitting & Crochet Guild as part of their Heritage Kits collection. It is interesting to see the three ridge rounds just above the hem as would have been worked for a traditional fisherman's gansey. The original garment aslo had gussets at the underarm and was possibly knitted in the round, as were most garments at that time – another indication that this was the inspiration for Aran designs.

In the days before software for charting, instructions would be written out round by round. If the crossings took place on several different rounds, this would entail every round being written out. Naturally, the pattern would then run to a number of pages. Commercial patterns have devised a way of cutting down on the number of pages by printing the instructions for each of the cable motifs separately. These days some patterns don't even include written instructions for the cables, just the charts.

The chart shows a copy of my original chart, complete with notes. It is quite possibly how the early Aran knitters might have constructed their patterns.

In September 2000 I recreated this Aran from Gladys Thompson's photograph and from Richard Rutt's charts in *A History of Handknitting* (1987). In those days I didn't have charting software and plotted the pattern on graph paper, which is perhaps the best way to visualize the finished object before beginning to knit.

The pattern on the sleeves is slightly different to that on the front. I am assuming here that the back and front are the same, although no-one has seen this garment to ascertain this, as it was lost some time after 1936. The central trellis pattern on the sleeves is smaller than that of the body and is outlined by a ribbed rope cable.

The rib has a small cable and is worked as follows:

Round 1: K3 (p1, k1, p1, k4) to end.
Round 2 and every alt round: Work sts as they present themselves.
Round 3 and every foll 8th round: K3 (p1, c3f, p1, k3) to end.

The first few rows above the rib are knitted in a ridge stitch of what is most likely a form of wager welt, although it could just be garter stitch:

Row 1: Knit.
Row 2: Purl.
Row 3: Purl on the right side.
Row 4: Purl.

The increased stitches to begin the cables can be placed evenly along the last purl row. There is no need to try to match up the cables of the rib with the cables of the body.

The side panels of the sweater are not cables but moss stitch diamonds, as would be found on a gansey. Next to the diamonds are zigzag lines of twisted stitches, resembling the marriage lines patterns of a gansey, but this time worked as twisted stitches and not purl stitches. The next panel in is a ribbed diamond pattern but smaller than the one described in Chapter 3. Then comes a rope, but if you look carefully at the illustration, you will see that it is sometimes crossed on the wrong row. Several of the early Arans had these types of misplaced crossings (There appear to be some in the cabled blanket in Chapter 1 too.) The rope here is made of five stitches, crossed three over two, which was a familiar way of working rope cables then as it didn't pull the stitches across as much as a rope with an even number of stitches would. The centre panel is made up of medallions joined together, sometimes filled with moss stitch and sometimes reverse stocking stitch. The straps on the shoulders are either in a similar ridge pattern to the one at the welt or in moss stitch. It is difficult to tell from Mary Thomas' illustration. Garter stitch would be looser but would probably fit more smoothly over the shoulders

The sleeves have similar patterns, but the centre one is narrower and, instead of the plain rope cable, this one is of twisted rib. There is no ridge pattern between the ribbed cuff and the sleeve and there don't appear to be any increased stitches before the pattern begins. If I were to knit it again, I would add the ridges, as the transition from k3, p2 rib to the cables looks untidy to me.

Back and Front
(work two pieces the same)

Using 3.75mm needles, and the yarn doubled, cast on 99 sts.
Break off one strand of yarn and continue in cable rib for 44 rounds.
Change to 4.5mm needles and knit 7 rounds, decreasing 1 stitch at centre of the first of these rounds.
Purl 1 round.
Work in pattern, following the chart and keeping a knit stitch at each end of the round.
Continue for 106 rounds altogether.
Cast off 30 sts, work 38 sts and leave them on a holder, cast off 30 sts.

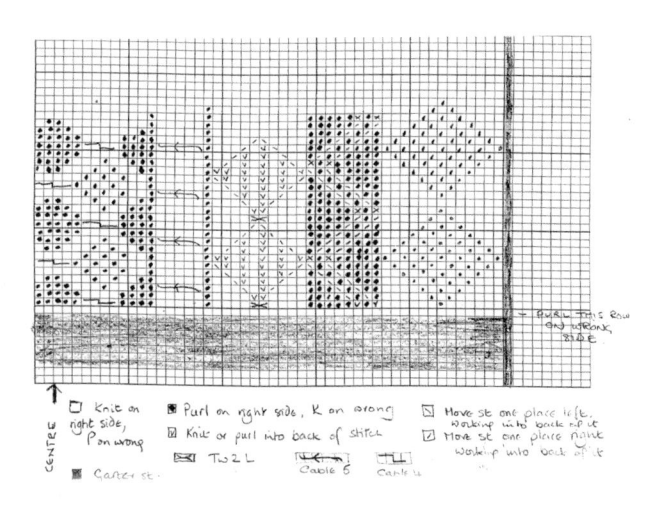

Chart for a replica of the 1936 jumper seen by Heinz Kiewe.

Sleeves

Using 3.75mm needles, cast on 60 sts and work in k3, p3 rib for 25 rounds.
Inc 14 sts evenly across the last round to 74 sts.
Change to 4.5mm needles and work in pattern following the chart and keeping one knit stitch at each end of the round.
The pattern for the sleeves is: knit 1, 8 zigzag, 10 ribbed diamond, 9 ribbed cable, 18 honeycomb, 9 ribbed cable, 10 ribbed diamond, 8 zigzag, knit 1.
Increase 1 st at each end of 9th then every following 8th round until there are 94 sts, working increased stitches in twisted rib.
When sleeve is required length, cast off 38 sts and patt to end of round.

Next row: Cast off 38 sts, change to 3.75mm needles and work 44 rows moss stitch on rem 18 sts for the shoulder strap.
Leave sts on a holder for the neckband.

Neckband

Join three of the shoulder seams.
Using 3.75mm needles, knit all of the stitches on the holders.
Work in rib for 3cm. Cast off.

ARAN KNITTING PATTERNS 127

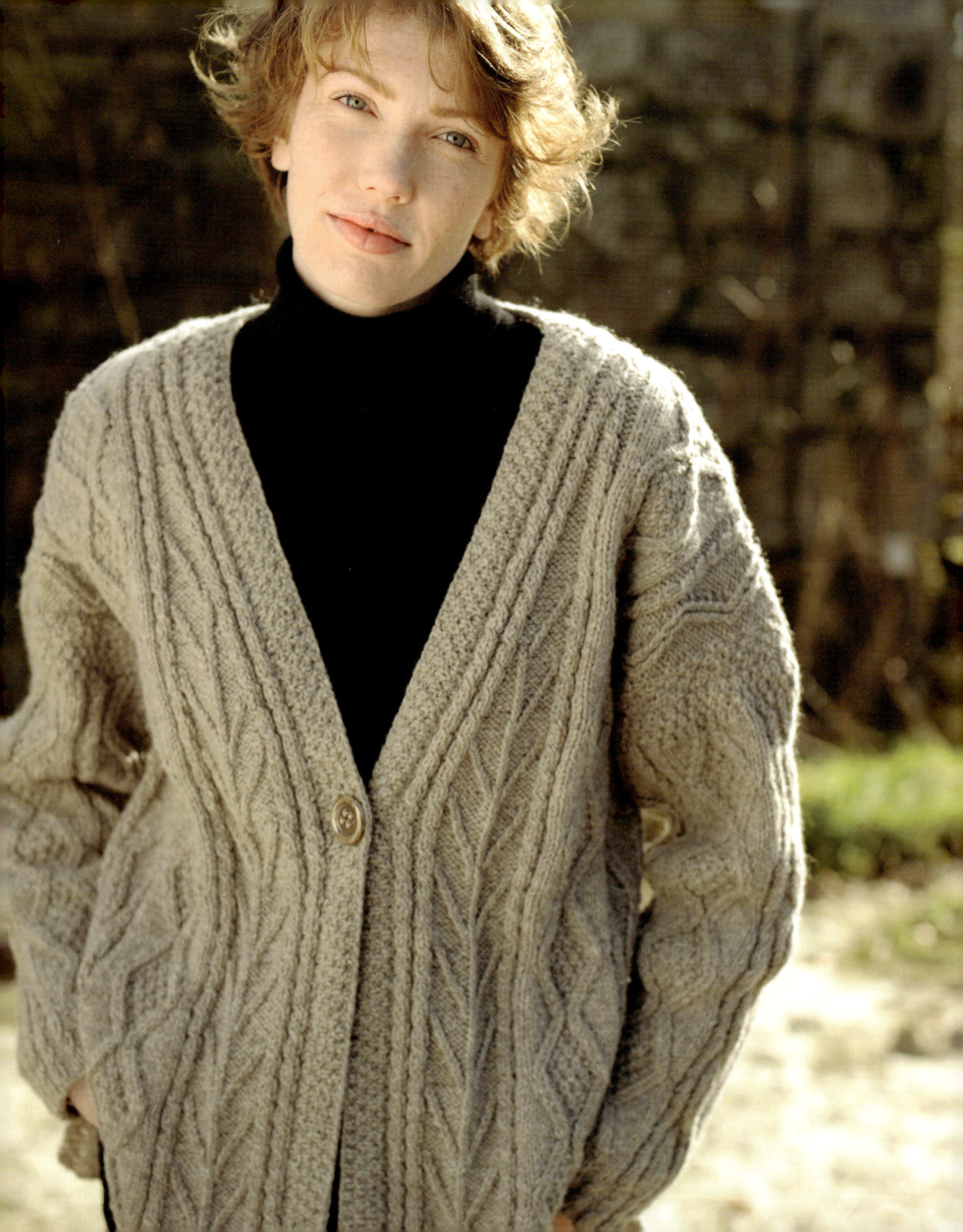

CHAPTER 6

TIPS AND TECHNIQUES

Picking Up Stitches

When picking up stitches for the neckband around the top edge of an Aran, it will usually be necessary to decrease stitches above the cables in the body of the garment to prevent the flaring out that occurs with the change of stitch from the cable pattern to the ribbing. The cables should end on a non-crossing row where the fabric is smooth. As you pick up the stitches, decrease one stitch for each of the times that the cables are crossed. Try to arrange a ribbed neckband so that the cables transition smoothly into it. If you have picked up the first row on the right side by knitting the stitches, you can probably fudge the first rib row a bit by increasing or decreasing at appropriate points.

OPPOSITE PAGE: *Cardigan incorporating cables and travelling stitches.*

Increasing

M1R and M1L
(also known as a lifted increase)

To make an almost invisible increase, work into the stitch of the row below. That is, knit to the stitch where the increase is to be made, insert the tip of the right needle into the right leg of the stitch in the row below it, lift it slightly and knit into that strand. This is known as 'make one right', abbreviated to

M1L – increase one stitch to the left by knitting into the left leg of the stitch on the row below.

129

M1R – increase one stitch to the right by knitting into the right leg of the stitch on the row below.

Increasing for Continuous or Closed Cables

Many of the newer, intricate cables are created by increasing a number of stitches at the beginning of the cable, usually by making 5 stitches out of one. The way to do this without making a rather ugly-looking hole, which you would get if you worked 5 times into the same stitch, is given in the Increasing and Decreasing Closed Cables panel.

M1R. For a 'make one left', knit the stitch where the increase is to be made, then insert the needle into the left strand of the stitch one row below it and knit it. The abbreviation for this is M1L.

Where a pattern states m1, you can use M1R or M1L instead of knitting into the back of the strand between the two stitches.

Increasing and Decreasing Closed Cables

Step 1: Lift the strand before the stitch and knit into the back of it.
Step 2: Insert the needle into the right leg of the stitch in the row below the next stitch (which will be the central one of the group) and knit it.
Step 3: Knit the central stitch.
Step 4: Insert the needle into the left leg of the stitch in the row below the central stitch and knit it.
Step 5: Lift the strand before the next stitch and knit into the back of it.

Following the completion of the cable, these stitches need to be decreased. A neat way of doing this is as follows:

Step 1: Slip the first 3 stitches from the left needle to the right needle knitwise, one at a time.
Step 2: Pass the middle stitch on the right needle over the one nearest the tip of the needle.
Step 3: Slip that stitch, which we will call the centre stitch, back to the left needle and pass the stitch to its left over it from left to right.
Step 4: Slip the centre stitch back to the right needle and pass the stitch to its right over it, from right to left, as in Step 2.
Step 5: Slip the centre stitch to the left needle and pass the stitch to its left over it from left to right, as in Step 3.
Step 6: Purl the centre stitch.

Celtic twist showing the open and closed cables.

Back of a waistcoat with bobbles.

Close up of the bobbles on the waistcoat.

Bobbles

Bobbles are a familiar sight on many Aran knits. There are a number of ways of making them, most of which are a little time-consuming, especially those methods where the work has to be turned back and forth.

The method most commonly used in Aran knitting is the 5-stitch bobble. There are a number of ways to work this, and I think the method described as for increasing in closed cables turns out the neatest.

An alternative method is to work the increases by knitting into the front and back of the stitch twice, then knitting it again, or by working k1, p1, k1, p1, k1 all into one stitch. The decreases can be worked in the same way as before or by simply knitting five stitches together, decreasing to three stitches and then knitting those together, or by knitting two stitches together twice, knitting the last stitch and passing the first two stitches over it.

In addition to stocking stitch, bobbles can also be worked in garter stitch or reverse stocking stitch.

Large bobbles can sometimes slip through to the back of the work, so either pull the yarn tight before making the next stitch and, on the wrong side row, knit into the back of the stitch that made the bobble; or, as you work the wrong side row, pick up the stitch at the base of the bobble and purl it together with the one at the top of it.

If you dislike turning the work backwards and forwards to work the five stitches, try knitting backwards. Insert the left needle into the back of the stitch nearest the point of the right needle, take the yarn from the back, clockwise, over the left needle and scoop it through the stitch. You have effectively worked a purl stitch.

Bobbles can look quite large and out of proportion to the rest of the stitches. For a smaller bobble, such as the one worked inside the diamond on the Diamond and Nosegay cable, k1, p1, k1 into the same stitch, slip the purl stitch over

TIPS AND TECHNIQUES

the last knit stitch, slip the two stitches to the left needle and slip the second stitch back over the first. Replace the resulting stitch back on the right needle.

Knots

Knots are made over one row, by increasing to as many stitches as are required and then decreasing them again by knitting all of the stitches together on the same row. Either decrease them in the same way as for bobbles, or by passing each stitch over the first stitch, starting with the second stitch from the point of the needle.

> ### Quantities
>
> Most ball bands these days state the number of metres to the ball. About 2000 metres is usually enough for a medium-sized Aran. It takes more yarn to make a sweater with cables than for a sweater of the same dimensions in a simple pattern.

Sewing Up

Mattress Stitch

Place the pieces side by side with the right sides uppermost. Join in a new piece of yarn, about 10 rows up from the bottom edge, leaving a long tail with a knot at the end to prevent it pulling through. Bring the sewing needle across to the corresponding stitch on the other piece and fasten it securely. Now take the needle back to the first piece and find the thread between the edge stitch and the second stitch. Pass it under the thread, cross to the other piece and do the same on that one. Continue in this way, working along the seam, zigzagging across to the matching stitches on each side. Every now and then pull gently on the thread to close the edges together. When you have completed this part of the seam, return to the long tail that was left at the beginning and work downwards to the cast-on edge. Starting part way along the seam makes it easier to handle the work than trying to hold the cast-on edges together.

If all of the edge stitches have been worked as knit stitches, take the sewing needle under the ridge of the first stitch instead of under the horizontal bar between the first and second stitches.

Sewing In a Set-In Sleeve

With the garment turned inside out, insert the sleeve head into the armhole so that its right side is facing the right side of the garment. Place the centre of the head of the sleeve, the straight cast-off edge, against the shoulder seam. Place the cast-off stitches at the base of the sleeve top against the cast-off stitches at the start of the armhole shaping. Adjust the rest of the sleeve around the armhole and pin it into position. Where possible, join the pieces with mattress stitch, especially at the straight edge at the head of the sleeve. Where this is awkward around the shaped sections, use back stitch working one stitch in from the edge. Check from time to time to make sure that there are no misaligned edges and the seam is neat and even.

Button Bands on Cardigans

Which look best: horizontal or vertical bands? Both of the cardigans described here have vertical bands. They seem to accord best with the vertical panels of the Aran patterns, but many people prefer knitted-on horizontal bands.

The front bands of a cardigan can be made in a number of different ways. They can be created at the same time as the fronts are being worked, they can be made separately and sewn on, or they can be picked up and knitted. They are best worked in a stitch that won't curl or distort, although they can be worked in a cable stitch, as in the ladies cardigan in Chapter 5. They should be firm enough to hold the shape of the garment and so are usually worked with needles one or two sizes smaller than those used for the body. Horizontal bands, picked up and knitted from the body outwards, give a firmer edge and have the advantage of vertical buttonholes, preventing the buttons from sliding towards the front edge. Vertical bands are less likely to stretch downwards than horizontal bands. They travel in the same direction as the ribbing at the hem and look more balanced than horizontal bands. However, they do have the disadvantage of buttonholes lying in the opposite direction, which can gradually stretch out, giving the bands a 'frilly' appearance. The way around this is to create vertical buttonholes.

Horizontal Bands

Pick up approximately three stitches for every four row ends along a straight edge, and one stitch for every two stitches on a diagonal such as a V neck. Pick up these stitches one stitch in from the edge through the centre of the stitch. Use a needle two sizes smaller than that used for the body and work enough rows so that the bands will overlap, with the top one covering the bottom one completely.

Vertical Bands

These can be made at the same time as you knit the garment, but this has the disadvantage of making them slightly baggy unless they are worked in garter stitch. For best results, knit them separately and then sew them on with mattress stitch. Slipping the first stitch on the right side will give the neatest edge.

Buttons

After all your hard work, don't spoil the garment with ill-chosen buttons. Bone, wood or horn always look appropriate, especially on a natural-coloured Aran. Leather buttons are suitable too, especially on a man's Aran.

Buttons and toggles. Toggles were especially favoured in the 1960s and 1970s.

Calculating Positions of Buttonholes

Buttonholes on an Vertical Band

Knit the button band first and mark the positions for the buttons. Then count the rows between the markers to identify the position of the buttonholes.

Buttons on a Horizontal Band

On a horizontal band the buttonhole placing needs to be worked out as soon as you have picked up the required number of stitches. This is done mathematically.

Step 1: Count how many stitches you would like before the first buttonhole and how many after the last one. Add these numbers together and subtract them from the total number of stitches in the band.

> **Example:**
> There are 110 stitches in the band and you want to leave 4 at both the top and bottom.
> 110 − 8 = 102

Step 2: Decide how many stitches you want in each buttonhole and how many buttonholes you need altogether.

> **Example:**
> Six 3-stitch buttonholes equals 18 stitches. Subtract this number from the total you got at Step 1;
> 102 − 18 = 84

Step 3: This number (84 in our example) needs to be divided by the number of spaces between buttonholes. If there are 6 buttonholes there will be 5 spaces between them.

> **Example:**
> 84 ÷ 5 = 16.8

TIPS AND TECHNIQUES 133

As it is not possible to work one eighth of a stitch, you will need to decide where to put the extra stitches. Work 16 stitches between each buttonhole and add the extra stitches to the stitches at the top and bottom, or work 17 stitches between each buttonhole and only 3 stitches at the top.

Working Buttonholes

The most commonly used buttonhole, worked over two rows, can often look untidy at the edges. A neater way of making a buttonhole over several stitches is to work it over one row.

One Row Buttonhole

Step 1: Bring yarn to the front of the work. Slip the first stitch from the left, purlwise. Take the yarn to the back. *Slip the next stitch from the left needle, purlwise. Pass the first slip stitch over it. Repeat from * twice more (3 stitches cast off). Slip the last stitch back to the left needle.

Step 2: Turn the work (left needle transfers to your right hand and right needle to your left hand). Move yarn to the back of the work. Cast on 3 stitches on the left needle using the cable cast-on. Pull the loop through for the another cast-on stitch and bring the yarn to the front before placing the loop on the left needle.

Step 3. Turn the work. Slip the first stitch from the left needle onto the right needle purlwise. Pass the last caston stitch over the slipped stitch to close the buttonhole.

Vertical Buttonhole

Step 1: Work across the row to the position of the buttonhole.

Step 2: Leave the yarn and join on a second ball to continue across the row.

Step 3: Work to the point where the first ball of yarn was left, pick it up and complete the row.

Step 4: Work back to the point where the second ball was left and complete the row with that one.

Step 5: Continue working in this way until the buttonhole is as long as required. Break off the second ball.

Step 6: Work across the row with the first ball of yarn.

Grafting

Stocking Stitch

To join two pieces of stocking stitch together, first of all you must have the same number of stitches on each needle.

Hold the knitting needles parallel in your left hand with the tips pointing towards the right and the wrong sides facing each other. If you don't already have a tail of yarn, join on a piece long enough to work across the whole row (about four times as long as the width of the piece) into the first stitch on the front needle. Thread this tail into a blunt-ended or tapestry needle.

Step 1: Bring the tapestry needle through the first stitch on the front needle as if to purl, leaving the stitch on the needle.

Step 2: Take the tapestry needle through the first stitch on the back needle as if to knit, leaving the stitch on the needle.

Step 3: Bring the tapestry needle through the first front stitch (the one that already has some yarn through it) as if to knit, and then slip this stitch off the knitting needle. Bring the tapestry needle through the next front stitch as if to purl and leave the stitch on the knitting needle.

Step 4: Take the tapestry needle through the first back stitch as if to purl, slip the stitch off, then take the tapestry needle through the next back stitch as if to knit and leave it on needle. Repeat steps 3 and 4 until all stitches are worked off.

Gently tug the yarn so that the tension of your grafted stitches matches the tension of the knitted ones. Pull the yarn through the last loop and weave it down the side edge.

Garter Stitch

If you need to graft garter stitch, end one side with a ridge row and the other side with a smooth one.

Step 1: Bring the tapestry needle through the front stitch as if to purl and leave it on the needle.

Step 2: Take the tapestry needle through the back stitch, also as if to purl and leave it on the needle.

Step 3: Bring the tapestry needle through the first stitch on the front as if to knit and slip it off the needle.

Step 4: Bring the tapestry needle through the next stitch on the front as if to purl and leave it on the needle.

Step 5: Take the tapestry needle through the first stitch on the back needle as if to knit and slip it off the needle.

Step 6: Take the tapestry needle through the next stitch on the back as if to purl and leave it on the needle.
Repeat from Step 3 until all stitches are worked off.

Uneven Stitches

Sometimes the left-hand knit stitch on cables looks looser than the others. To prevent this, work the purl stitch after it in a different way to normal. On right side rows, work the last knit stitch in the cable. Then, to work the purl stitch immediately to its left, insert the right needle into the stitch purlwise as normal but wrap the yarn around the needle in the opposite direction – clockwise instead of anticlockwise – before purling it. On the next row, the stitch will present as a twisted stitch, so knit it through the back loop to untwist it. Because working the purl stitch in this way uses a shorter length of yarn, it pulls the on the knit stitch before it and helps to even up the tension.

Following a Chart

It is possible to work a cabled garment by ignoring the written instructions and simply following the chart. It looks like the piece of knitting on your needles and it is easier to see which row you are on than when following written text, especially where there are several different cables across the row with different numbers of stitches in each and with the crossings worked at different intervals. Charts are also useful where there are increases and decreases to be made. You can see how this would affect the shape of a motif if you photocopy the chart and then draw on it where the stitches are to added or removed.

Charts show how the knitting appears when it is viewed with the right side of the work facing. This means that right side rows are worked from right to left, the opposite way to reading text. The wrong side rows are worked from left to right – imagine that you are working with the wrong side facing you. If you are working in the round, all of the rows are read from right to left.

Most charts have a vertical line of numbers running alongside from bottom to top with row 1 at the bottom right and row 2 on the next line up at the left of the chart. Along the top and bottom of the charts in this book are the stitch numbers; these will often only be along the bottom of the chart in many other books and stitch dictionaries.

Alongside the chart is a key to the symbols that appear in that chart only. Each chart will have its own set of symbols. If there is a red outline around some of the stitches, this signals that those stitches are repeated as many times as are required to complete the motif.

Where the knit and purl stitches are worked as they are presented on wrong side rows, some stitch dictionaries will only show the right side rows. In this book both right and wrong side rows are shown on the chart, so the chart shows you exactly how the piece of knitting will look. The chart shown here has 12 stitches and 16 rows. Row 1 is a right side row, so is worked as follows, reading from right to left: purl 2, knit 8, purl 2. Row 2 is a wrong side row and is read from left to right: knit 2, purl 8, knit 2.

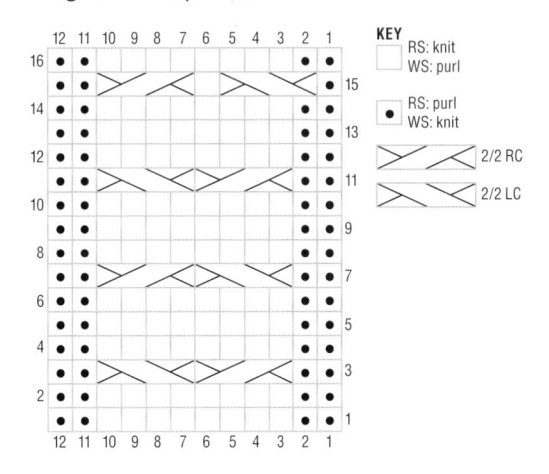

The next row has 2 purl stitches followed by symbols for cables, the first one meaning cross the stitches so that the second two pass over the first two from left to right. This is shown in the key as 2/2RC, meaning cross 2 stitches over the 2 stitches to the right. The next symbol on row 3 crosses them in the opposite direction: 2/2LC. Three rows without cables are then worked, followed by row 5 with the stitches crossing first to the left and then to the right. The rest of the chart is a repeat of the first 6 rows.

If you find it difficult to follow some of the more intricate cable charts, try marking all of the same symbols in a different colour. Colour the ones in the key too and they will be easier to follow. It is useful to make an enlarged photocopy of the chart in order to mark your place on it. You can simply mark it in pencil or use a chart holder, placing the magnetic strip just above the row you are on so that you can see how it fits with the row just finished.

The symbols used in this book closely match the appearance of the actual knitted stitches. The diagonal lines are made with their slope going from left to right or right to left, in the same direction as the stitches themselves will move. If any of the stitches are purled, the symbol will have a dot to the right or left of the diagonal.

Working in the Round

A pair of cabled wristwarmers.

As I have said earlier, if you are working in the round, make your swatch in the round too for the most accurate measurements. Many knitters work purl stitches at a looser tension than knit ones. Remember that you don't need to incorporate edge stitches when working in the round.

For a first attempt at working in the round, try this pattern for a pair of wristwarmers. There is no shaping to do, but the actual method of working might feel a little awkward at first. Because of the small number of stitches, it might be best to use a set of 4 double-pointed needles.

Materials

About 50g of any Aran weight wool

Needles

4mm and 4.5mm needles

Special abbreviation

Sl2 = slip 2 sts purlwise

Instructions

Using 4mm needles, cast on 40 sts.
Work 11 rounds of k2, p2 rib.

Change to 4.5mm needles and work in pattern as follows:
Round 1: (P2, k8) to end of round.
Round 2: (P2, 2/2RC, 2/2LC, p2, k3, sl2, k3) to end.
Round 3: (P2, k8, p2, k3, sl2, k3) to end.
Round 4: (P2, k8, p2, 1/3LC, 1/3RC) to end.
Round 5: As round 1.
Round 6: (P2, 2/2LC, 2/2RC, p2, k3, sl2, k3) to end.
Round 7: (P2, k8, p2, k3, sl2, k3) to end.
Round 8: As round 4.
Round 9: As round 1.
Round 10: As round 6.
Round 11: As round 3.
Round 12: As round 4.
Round 13: As round 1.
Round 14: (P2, 2/2LC, 2/2RC, p2, k3, sl2, k3) to end.

Round 15: As round 3.
Round 16: As round 4.
Round 17: As round 1.
Round 18: As round 14.
Round 19: As round 3.
Round 20: As round 4.
Round 21: As round 1.
Round 22: (P2, 2/2LC, 2/2RC, p2, k8) to end.
Round 23: As round 1.
Change to 4mm needles and work 5 rows k2, p2 rib. Cast off loosely.

Working Top-Down

Raglan shaped sweaters are the easiest to work top-down, but it is possible to make them with a variety of shaped necklines and sleeves. The following calculations are based on the pattern for the cabled raglan which has a crew neck. An even easier version is to work the sweater back and front the same with no neck shaping.

Top-Down Raglan Sweater

Cast on 1 st for the front, 1 st for a seam stitch, 10 sts for the left sleeve, 1 st for the seam, the 48 sts for the back of the neck, 1 st for the seam, 10 sts for the right sleeve, 1 st for the seam and 1 st to begin the fronts. Place a stitch marker each side of all the seam stitches.

Working back and forth, increase each side of the seam stitches on alternate rounds, and at the beginning and end of the round on every round for the front neck. Work in pattern from the chart and when you have increased to 20 sts, cast on 14 sts for the front neck and join to work in the round.

Continue in pattern, increasing on alternate rounds at raglan edge until you have enough stitches for the chest measurement. Cast on 6 sts for the underarm and leave the sleeve stitches on holders.

Continue to work the body to the length required, remembering to decrease before starting the ribbed hem.

Return to the stitches left for the sleeves, pick up 6 sts from those cast on and work the sleeves downwards, decreasing before the ribbed cuff.

With this method you can keep trying on the sweater as you knit, but you will need to slip the stitches onto two long circular needles or a long length of cord to do so.

Raglan sleeved round neck sweater could easily be worked top-down.

Blocking

It is important to block your swatches and your garment after they have been knitted in order to assess the finished appearance as well as the changes in measurements that can occur. Cables can sometimes spread out when wet, making the piece slightly larger than when it was first knitted.

Wet Blocking

Step 1: Fill a bowl with lukewarm water. There is no need to add soap or wool wash, but the latter can give the knitting a pleasant smell.

Step 2: Immerse the piece(s) in the water and let them soak for a few minutes. Lift them out and give them a gentle squeeze to remove excess water. Don't wring or rub them.

Step 3: Lay them on a towel, roll it up and give it another gentle squeeze.

Step 4: Unroll the towel, remove the pieces and lay them out flat on a slightly padded surface – another dry towel will suffice. You could cover this with a piece of checked fabric to help keep the edges of the knitting straight. Pin the pieces out to the required measurements and leave them to dry naturally, preferably overnight.

Steam Blocking

Step 1: Place the dry items on a padded board or a pile of towels. Pin them out to the required measurements using rustless pins.

Step 2: Hover a steam iron just above the pieces and let the steam penetrate the fabric. Don't press down or you will flatten the cables and spoil the texture of the piece.

Step 3: Leave the piece to dry for at least half an hour.

Mistakes

Check your knitting regularly for any dropped stitches, miss-crossed or forgotten cables. It is much easier to correct mistakes if they are only a few rows or rounds down. Mark them with a split ring marker or safety pin if you are unable to correct them straight away. A crochet hook is useful for picking up stitches.

If a dropped knit stitch is several rows down, insert the hook into the loose stitch, making sure that the strands to be picked up lie behind it. Pull each strand through the stitch in the correct vertical order, then slip the stitch back onto the right needle. If the dropped stitch is in a purl column, turn the work so that the wrong side is facing you and work as for a knit stitch. If the dropped stitch is in a row of moss stitch, make sure that the strands lie alternately behind and in front of the loose stitch when picking them up.

If you notice a cable with a mistake in it, work to the start of the cable, then remove the left needle and let the stitches ladder down to where the mistake is. Place the 'live' stitches on a double-pointed needle in the order that they are meant to be worked. Using your crochet hook work each stitch, one at a time, back over the loose strands as for a dropped stitch. It is tempting to place each stitch back onto the right needle when you have worked it, but I have found that they often fall off again, especially if you have had to unravel a number of rows. So I use a safety pin or a stitch marker to hold them while I pick up the next stitch.

Alternatively, if the mistaken cross is a long way down and there are other crossings above it, it is possible to correct it by unravelling that row only, as follows:

Step 1: Run waste yarn through the stitches of the row below the mis-crossed cable.

Step 2: Carefully cut through the centre stitch of the cable and unpick the stitches each side of it.

Step 3: Slip one half of the stitches onto one cable needle or double-pointed needle and the other half onto another needle.

Step 4: Cross the stitches in the correct direction.

Step 5: Using separate strand of yarn, graft the stitches together.

Step 6: Firmly darn in all the ends.

If you have made a number of mistakes in an intricate cable, it is much better to unravel the work and start again. When you reach the point where the work is correct, don't slip the live stitches onto the knitting needle, but insert it into each stitch of the row below. It is easy to split or twist a live stitch as you replace it on the needle.

> **Tip**
>
> If you have worked a knit instead of a purl stitch, or vice versa, and notice it when you are half way through the row, don't take the row back, but correct the stitch on the return row by letting it drop off the needle and then picking it up the correct way round.

Pockets

Because you don't want to cover the decorative section of your Aran garment, pockets are best inserted as linings, and not applied on the surface as patch pockets. The first way described here is an afterthought pocket and is placed in the side seams.

Side Seam Pockets

Place markers at the top and bottom edge on the back where you want the pocket to be. Pick up stitches between those markers and work in stocking stitch for the depth you would like the pocket. Cast off. Hold the back and front piece together and place markers for the pocket placement at the same points on the front edge. Pick up the same number of stitches along the front edge, and using smaller needles, work a few rows of rib. Cast off. Place the front section over the top of the pocket lining and stitch it into place on the front, being careful not to pull either piece of fabric out of shape. Stitch down the side edges of the ribbed section.

Front Pockets

For pockets placed directly on the front of a cardigan or sweater, make the pocket lining first in stocking stitch. Remember that, because cables pull the fabric in, it is best to work the lining on a needle at least two sizes smaller than the one used for the body. Leave the stitches on a stitch holder.

Work the front as far as the top of where you would like the pocket to be. The usual position is approximately 15cm up from the top of the ribbing for a medium-length cardigan and between 7cm and 10cm in from the front edge. This last measurement will depend on where your cable panels are, as you will also be working a ribbed top to the pocket, and this will look more professional if it fits precisely across one or more cables rather than cutting into them.

Work the required number of stitches from the front edge, then place the stitches that will constitute the front of the pocket onto another stitch holder. In their place, work in pattern across the stitches of the pocket lining, then work across the rest of the stitches of the front. When the front is finished, return to the stitches left on the holder and make a ribbed hem, preferably in the same pattern as was used for the other edgings. Make it straight or shaped, as in the one on a man's cardigan shown here..

When all of the work is finished, stitch the pocket lining to the inside of the front, again taking care that it is not lopsided or pulled out of shape. A way to make sure that pocket stays parallel to the other edges is to run a contrasting thread or a double-pointed needle along those stitches of the front that the sides of the pocket should meet. Finally, stitch the edges of the ribbed section in place.

A man's cardigan with unusual pocket tops.

Work the lining and leave it on a holder. Work as far as the position of the top of the pocket, but instead of working the row in pattern, work a border over the same number of stitches as in the pocket lining, working the rest of the row in pattern. Work the border in the same stitch as the hem of the garment unless it is very ornate, in which case a simple rib will be best. When the border is the required depth, cast off its stitches and work to the end of the round in pattern. On the next round, work to the cast-off stitches and work across the stitches of the pocket lining in their place, in pattern. Using this method there is no need to sew the edges of the border in place, giving a neater finish.

> An alternative method for finishing the top edge of a pocket is to work a border of rib or garter stitch in place of the pattern stitches of the body.

TIPS AND TECHNIQUES 139

BIBLIOGRAPHY

The Harmony Guide to Aran Knitting
(Lyric Books Limited, 1991)

Lavold, Elsebeth, *Viking Patterns for Knitting*
(Trafalgar Square, 1998)

Rutt, Richard, *A History of Handknitting* (Batsford, 1987)

Starmore, Alice, *Fishermen's Sweaters*
(Collins and Brown, 1994)

Thomas, Mary, *Mary Thomas's Knitting Book*
(Hodder and Stoughton, 1938)

APPENDIX

Number of stitches in each chart:

4 – rope 4-stitch
5 – small chain
6 – asymmetrical cable
6 – gullwing
6 – irregular crossings
6 – ribbed cable cross
6 – rope 6-stitch, crossed every 6th or 8th row
6 – snake cable
8 – cups
8 – enclosed rope
8 – honeycomb
8 – horseshoes
8 – medallions
8 – oxo
8 – rope 8-stitch
8 – wishbone and moss
9 – chain cable
9 – claw
9 – small plait
12 – arrowheads
12 – trellis
13 – medallion moss
13 – small diamond
14 – diamond with twisted rib
14 – nosegay
14 – ribbed braids
15 – 20-row diamond
15 – diamond and nosegay

15 – ribbed cable
16 – crossed ropes
16 – garter band
16 – goblets
16 – overlapping diamonds
16 – staghorn
18 – diamond and cross
18 – diamond with cables
18 – nutcracker
18 – ribbed braid
19 – diamond and moss
19 – Celtic twists
19 – half diamond
20 – nautical cable
22 – branches
22 – outlined diamonds
22 – triple cable
24 – Celtic braid
26 – bobbles and diamond
26 – diamond eight
26 – triple cross
27 – interlocking twist
28 – double cross
32 – double diamonds

Several of these charts can be made larger by inserting an extra stitch at the centre, as in Gullwing, for example. Most of the diamonds can also be enlarged, even though they may have other patterns within them.

INDEX

abbreviations 8
asymmetric design 92

bainin 17, 22
blocking 98
bobbles 22, 37, 141
braids 49, 51, 52, 56, 76
buttonholes 143, 144
buttons 143

cable needles 38
Celtic 24, 45, 51, 52, 90
charts; how to follow 145
circular knitting 100
converting patterns 50, 119, 125
cushion cover 110

decreasing 139, 140

filler stitches 46, 47, 87, 94

Gahan, Muriel 17
ganseys 15, 18
grafting 144
graph paper 39, 97, 103

increasing 139, 140
   increasing in cable 98

Kiewe, H.K. 16
Knitting Guilds 13
Knots 142

measurements table 89
measuring 87, 100
mistakes 148
myths and meanings 18, 26, 27, 52

naalbinding 13
necklines 96
needles 36-38

picking up stitches 139
plaits 49
planning 92, 96, 102
ply 33
pockets 149

reversible stitches 24, 85
rope cables 48

sewing up 142
shapes and styles 89, 96
sheep 34
stitch dictionary 45
stitch markers 39
swatching 41

tension 99
top down 130, 147
twisted stitches 14, 25, 41, 49, 86

worsted 15, 32, 33

yarns 29

OTHER KNITTING TITLES FROM CROWOOD

978 1 78500 455 1

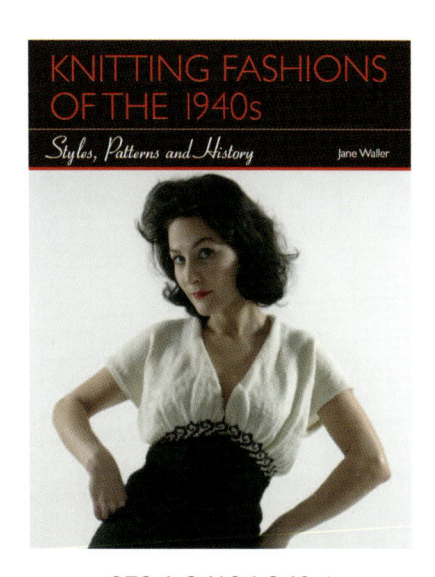

978 1 86126 862 4

978 1 84797 217 0

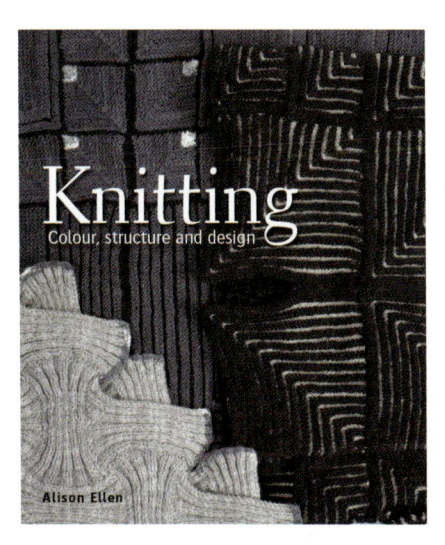

978 1 84797 284 2

987 1 78500 029 4

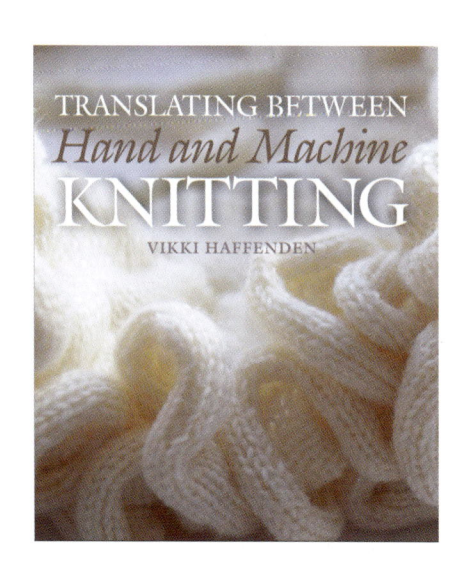

978 1 78500 431 5